Online Survey Design and Data Analytics:

Emerging Research and Opportunities

Shalin Hai-Jew
Kansas State University, USA

A volume in the Advances in Data
Mining and Database Management
(ADMDM) Book Series

Published in the United States of America by
    IGI Global
    Engineering Science Reference (an imprint of IGI Global)
    701 E. Chocolate Avenue
    Hershey PA, USA 17033
    Tel: 717-533-8845
    Fax: 717-533-8661
    E-mail: cust@igi-global.com
    Web site: http://www.igi-global.com

Library of Congress Cataloging-in-Publication Data

Names: Hai-Jew, Shalin, author.
Title: Online survey design and data analytics: Emerging research and
  opportunities / by Shalin Hai-Jew
Description: Hershey, PA : Engineering Science Reference, [2020]
Identifiers: LCCN 2018055427| ISBN 9781522585633 (hardcover) | ISBN
  9781522585657 (eISBN) | ISBN 9781522585640 (softcover)
Subjects: LCSH: Social surveys--Methodology. | Quantitative research. |
  Qualitative research.
Classification: LCC HM538 .Q34 2020 | DDC 300.72/3--dc23 LC record available at https://lccn.
loc.gov/2018055427

This book is published in the IGI Global book series Advances in Data Mining and Database Management (ADMDM) (ISSN: 2327-1981; eISSN: 2327-199X)

British Cataloguing in Publication Data
A Cataloguing in Publication record for this book is available from the British Library.

All work contributed to this book is new, previously-unpublished material.
The views expressed in this book are those of the authors, but not necessarily of the publisher.

For electronic access to this publication, please contact: eresources@igi-global.com.

Advances in Data Mining and Database Management (ADMDM) Book Series

ISSN:2327-1981
EISSN:2327-199X

Editor-in-Chief: David Taniar, Monash University, Australia

MISSION

With the large amounts of information available to organizations in today's digital world, there is a need for continual research surrounding emerging methods and tools for collecting, analyzing, and storing data.

The **Advances in Data Mining & Database Management (ADMDM)** series aims to bring together research in information retrieval, data analysis, data warehousing, and related areas in order to become an ideal resource for those working and studying in these fields. IT professionals, software engineers, academicians and upper-level students will find titles within the ADMDM book series particularly useful for staying up-to-date on emerging research, theories, and applications in the fields of data mining and database management.

COVERAGE

- Decision Support Systems
- Customer Analytics
- Web Mining
- Data Warehousing
- Text Mining
- Data Mining
- Factor Analysis
- Database Security
- Quantitative Structure–Activity Relationship
- Profiling Practices

IGI Global is currently accepting manuscripts for publication within this series. To submit a proposal for a volume in this series, please contact our Acquisition Editors at Acquisitions@igi-global.com or visit: http://www.igi-global.com/publish/.

Titles in this Series

For a list of additional titles in this series, please visit:
https://www.igi-global.com/book-series/advances-data-mining-database-management/37146

Managerial Perspectives on Intelligent Big Data Analytics
Zhaohao Sun (Papua New Guinea University of Technology, Papua New Guinea)
Engineering Science Reference • ©2019 • 335pp • H/C (ISBN: 9781522572770) • US $225.00

Optimizing Big Data Management and Industrial Systems With Intelligent Techniques
Sultan Ceren Öner (Istanbul Technical University, Turkey) and Oya H. Yüregir (Çukurova University, Turkey)
Engineering Science Reference • ©2019 • 238pp • H/C (ISBN: 9781522551379) • US $205.00

Big Data Processing With Hadoop
T. Revathi (Mepco Schlenk Engineering College, India) K. Muneeswaran (Mepco Schlenk Engineering College, India) and M. Blessa Binolin Pepsi (Mepco Schlenk Engineering College, India)
Engineering Science Reference • ©2019 • 244pp • H/C (ISBN: 9781522537908) • US $195.00

Extracting Knowledge From Opinion Mining
Rashmi Agrawal (Manav Rachna International Institute of Research and Studies, India) and Neha Gupta (Manav Rachna International Institute of Research and Studies, India)
Engineering Science Reference • ©2019 • 346pp • H/C (ISBN: 9781522561170) • US $225.00

Intelligent Innovations in Multimedia Data Engineering and Management
Siddhartha Bhattacharyya (RCC Institute of Information Technology, India)
Engineering Science Reference • ©2019 • 316pp • H/C (ISBN: 9781522571070) • US $225.00

Data Clustering and Image Segmentation Through Genetic Algorithms Emerging...
S. Dash (North Orissa University, India) and B.K. Tripathy (VIT University, India)
Engineering Science Reference • ©2019 • 160pp • H/C (ISBN: 9781522563198) • US $165.00

For an entire list of titles in this series, please visit:
https://www.igi-global.com/book-series/advances-data-mining-database-management/37146

701 East Chocolate Avenue, Hershey, PA 17033, USA
Tel: 717-533-8845 x100 • Fax: 717-533-8661
E-Mail: cust@igi-global.com • www.igi-global.com

This is for R. Max, Lily, and Asher, who embody hope, integrity, ambition, and grace.

Table of Contents

Section 3
Analyzing Online Survey Data

Preface

Online survey research suites have been in broad public usage for many years, and they have had a formal place in English books since about the 1990s. Computer assisted interviewing, a precursor research approach, hails from the 1980s (Figure 1).

Online survey research suites enable a wide range of capabilities not even conceptualized in early days. They enable the presentation of virtually every type of digital data—text, imagery, audio, video, and multimedia forms. They enable interactive elements. They enable off-line data collection. They enable translations of surveys into hundreds of different languages. They are integrated with social media and crowd-sourced work platforms and content platforms. They function well on a wide range of mobile devices. They have accessibility accommodations. They enable rich scripted actions and behaviors, the uses of randomizers, the surveillance of user behaviors, and other capabilities. There are built-in data analytics, including quantitative cross-tabulation analyses, text analyses, and other enablements that extend the capabilities of researchers and data analysts. There are built-in data visualization capabilities. With some researcher sophistication, these online survey research suites enable a wide range of quantitative, qualitative, and mixed methods research. *Online Survey Design and Data Analytics: Emerging Research and Opportunities* is the result of the exciting possibilities of these technologies.

This work was started in early May 2018 under a different title, with a slightly different ambition. The initial objective was to collect a wide-ranging list of works by different authors about their different usages of online survey platforms in their academic research work. Over time, it became apparent that some of the available works making the rounds were based on known approaches, without new insights. And while there were some excellent draft chapters, they were too few to cobble into a coherent collection. (These works later found homes in other excellent publications.) Ultimately, nine months later, this work became an authored one, in three parts, roughly about setting up surveys for particular ends, eliciting data in in-depth ways, and applying creative analytics methods to online survey data. And it is going out into the world with a more apt title.

An extended Table of Contents follows:

Figure 1. An exploration of different types of survey techniques as referenced in book texts as big data (Google Books Ngram Viewer)

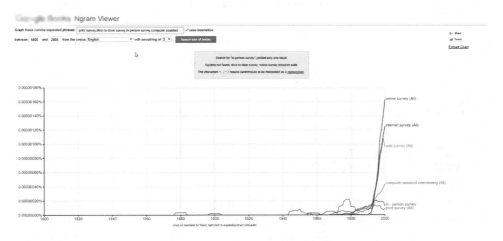

SECTION 1: ONLINE SURVEY SETUP

Basics to Branching Logic in Self-Administered Online Surveys (Chapter 1)

Essentially, the "branching logic" feature enables survey developers to create one survey and deploy it in different ways to different respondents; this enables survey developers to create one survey with variant question elicitations among different respondents, based on a wide variety of variables. This work provides a basic overview of some common types of branching logic in self-administered online survey design, development, and deployment, and highlights some considerations in effective branching logic and some precautions related to survey taker trajectories and experiences, proper survey setups for desired data collection and data analysis, survey pilot testing, and other aspects.

Setting Up an Online Survey Instrument for Effective Quantitative Cross Tabulation Analysis (Chapter 2)

The building of an online survey instrument involves sophisticated understandings of the research context, research design, research questions, and other elements. A lesser observed need is to consider what types of data analytics will be applied to the findings. With beginning-to-end online survey research suites, it becomes all the more necessary to think through the process from beginning to end in order to create an instrument that achieves all the necessary aims of the research. After all, improper online survey instrument designs will result in makework when it comes time to analyze data and will foreclose on particular data analytics opportunities. (Such instruments also will not have second or third uses after the first one-off.) This work explores how to build an effective online survey instrument to enable a quantitative cross tabulation analysis with the built-in analysis Qualtrics.

SECTION 2: IN-DEPTH DATA ELICITATIONS

Designing, Deploying, and Evaluating Open-Access Online Delphi Studies (Chapter 3)

This chapter describes the work of creating multimodal Open-Access Online Delphi Studies (OAODS). These are Electronic Delphi Studies that do not begin with an invited group of identified experts to seat a Delphi panel but rather with self-identified domain-specific authorities active on the Social Web, with post-data-collection vetting of the participants (when knowable) and their responses. This work explores how to design such instruments with efficacy and nuance, and built-in tests of respondent expertise...and fraud detection...and further, how to test such instruments for efficacy, reliability, and validity, while using some of the latest features available in online survey research platforms. The platform used in this work is the Qualtrics Research Suite.

Conducting a Basic Self-Explicated Conjoint Analysis Online With Qualtrics® (Chapter 4)

A recent feature in the Qualtrics® Research Core Platform 2018 (or Qualtrics Research Suite) is a basic self-explicated conjoint analysis, which is a research method to understand respondent preferences in a real-world context with limited available features and selection tradeoffs at respective price points. This chapter will introduce the basic self-explicated conjoint analysis tool and how to design questions for this, how to deploy the conjoint analysis (as either part of a larger survey or as a stand-alone survey), and how to analyze and use the resulting data. This chapter will describe the assertability of the findings based on the back-end factorial statistical analysis and suggest ways to explore beyond the initial conjoint analysis.

Setting Up Education-Based "Crosswalk Analyses" on an Online Survey Platform (Chapter 5)

Practically, crosswalk analyses in education may be used to identify gaps for decision making and program planning, enable cross-system comparisons, promote cross-disciplinary work, and others. Often, crosswalk analyses require the expertise of a cross-disciplinary and / or distributed team. Setting up a crosswalk analysis on an online survey platform stands to benefit this collaborative work in ways that are more powerful than a co-edited shared online file. This work describes some ways to set up education-based crosswalk analyses on an online survey platform and highlights some online survey features that can enhance this work.

Setting Up and Running a Q-Methodology Study in an Online Survey Research Suite (Chapter 6)

The q-method, as a graphic (visual) elicitation, has existed since the mid-1930s. Setting up a q-method, with q-sort capabilities, in an online survey platform, extends the reach of this method, even as data has to be processed in a quantitative data analytics suite. This work describes the setting up of a visual q-sort and the related debriefing on the Qualtrics Research Suite. The available data may be extracted and analyzed in a basic statistical analysis tool for factors and preference clusters.

SECTION 3: ANALYZING ONLINE SURVEY DATA

Using Computational Text Analysis to Explore Open-Ended Survey Question Responses (Chapter 7)

To capture a broader range of data than close-ended questions (often defined and delimited by the survey instrument designer), open-ended questions, such as text-based elicitations (and file-upload options for still imagery, audio, video, and other contents), are becoming more common because of the wide availability of computational text analysis, both within online survey tools and in external software applications. These computational text analysis tools—some online, some offline—make it easier to capture reproducible insights with qualitative data. This chapter explores some analytical capabilities, in matrix queries, theme extraction (topic modeling), sentiment analysis, cluster analysis (concept mapping), network text structures, qualitative cross-tabulation analysis, manual coding to automated coding, linguistic analysis, psychometrics, stylometry, network analysis, and others, as applied to open-ended questions from online surveys (and combined with human close reading).

Applying Qualitative Matrix Coding Queries and Qualitative Crosstab Matrices for Explorations of Online Survey Data (Chapter 8)

Two computation-enabled matrix-based analytics techniques have become more available for the analysis of text data, including from online surveys. These two approaches are (1) the qualitative matrix coding query and (2) the qualitative crosstab matrix, both in NVivo 12 Plus. The first approach enables insights about the coding applied to qualitative data, and the second enables the identification of data patterns based on case (ego or entity) attributes of survey respondents. The data analytics software has integrations with multiple online survey platforms (Qualtrics and Survey Monkey currently), and the automated coding of the data from these respective platforms and other software features enable powerful data analytics. This chapter provides insights as to some of what may be discoverable using both matrix-based techniques as applied to online survey data.

It is assumed that the readers of this text have basic foundational knowledge of survey design, including sampling methodologies, some basic statistics, and a strong foundation in human subjects research ethics and necessary human protections and data privacy protections, among others. It is beyond the purview of this work to cover the fundamentals. Also, as to the history of surveys, the first questionnaire was deployed by the Statistical Society of London in 1838 (Gault, 1907), and the first censuses are mentioned from Biblical times. There are excellent published works available on basic survey design methodologies (with complex decision-making and design tradeoffs) and histories of survey use to understand human subjectivities. Many contemporaneous works address issues of shoring up survey design and deployment precision, with proper population sampling (and addressing non-response biases), minimization of error biases, survey sequencing and randomization, and data analytics. In the space, researchers are continuously exploring novel survey research approaches. This is a dynamic space even as some question whether surveys are relevant anymore given the drop in response rates (Miller, 2017).

I hope that this work helps inspire others' research and that these may extend the uses of the online survey research suites available in the world today.

Shalin Hai-Jew
Kansas State University, USA
March 2019

REFERENCES

Gault, R. H. (1907). A History of the Questionnaire Method of Research in Psychology. *The Pedagogical Seminary*, *14*(3), 366–383. doi:10.1080/08919402.1907.10532551

Miller, P. V. (2017). Is there a future for surveys? *Public Opinion Quarterly*, *81*(S1), 205–212. doi:10.1093/poq/nfx008

Acknowledgment

Thanks to Jan Travers, Director of Intellectual Property and Contracts, at IGI Global, for her flexibility in adjusting to a changing book editing environment. Thanks to Jordan Tepper, Development Coordinator at IGI Global, Mike Brehm, Assistant Production Editor at IGI Global, and all the other excellent and supportive staff at IGI Global, for helping this book come to fruition. Thanks also to the two anonymous reviewers of the manuscript for their excellent suggestions.

Section 1
Online Survey Setup

Chapter 1
Basics to Branching Logic in Self-Administered Online Surveys

ABSTRACT

Essentially, the "branching logic" feature enables survey developers to create one survey and deploy it in different ways to different respondents; this enables survey developers to create one survey with variant question elicitations among different respondents, based on a wide variety of variables. This chapter provides a basic overview of some common types of branching logic in self-administered online survey design, development, and deployment, and highlights some considerations in effective branching logic and some precautions related to survey taker trajectories and experiences, proper survey setups for desired data collection and data analysis, survey pilot testing, and other aspects.

INTRODUCTION

Online survey systems have expanded the reach of many researchers who engage with people—their perceptions, their experiences, their attitudes, their preferences, their thinking—through a wide range of enablements:

- geographical distributions of respondents
- integrations with social media platforms for crowd-sourcing "human intelligence"

DOI: 10.4018/978-1-5225-8563-3.ch001

- uses of digital resources (text, audio, video, slideshows, simulations, multimodal objects, and others) to elicit questions
- types of data collected (closed-ended questions, open-ended questions, file upload question types, screen captures, audio collection, video collection, and others)
- ability to use high-level computer languages for scripted behaviors
- ability to set triggers for information collection and survey monitoring
- security features to try to prevent malicious responses and "ballot box stuffing"
- delivery on a variety of digital devices, operating systems, web browsers, and applications
- respondent behavior tracking (on the survey)
- efficient digital data collection
- coding and recoding of values based on particular closed-ended question responses
- scoring to enable totaling of "performance" by survey respondents
- built-in data analytics (textual, cross-tabulation analyses, variable creation),
- efficiencies of automation, and much more.

Of the many advanced affordances and enablements of online survey systems, one of the most important capabilities affects possible (1) data collection in self-administered surveys for the researcher and (2) the self-administered survey experience for the respondent: branching logic.

Branching logic enables survey developers to create one survey to capture data from a wide variety of respondents. "Branching logic," in the online survey context, refers to conditionals that determine the paths of respective survey respondents. [Other tools enable survey takers of the same survey to have different experiences. These include piped text for unique information to be used in salutations and prompts and directions and questions. There is "display logic," which enables some survey respondents to see some contents—questions, sections of questions (blocks), and other contents—but others not. From the survey respondent side, branching logic enables a different range of customized survey experiences. (Table 1)

Table 1. Some enablements of branching logic for survey developers and researchers... and survey respondents

Survey Developers and Researchers	Branching Logic	Survey Respondents
• Wide range of data collection		• Customized survey experiences

To better understand how branching may work, this chapter offers an abstract view of how branching is applied in academic research contexts, to provide a sense of the possibilities for new users of this feature. This work is built off of years of experiences using the Qualtrics™ Research Suite in a higher education context. [Online surveys have come a long way from when researchers had to use "canned" surveys or build their own websites using webpage-building tools. (Gordon & McNew, 2008)]

REVIEW OF THE LITERATURE

Online survey systems have already been in use for some three decades. They were harnessed for use in computer-aided personal interviewing (CAPI) since the 1990s (Leisher, 2014). Some works have focused on the enhanced efficiencies of replacing paper surveys with online ones. These can limit "methodological difficulties that prevented generation of the necessary evidence" such as "by adding automating controls and skip or branching logic" (Touvier, Méjean, Kesse-Guyot, Pollet, Malon, Castetbon, & Hercberg, 2010, p. 288). Conditional branching is more efficient in electronic automatic branching as compared to paper surveys and much less onerous than directing respondents in paper surveys to move to particular segments based on their responses (Vergnaud, Touvier, Méjean, Kesse-Guyot, Pollet, Malon, Castetbon, & Hercberg, 2011, p. 409).

Their capabilities have grown over the years, and while the affordances work well when the systems are used correctly, the skills needed to use the systems effectively require a fair amount of training and sometimes some scripting know-how. The learning curve may be fairly steep. There is the sense that "developing web based surveys can be extremely high when questions are complex (eg., when they entail branching logic), and when graphics, video, and audio are included" (Carbonaro, Bainbridge, & Wolodko, 2002, p. 276). Further, such online surveys also require prototyping before use with the target survey respondents. One research team observes the criticality of proper survey design—the question design, the overall questionnaire structure, and "guidelines for the process of testing questionnaires formatively, as a means to prototype and improve the questionnaires before going live in a full-scale survey" (Sjöström, Rahman, Rafiq, Lochan, & Ågerfalk, 2013, p. 511).

At a simple level, branching logic enables respondents not to have to see the full range of options if the questions do not directly pertain to them (Wasson, MacKenzie, & Hall, 2007). Cross-cultural online surveys have been used to localize surveys to target respondents based on the respondents' cultural backgrounds (Walsh, Nurkka, Koponen, Varsaluoma, Kujala, & Belt, 2011; Walsh, Petrie, & Zhang, 2015). The ability to "version" different forms of an online survey speaks to another application of branching logic.

Some online surveys use gamification features to make surveys more interesting and engaging for respondents (Harms, Wimmer, Kappel, & Grechenig, 2014).

With the popularity of crowd-sourced surveying, with respondents taking surveys for micropayments, researchers employ various means to protect against malicious respondents (Gadiraju, Kawase, Dietze, & Demartini, 2015). Online survey systems have security features to prevent scripted agent or robot access to surveys, to hide surveys from web search engine "spiders," to prevent multiple access to a survey from a particular Internet Protocol address, and other protections.

Many systems enable the logging of respondent behaviors in the online survey, which may inform on the survey design and on the respondents themselves (Sjöström, Rahman, Rafiq, Lochan, & Ågerfalk, 2013). (The modern equivalent of this involves "hidden questions" that may monitor how long respondents take to answer a particular question or group of questions or survey. There are other hidden questions that capture other respondent behavioral data of interest, such as when they drop out of a survey, how they engage with particular questions in a survey, and so on. These data may be used for item analysis and survey analysis, among other applications.)

Finally, even though one online survey may be used to collect data from large disparate groups of people, it is possible to move people from one survey to another invisibly, in an experience that may seem all of a piece…or to conduct longitudinal research over multiple years…using one online survey system and interlinked surveys. Hyperlinks are "loosely defined as branching mechanisms that reference other web pages both inside and outside the web page" (Postoaca, 2006, p. 84), and this linking capability may be used creatively in online survey research.

BASICS TO THE LOGIC OF BRANCHING IN AN ONLINE SURVEY

A basic summary of steps required to create and deploy a research survey is described in Figure 1. This is conceptualized as including nine basic steps: Research Design (1), Survey Design (2), Survey Development (with requisite testing) (3), Deployment (with light monitoring) (4), Data Collection (5), Data Cleaning (6), Data Analysis (7), Write-up (8), and Presentation (09). This process is depicted as somewhat linear, but the understanding is that this process can be quite recursive depending on work needs. Also, in Step 3, alpha testing, beta testing, instrument construct validity, instrument reliability, and revision…are a part of the development cycle. This extended cycle is followed usually only for high-end grant-funded projects. In many cases, research surveys may garner less attention in terms of rigor.

Figure 1. A typical sequence of online survey design, development, testing, and deployment (in academia)

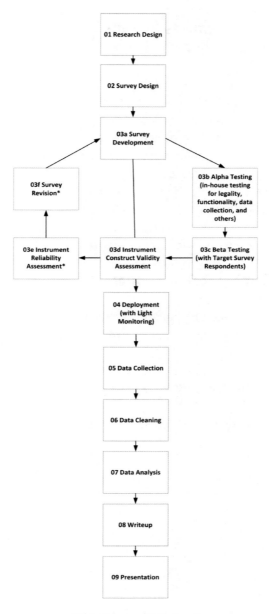

A Typical Sequence of Online Survey
Design, Development, Testing, and Deployment
(in Academia)

The * in Step 03e and 03f indicates that that testing is more typical for
high-end well-funded academic survey instruments.

Given the attention testing has in the sequence, some observations will be made after the branching is addressed

Some Branching Junctures in Self-Administered Online Surveys

So what are some branching junctures in self-administered online surveys? One common one is by validation or pre-screening based on any number of criteria. (Figure 2) One common one is "informed consent," which the survey respondent has to read and indicate that he or she has understood and has legal standing to accept. Another type of authentication may be workplace membership, such as through the Authenticator validation by comparison against a contact list or security middleware against a database of identities. Technologically, there may be other types of validation and combinations of validations: through signature, password, reverse Turing (non-bot human test) test, originating IP address, and others. These validations may be applied in various layers and in various parts of a survey.

Needs of the Survey Respondents

Several other types of branching junctures involve the respective actual and / or felt needs of the survey respondents. Perhaps the respondents have particular accessibility accommodations (Figure 3).

Preferences of the Survey Respondents

Perhaps there are preferences, such as in cross-cultural surveys and mass-scale ones (Figure 4).

Figure 2. Branching by validation / pre-screening

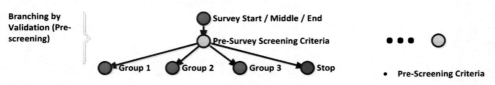

Branching by Validation / Pre-Screening

Figure 3. Branching by accessibility needs

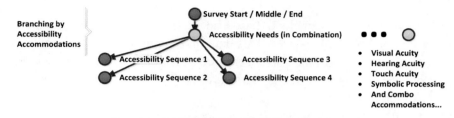

Branching by Accessibility Needs (incl. Preferences)

Figure 4. Branching by language preference(s) and / or cultural preference(s)

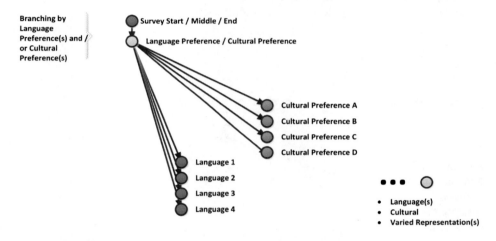

Branching by Language Preference(s) and / or Cultural Preference(s)

Figure 5. Branching by demographics or other group membership features (including thin slicing)

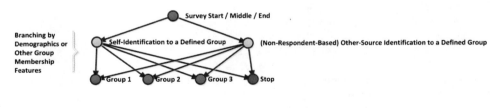

- Demographic (any of a variety of dimensions like age, class, education, gender, and / or others)
- Membership Type
- Role Type
- Technology Use / Device Use
- Application Use
- Location, or Other

- Thin Slicing (by Mix of Identity Requirements)

Branching by Demographics or Other Group Membership Features (including Thin Slicing)

Branching by Respondent Features

There can be branching junctures based on survey respondent demographics or other group membership features. This data may come from the respondent, or it may come from another data source. (Figure 5) Membership may be understood at a broad-scale or zoomed-out or coarse level, or it may be understood at a meso-scale level, or at a micro-scale or zoomed-in or granular level. For example, it is possible to design questions just for a particular group of a particular age, ethnic background, class level, and geographical location—through thin slicing and fairly simple scripting. As long as the data is available to the system, it is possible to filter and split the data in particular ways and then enable the visibility of the unique target questions through display logic or branching logic.

Figure 6. Branching by respondent choices, discretion, and will

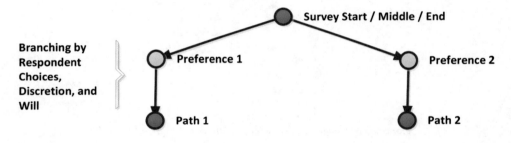

- Personal Taste (including tacit)
- Personal Preference (including tacit)
- Other

  FOR
- Respondent Motivation
- Respondent Pleasure
- Respondent Satisfaction
- Respondent Agency and Empowerment

Branching by Respondent Choices, Discretion, and Will

Branching by Respondent Choices, Discretion, and Will

If it is important to motivate survey respondent participation (and it is), then it may be helpful to empower them to make choices about what they want to respond to, at least in some surveys. Respondent agency may support their motivation to engage and to share. (Figure 6). The path respondents choice enables other data points.

Branching by Respondent Responses and Performance

There can be branching junctures based on respondent responses (say, to a particular question) or to their performance in a block or a series of questions. (Figure 7)

Branching by Research Design Needs

The first step of the survey design sequence in Figure 1 pointed to the Research Design. The design of the research informs the design of the survey instrument and the standards it must be designed to. (Figure 8) If there are quotas that need to be

Figure 7. Branching by responses and /or performance

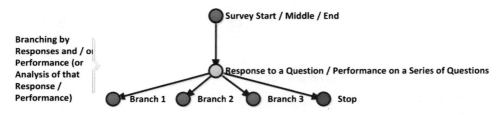

- **Expressed Opinion / Sentiment**
- **Demonstrated Awareness, Capability, Skill, Knowledge, or Ability**
- **Experience**
- **Performance (including Scored Cumulative Performances)**
- **(Scored) Personality Trait**
- **Demonstrated Skill**
- **Latent Features**
- **Expressed Interest(s), or Other**

  FOR
  - **Elaboratory Elicitation**
  - **Respondent Pooling for Additional Survey Tracks**

Branching by Responses and / or Performance

Figure 8. Branching by research design needs

Branching by Research Design Needs (such as Pre-Set Quotas or Pre-Set Memberships, and others)

Survey Start / Middle / End

Pre-established Quota / Limit

Group 1   Group 2   Group 3   Stop

• • • ○

- Quotas
- Memberships, and others

Some Possible Divergent Survey Respondent Experiences

Sequences
- Question
- Block / Sequence
- New Survey / Sequence
- Skip Logic
- Display Logic
- Conclusion / Bye

Customized (Piped) Data
- Dynamic Data
- Pre-designed Messaging or Emails

Some Sample Versioned Sequences
- Select Language Sequence
- Presentational Variance (for specialized accessibility)

Some Possible Divergent Survey Creator Options

New Groups
- New Panels / Groups

Data
- User-grouped Data
- Data Extractions
- More Granular Data for Data Analytics (More Queryable)

- Class   Gender   Mobile Device
- Geolocation   Some Experiential Descriptor
- Sentiment   Skill   Membership

Branching by Research Design Needs

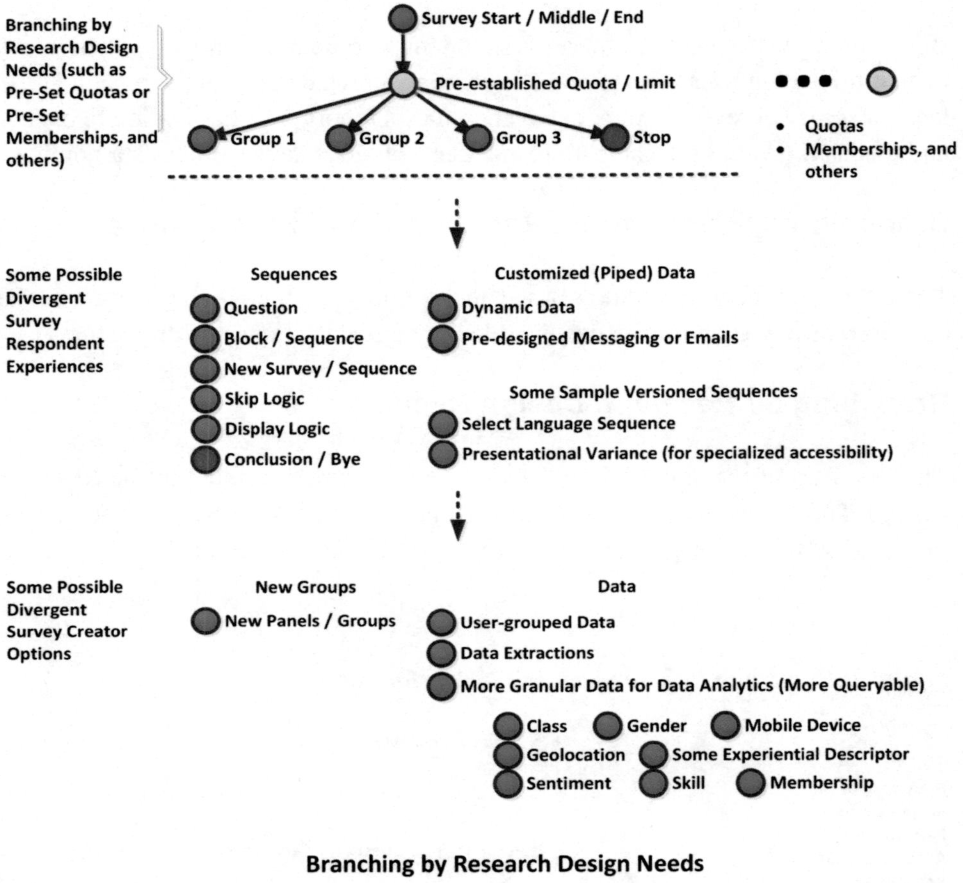

met or certain ways to separate out the survey respondent population, then those rules may be built into an online survey.

Branching to Ensure Anonymized Data

A common branching logic move at the end of a survey is to branch respondents off who want to share their contact information for some follow-on service, information, resource…or random prize draw (part of the survey response incentive, sometimes). The idea is to separate the respondents' data in the prior survey from his or her personally identifiable information (PII). Professional researchers do their best to control their own subjective influences on the research work. (Depending on the

Figure 9. Branching to ensure anonymized data

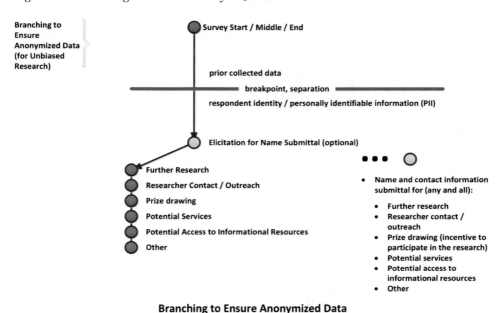

Branching to Ensure Anonymized Data

density of responses, time stamps may be used to reidentify survey respondents. This would require small effort to achieve.) (Figure 9)

There are certainly other types of general branching junctures, but these are some of the more common ones. Finally, these junctures generally appear in certain points in the sequence of a survey to achieve the respective objectives. (Figure 10) For example, no survey respondent should be able to sign up for a randomized prize drawing until they have actually done the survey to satisfaction (with some forced response questions or some auto-validation of sufficient contents in an open-ended text response question, for example). In typical surveys, there may be a number of needs, and there may be multiple designed branching junctures. This aspect is indicated by having a potential for multiple start points and multiple end points in Figure 10.

TESTING THE SURVEY FOR SOME QUALITY STANDARDS

Figure 1 provided a simplified sequence of work required to design and develop a research survey (using branching logic, potentially). Step 3 referred to various types of testing: alpha, beta, construct validity, and reliability. Each of those will require

Figure 10. Some typical placements of branching junctures in survey flows

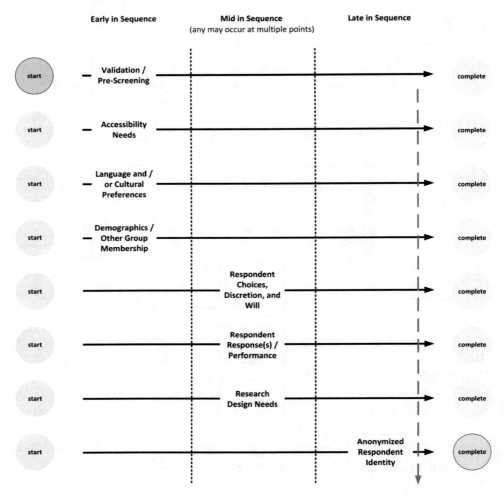

Some Typical Placements of Branching Junctures in Survey Flows

plenty of work to explain. However, it would be helpful to identify a few important aspects of survey design that are practically relevant.

A Non-Biased Survey Instrument: A number of studies have shown how survey respondents may be sensitive to how questions are asked, the sequence of elicitations, the framing of the questions, the priming based on even something as simple as the order of a Likert scale. The gold standard of survey research is to sample randomly and to sufficient numbers of respondents for statistical power. No part of the survey should introduce bias. None of the questions should be leading ones. Closed-answered questions need to apply boundary logics appropriately and not force responses which are inaccurate to the respondent. Opt-outs should be designed into closed-answered questions. The construct validity of the reliability of others' instruments do not apply when only segments have been borrowed, either.

Legal Fundamentals: Online surveys are deployed in a legal context. First, survey participants' well-being has to be protected. This is enforced in part through human subjects review oversight. Survey participants have to be given sufficient information about the study and how their data will be used, and they have to give their informed consent early on in a survey. The respondent has to have legal standard to sign their consent. Also, human subjects' private data should be protected and carefully held for a number of years after the end of the research study. The survey instruments should also be original, and they should not borrow liberally (or at all) from others' instruments without permission. Online surveys should not contravene others' intellectual property rights. Online surveys should also be accessible, based on web accessibility standards. One other note: Anything illegally attained cannot be legally used.

Technological Functioning: Online surveys function in complex environments, and the setting in one area may contravene that in another. In terms of branching logic, changes in one area may have repercussions on another. Building a clean survey that functions as desired requires very close attention to details…and getting the fundamentals right.

Survey Respondent Experiential Trajectories: When testing, it is important to test for survey respondent fatigue. While the survey design team is familiar with the topic, respondents may be less familiar, or they may not be in the mindset of addressing the questions. They may experience respondent fatigue much faster than the design team may have anticipated. When respondents answer from tiredness, that will likely harm the quality of their responses.

Branching Logic and Data: The way the data are collected from branches often means a lack of comparability across groups taking different paths. To compare their responses, it is necessary for the researchers to be able to re-collate the data in a meaningful and accurate way. (In some cases, the way the data is reported out in the data table makes it difficult or impossible to compare.) If the output data is not tested prior to launch, then the online survey setup may end up creating a lot of make-work. (Also, if the responses to various close-ended questions are coded at certain values, they should be coded the same way across all the data.) In some cases, Embedded Data variables need to be set up to capture relevant data for analysis. If randomizers are used to create particular questions, Embedded Data is needed to capture the output numbers for each respondent, for example. Or if a lot of text entry questions are used and then referred to in subsequent questions (using Loop & Merge), then Embedded Data variables are needed to log the respective text entries

13

used by the respondent. It is wholly possible for a survey to look like it makes sense on the survey respondent side…and for the survey designer to think everything looks right…but to have the data garbled and irretrievable for meaningful analysis.

Beyond these basics, there are other requirements for effective online survey usage for research. For example, the efficacy of the surveys as research instruments (with construct validity, with reliability, and other features) will be important if the findings are to be treated with confidence, and if the instruments will be re-used in other research contexts by other researchers.

Also, in terms of transferability, online surveys vary in terms of how portable they are. In the Qualtrics Research Suite, it is possible to download surveys as .qsf (Qualtrics Survey Format) files. These may be re-uploaded into other Qualtrics instances and deployed there with most (or all) of the back-end scripting intact. It is possible to export surveys as Word files, but the nuances of the scripting are not as obvious, and some of the branching may be un-described and un-captured. The hosted survey system uses a basic top-to-bottom sequence of "blocks" to describe the branching logic, and the more complex the branching is, the easier it may be to misconstrue the sequences. If handoffs are possible, it may be beneficial to have a fully explicated branching logic "tree" that shows every juncture and that has labeled blocks and nodes to coincide with the respective question blocks and questions. (Auto-numbering the finalized survey first would be helpful. Otherwise, the default question numbering in Qualtrics is based on when questions are created.)

DISCUSSIONS

This work has proposed a number of branching logic junctures in a typical survey. This work suggests that in the early sequence, branching logic may be applied for the following: validation / pre-screening, accessibility needs, language and / or cultural preferences, demographics and other types of group membership. In the mid-in-survey sequence, there may be branches for respondent choice, discretion, and will; response / performance, and research needs. Then, in the late part of the survey sequence, there may be branching to anonymize respondent identities (but still enable them to sign up for more resources or incentive prize drawings by contactable name and information).

FUTURE RESEARCH DIRECTIONS

What are some approaches to build on this work? It may help to identify other branching junctures in self-administered online surveys. After all, this initial approach is not likely comprehensive.

What about branching logic in other-administered online surveys? Face-to-face interviews using online survey systems? In research based on human interactions, the branching logic may manifest differently and deal with junctures that are more complex than anticipated in self-administered online surveys.

Are there particular cases of self-administered online surveys using branching logic and effective outcomes there? Particular cases often raise insights not anticipated in a generalist approach (taken in this chapter).

Also, there may be ways to learn from the various trajectories, timings in the trajectories, and revelatory insights from the respective decision junctures in self-administered online surveys. Perhaps these approaches to mining data may be explored.

CONCLUSION

"Branching logic" is one of many enablements in state-of-the-art online survey systems, and its use can be harnessed for powerful research outcomes in self-administered online surveys. This work provides a basic introduction to branching logic, which has little guidance otherwise in the research literature.

REFERENCES

Carbonaro, M., Bainbridge, J., & Wolodko, B. (2002). Using Internet surveys to gather research data from teachers: Trials and tribulations. *Australian Journal of Educational Technology*, *18*(3), 275–292.

Gadiraju, U., Kawase, R., Dietze, S., & Demartini, G. (2015). Understanding malicious behavior in crowdsourcing platforms: The case of online surveys. *Proceedings of CHI 2015*, 1631 – 1640.

Gordon, J. S., & McNew, R. (2008). Developing the online survey. *The Nursing Clinics of North America*, *43*(4), 605–619. doi:10.1016/j.cnur.2008.06.011 PMID:18940417

Harms, J., Wimmer, C., Kappel, K., & Grechenig, T. (2014). Gamification of online surveys: Conceptual foundations and a design process based on the MDA framework. *Proceedings of NordiCHI'14*, 565 – 568.

Leisher, C. (2014). A comparison of tablet-based and paper-based survey data collection in conservation projects. *Social Sciences*, *3*(2), 264–271. doi:10.3390ocsci3020264

Postoaca, A. (2006). Launching the bottle: The rhetoric of the online researcher. *The Anonymous Elect: Market Research through Online Access Panels*, 67-107.

Sjöström, J., Rahman, M. H., Rafiq, A., Lochan, R., & Ågerfalk, P. J. (2013). Respondent behavior logging: An opportunity for online survey design. In *DESRIST 2013, LNCS 7939, 511 – 518*. doi:10.1007/978-3-642-38827-9_44

Touvier, M., Méjean, C., Kesse-Guyot, E., Pollet, C., Malon, A., Castetbon, K., & Hercberg, S. (2010). Comparison between web-based and paper versions of a self-administered anthropometric questionnaire. *European Journal of Epidemiology*, *25*(5), 287–296. doi:10.100710654-010-9433-9 PMID:20191377

Vergnaud, A.-C., Touvier, M., Méjean, C., Kesse-Guyot, E., Pollet, C., Malon, A., ... Hercberg, S. (2011). Agreement between web-based and paper versions of a socio-demographic questionnaire in the NutriNet-Santé study. *International Journal of Public Health*, *56*(4), 407–417. doi:10.100700038-011-0257-5 PMID:21538094

Walsh, T., Nurkka, P., Koponen, T., Varsaluoma, J., Kujala, S., & Belt, S. (2011). Collecting cross-cultural user data with internationalized storyboard survey. *Proceedings of OZCHI '11*, 301 – 310. 10.1145/2071536.2071584

Walsh, T., Petrie, H., & Zhang, A. (2015). Localization of storyboards for cross-cultural user studies. *The 14ᵗʰ International Conference on Mobile and Ubiquitous Multimedia (MUM 2015)*, 200 – 209. 10.1145/2836041.2836061

Wasson, J. H., MacKenzie, T. A., & Hall, M. (2007). Patients use an internet technology to report when things go wrong. Error Management. *Quality & Safety in Health Care*, *16*(3), 213–215. doi:10.1136/qshc.2006.019810 PMID:17545349

KEY TERMS AND DEFINITIONS

Branching Logic: Conditionals that determine the differentiated sequential paths of different survey respondents.

Display Logic: Conditionals that determine whether particular survey respondents are able to view particular blocks or questions (or other parts of an online survey).

Chapter 2
Setting Up an Online Survey Instrument for Effective Quantitative Cross-Tabulation Analysis

ABSTRACT

The building of an online survey instrument involves sophisticated understandings of the research context, research design, research questions, and other elements. A lesser observed need is to consider what types of data analytics will be applied to the findings. With beginning-to-end online survey research suites, it becomes all the more necessary to think through the process from beginning to end in order to create an instrument that achieves all the necessary aims of the research. After all, improper online survey instrument designs will result in makework when it comes time to analyze data and will foreclose on particular data analytics opportunities. (Such instruments also will not have second or third uses after the first one-off.) This chapter explores how to build an effective online survey instrument to enable a quantitative cross tabulation analysis with the built-in analysis Qualtrics.

INTRODUCTION

A basic cross tabulation analysis (aka "contingency table") is comprised of a data table or matrix in which variables are placed in the column headers and the row headers, and the corresponding intersecting values for those variables are in the respective column and row cells. These tables represent a joint frequency distribution,

DOI: 10.4018/978-1-5225-8563-3.ch002

and these "multi-dimensional table(s) (are) used to compare the correlation between two variables (Cross-Tabulation Analysis, 2011, as cited in Lee, Aug. 15, 2015, p. 28) at a time, in a dyadic way. Even two variables being compared may be fairly complex, with scale values in some cases, and other related observations. Multiple variables may be explored at a time in a cross tabulation analysis. At the most basic, a cross tabulation analysis table contains at least two variables, in a 2x2 table. This may be seen in the bolded section at the top left of Table 1.

In qualitative cross tabulation analyses, the intersecting cells may be comprised of frequency counts, common shared terms (words from the respective text sets), or other measures. Some qualitative cross tabulation analyses enable clustering of textual responses to survey (interview, focus group, and others) data by demographic features, responses to particular questions (all those who expressed something), and others.

In a quantitative cross tabulation analysis, the respective intersecting or crossover cells (where the row and column intersect) usually contain a percentage calculation from the observed values / expected values. The "observed values" are the data collected from the research. The "expected values" are calculated based on the potential ranges of values given the numbers of cells (based on the available numbers of variables). The "degrees of freedom" (df) in the construct is calculated based on the number of variables minus one (n – 1). The chi-squared calculation is based off of an expected chi-squared distribution that would exist if the null hypothesis is true (only random chance is acting on the observed data and not some other influence). This chi-squared calculation is applied to each cell.

The p-value (probability value) is a threshold value at which the null hypothesis may be rejected, usually at $\leq$ .05 or $\leq$ .01; the lower the p-value, the rarer the observed data has to be before the null hypothesis may be rejected. A p-value (or "alpha value") of < .05 means that the observed results may fall on either end of the tails of the bell curve distribution at .025 at either end (extreme standard deviations from the center), and a p-value of < .01 means that the observed results may fall on either end of the tails at .005. (The assumption of a normal bell curve distribution

Table 1. Depiction of a basic cross tabulation analysis table

applies to some data but not necessarily to categorical data analyzed using a cross tabulation analysis, with the chi-squared statistic.) The calculations in each cell point to possible (non)associations between each pairing (of the variables in the particular row/stub and the column/banner header). In some research, the rows and the columns may contain a mix of variables; in others, one contains the independent variable(s) and the other the dependent variable(s). [The independent variables (IVs) are theorized or hypothesized to have effects on the dependent variables (DVs). The dependent variables are the ones being tested or explored in research.]

Some online survey research suites, like Qualtrics, enable an end-to-end process, including built-in cross tabulation analysis. While many survey designers and researchers do not consider how they will analyze the data from a survey until the data have been collected, it is important to consider requirements for cross tabulation-based data analytics, so that the way the data is collected does not forestall usage of this technique. While values for responses may be coded/recoded before the data download, if the data are collected inappropriately early on, there are some issues that cannot be corrected even with post-collection data cleaning, recoding, or other data processing. On Qualtrics, "only multiple choice questions, matrix questions, and embedded data can be added to a Cross Tabulation" (Qualtrics research suite software).

This work explores some basic effective practices for building online surveys with cross tabulation analysis in mind.

REVIEW OF THE LITERATURE

The earliest cross tabulation analysis was proposed by Karl Pearson in "On the Theory of Contingency and its Relation to Association and Normal Correlation" in *Drapers' Company Research Memoirs Biometric Series* (1904) ("Contingency table," Dec. 3, 2018). [This is the Pearson in the Pearson's Chi-Square.] Cross tabulations are "a joint frequency distribution of cases based on two or more categorical variables" (Michael, 2001). Categorical or nominal variables are those with categories or classifications; they are generally without a numeric value. For example, the geographical location of a person's home may be a categorical variable (even as the various locations may be labeled / rendered with numeric labels: Region 1, Region 2, etc.). By contrast, a person's age may be conceptualized as a continuous variable, which may be represented numerically. Cell data in a cross tabulation analysis may involve binary or dichotomous cell data (including yes or no, present or not-present), frequency cell data (counts of occurrences in various categories or classes), content data (text from open-ended questions), and others (Hai-Jew, Fall 2016 – Winter 2017).

Given the computational complexity of cross tabulation analyses, most of these are not manually calculated but achieved through computers. (There are online chi-squared tables for usage for those who want to compute "by hand" with handheld or online calculators.) Cross tabulation analyses are usually conducted using quantitative data analytics software packages because these would be unwieldy to do by hand. For online surveys, the data is exported, cleaned, and run through the respective programs. One popular package for analyzing Qualtrics research data is IBM's Statistical Package for Social Sciences (SPSS) (Small, Porterfield, & Gordon, 2015), and there are others like SAS and R and Python. Certainly, others also export the online survey data to conduct double checks on the cross tabulation analysis from the extracted data in Qualtrics using additional software tools (Farkas, Hinchliffe, & Houk, March 2015, p. 157).

A cross tabulation analysis may be based on hypotheses in a research study (Are there any associations between the independent and dependent variables? Is there evidence for a particular hypothesis?). Or it may be exploratory (Are there any associations between the variables in the study?), with post-hoc hypothesizing (after the data has been collected and analyzed).

Cross tabulation analyses may be run without the finding that there are any statistically significant associations between variables. And even when there are, there may be additional caveating based on the available information and the degrees of freedom. (Anomalies to numeric ranges serve as red flags that the underlying assumptions of the research approach may not be valid.) Or, even if there are statistically significant associations between variables, the association may not be particularly relevant or novel or unknown (in prior research).

BUILDING AN INTEGRATED SURVEY FOR ONLINE CROSS TABULATION ANALYSIS

There is plenty of research about how to set up online survey instruments in the most research-effective ways. The instruments should be supported by the research literature and proper theorizing. The questions should be neutrally phrased and non-leading and non-biasing. The survey respondents should be randomly selected for representativeness. The survey experience should not lead to respondent fatigue, which can bias responses. The survey respondents also should have the knowledge in order to be able to respond to particular questions, or they should be able to opt-out of what they cannot respond to. The questions should achieve "saturation" or coverage of the constructs of interest. The research should adhere to human subjects review and provide informed consent to the survey respondents. The respondents (and humanity) should ultimately benefit from the research. Those are some basics.

Figure 1 suggests that online survey instruments do not exist in isolation but are a part of a research design and research and world context. The prior steps leading up to the instrument design inform it as well as the follow-on steps. Throughout the focus is on operationalizing constructs and abstract ideas into something observable and trustworthy. This research here focuses on Step 4 and Step 8a.

Similarly, there are some basic best practices that can benefit setting up an online survey instrument for cross tabulation analyses in particular. To run an effective cross tabulation analysis from survey data, several things are needed.

- **Single-Barreled Variables (Questions):** First, the respective survey questions need to be single-barreled. They should represent one variable in one dimension. Anything that is double-barreled or multi-barreled will introduce noise into the data and make it unclear what the survey respondent was responding to when indicating a particular response to the particular question. This single-barreled-ness is a basic requirement in survey research design, but it is one that is missed by researchers. (Single-barreled questions can be combined into compound variables later through various data cleaning methods, but a combined multi-barreled question cannot be decomposed to the constituent parts per se to understand the weighting of each element in the survey respondent's answer.)

Figure 1. Role of an online survey instrument in a research context

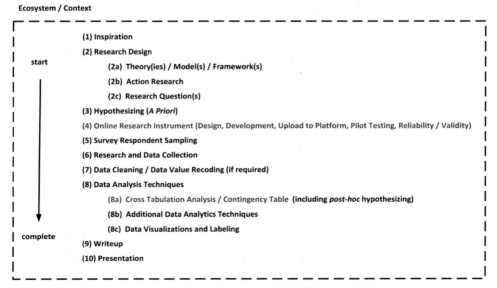

Ecosystem / Context

(1) Inspiration
(2) Research Design
  (2a) Theory(ies) / Model(s) / Framework(s)
  (2b) Action Research
  (2c) Research Question(s)
(3) Hypothesizing (*A Priori*)
(4) Online Research Instrument (Design, Development, Upload to Platform, Pilot Testing, Reliability / Validity)
(5) Survey Respondent Sampling
(6) Research and Data Collection
(7) Data Cleaning / Data Value Recoding (if required)
(8) Data Analysis Techniques
  (8a) Cross Tabulation Analysis / Contingency Table (including *post-hoc* hypothesizing)
  (8b) Additional Data Analytics Techniques
  (8c) Data Visualizations and Labeling
(9) Writeup
(10) Presentation

start

complete

Role of an Online Survey Instrument in a Research Context

- **Sufficient Variables for the Constructs:** The online survey should be constructed in way such that the variables support the respective constructs being studied (and these may be used to verify "construct validity" in a follow-on factor analysis and / or principal components analysis. If there are gaps, those will often show up in the factor analyses and the respective explanatory powers of the respective factors.)
- **Question Types, Answer Types, Answer Coding Values, and Export Data Value:** Next, the types of questions that enable cross tabulation analysis in Qualtrics are the following: multiple choice questions, matrix questions, and embedded data (captured variable information). To enhance the usability of such answers, the scalar responses have to be recoded to align with intensities, and text data have to be converted to numeric data (dummy variables)… for online data processing and for exporting for analyses in other software tools. Other data—such as text data from open-ended questions—may be run through qualitative data analytics software tools (like NVivo 12 Plus), but these will require additional skills and additional capabilities.
- *A Priori* **Hypothesizing**: It is generally good practice to do some preliminary work hypothesizing about what the research may found, document the hypotheses in contemporaneous ways, and then proceed with the research work.
- *Post Hoc* **Hypothesizing:** After the online survey data have been collected, then post hoc hypothesizing may be done once the results have come in. It is not ethical nor professional to engage in post hoc hypothesizing and then pretend that those hypotheses were done *a priori*. Also, it is important to avoid "data dredging," "data fishing," "data snooping," or "p-hacking" to suggest something is significant through any sort of manipulation instead of indicating an actual (real-world) underlying phenomenon or effect ("Data dredging," Nov. 29, 2018).
- **Sampling**: Who responds to a survey will affect the available data to some degree. How the respondents are identified and encouraged to participate will be important to the success of the online survey research.
- **Exploratory Analyses in Cross Tab Analyses:** In general, in structured research, cross tab analyses are set up in alignment with the *a priori* hypothesizing, the identified independent variables and dependent variables, for example. A more exploratory (zoomed-out) approach is to put up the respective variables in the study, see if there are statistically significant associations, and then re-run based on particular selected variables to see if there is still significance with lower degrees of freedom (fewer variables at play). Certainly, it would be important to explain the work sequences and purposes as well.

- **Validating Findings:** It would be helpful to test findings in other software data analytics tools outside of Qualtrics as well, not because there have been any problems found, but because having the data in another analytics tool enables a wide range of additional other analyses like factor analyses and different data visualizations. Data analytics software programs themselves may inspire thinking in new data analytics directions.
- **Complementary Data Analyses:** Also, the cross tabulation tables or matrices may be enhanced with additional other research. Open-ended questions from a survey that were not analyzed in the cross tabulation may do well being analyzed "manually" with a uniquely created or inherited codebook. Or the text data may be autocoded (topic modeling, sentiment analysis, and others). What may be applied will depend on the research, the research design, the domain, the research team's expertise, and other aspects.
- **Interpreting:** Then, a critical element involves looking at the statistically significant associations and to interpret what those could mean (while not confusing association or correlation with causation). It would be helpful to understand if there might be a "direction" to the variable relationship or association. Not all data patterns may be relevant. Still, discussing the findings and implications is important in research work. Also, for researchers, what is not seen may be as relevant as what is seen, so there should be sufficient exploratory depth applied to the cross tabulation analyses findings. Also, are there surprises or sharp differences or sharp similarities?
- **Planning for Follow-On Research**: In many ways, cross tabulation analyses are somewhat provisional. The findings may indicate associations between variables, that may suggest the need for additional research. If the cross tabulation analysis is solidly achieved, it can be the basis of more solid research in the future.

In some cases, cell data in cross tabulation analyses is suppressed in order to "mask" information for privacy protections and / or analytical needs. This cell data suppression capability does not seem to be included in Qualtrics.

DISCUSSION

Basically, a cross tabulation analysis involves the intersection of variables and looking to see if there are statistically significant intensifications of data in those overlaps (as compared to other variables). To effectively use the built-in cross tabulation analysis tool in the Qualtrics research suite, it helps to think about this data analytics method and the types of questions it can handle and build and test accordingly.

FUTURE RESEARCH DIRECTIONS

This short chapter only suggests some basic ideas for online survey design for cross tabulation analyses. Additional work in this area would benefit the field.

Qualtrics as a leading online survey / research platform enables other built-in data analytics methods, including text analysis (a feature in its early phases) and weighting of variables (for compound or composite variables).

This approach of designing and testing online survey instruments by first considering the likely forms of collected data and how the data will represent in the respective data analytics methods is not new, but it is not commonly practiced. There are a wide range of data analytics methods—manual and computational—that would bear analyzing for their implications on online survey design.

CONCLUSION

This brief work describes some approaches to designing an online survey instrument based on the needs of a cross tabulation analysis. Thinking about how survey data will be analyzed enhances survey design and development, and it can result in more useful data analysis.

REFERENCES

Chi-squared test. (2018, Nov. 13). In *Wikipedia*. Retrieved Jan. 7, 2019, from https://en.wikipedia.org/wiki/Chi-squared_test

Contingency table. (2018, Dec. 3). In *Wikipedia*. Retrieved Jan. 7, 2019, from https://en.wikipedia.org/wiki/Contingency_table

Data dredging. (2018, Nov. 29). In *Wikipedia*. Retrieved Jan. 7, 2019, from https://en.wikipedia.org/wiki/Data_dredging

Farkas, M. G., Hinchliffe, L. J., & Houk, A. H. (2015, March). Bridges and barriers: Factors influencing a culture of assessment in academic libraries. *College & Research Libraries*, 76(2), 150–169. doi:10.5860/crl.76.2.150

Hai-Jew, S. (2016). *Conducting a Cross Tabulation Analysis in the Qualtrics Research Suite*. Retrieved Jan. 7, 2019, from http://scalar.usc.edu/works/c2c-digital-magazine-fall-2016--winter-2017/conducting-a-cross-tabulation-analysis-qualtrics-research-suite

Lee, D. (2015, Aug. 15). *The effects of mobility on youth employment in the European Union: The Case of the Netherlands* (Master thesis). Utrecht University.

Michael, R. S. (2001). *Crosstabulation & chi square*. Indiana University.

Small, C. R., Porterfield, S., & Gordon, G. (2015). Disruptive behavior within the workplace. *Applied Nursing Research, 28*(2), 67–71. doi:10.1016/j.apnr.2014.12.002 PMID:25908540

KEY TERMS AND DEFINITIONS

Cross-Tabulation Analysis: A data table or matrix that compares measures of the included variables (and that may be used to identify associational data patterns in a joint frequency distribution).

Data Pattern: Descriptive features and tendencies of focal data.

Degrees of Freedom: The number of variables in a system (including in a cross-tabulation analysis or contingency table).

Null Hypothesis: The assertion that the observed results of the research may be a result of random chance than anything else acting on the variables.

P-Value: A probability (p) value between 0 and 1 indicating a standard for statistical significance.

APPENDIX A: PREPARING THE COLLECTED SURVEY DATA IN QUALTRICS THROUGH RECODED VALUES AND RE-NAMED VARIABLES

Once data has been collected, it is important to check the data coding to ensure that it is correctly done. Log into Qualtrics. From the Projects list, find the proper online survey. In each of the multiple choice or matrix questions, check the Recode Values, and set those up correctly. In Figure 2, the numbers are only used as differentiators, not intensity indicators.

Figure 4 shows the recoding of variable names for less unwieldiness in handling the data when it is output in text format.

This processing is done on the cloud-hosted Qualtrics system. These changes will also affect the data exported from this system (when the data is exported in numerical format).

Be sure to "publish" changes to make sure that the renaming and such populate through the data.

Figure 2. Recoding values (as labels and dummy variables)

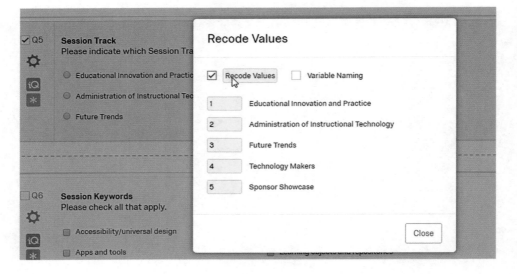

Figure 3. Recoding values (as intensity indicators)

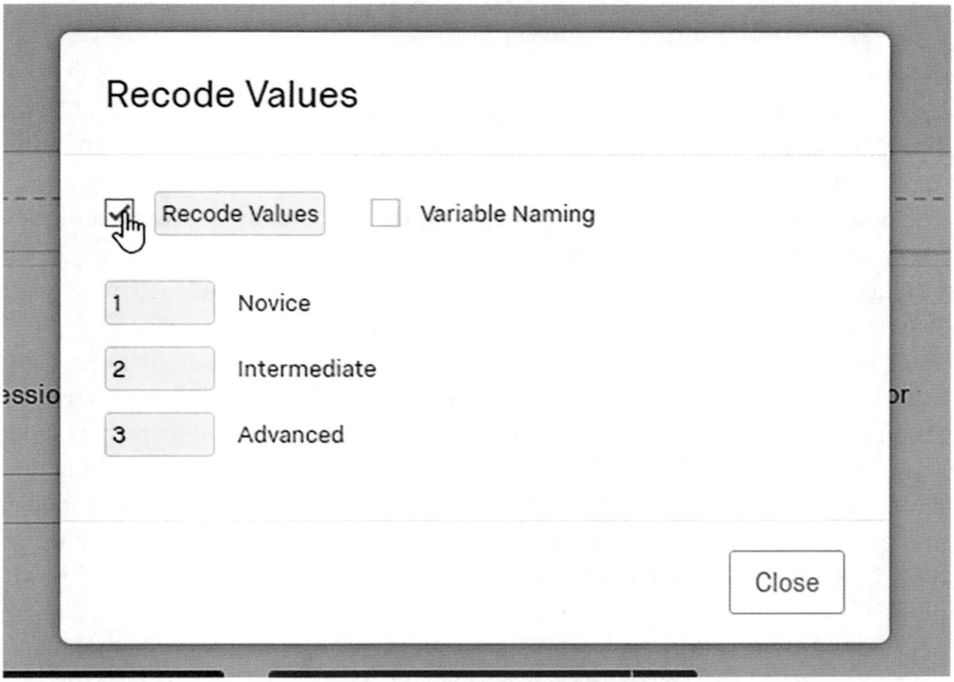

Figure 4. Renaming answers with new variable names

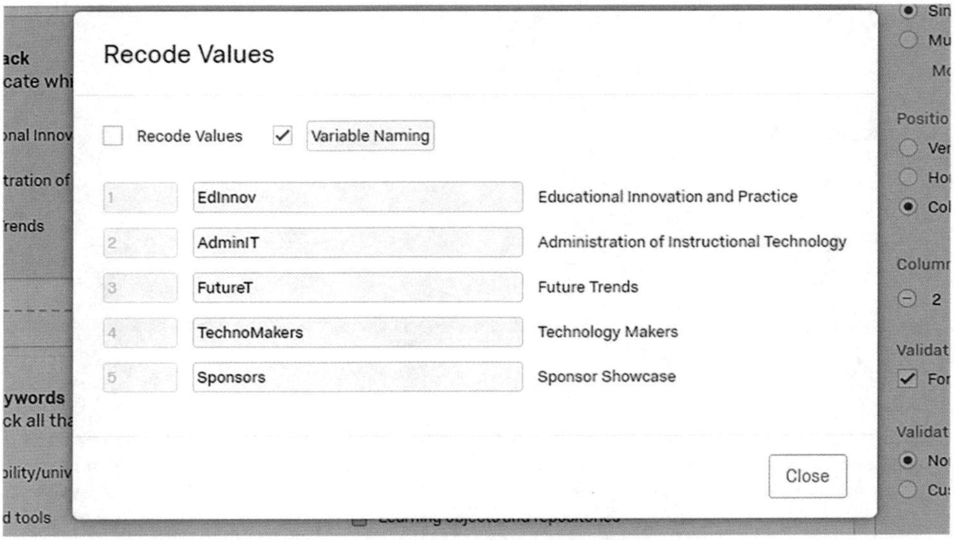

APPENDIX B: CONDUCTING A CROSS TABULATION ANALYSIS IN QUALTRICS

Once a survey has been deployed, the data collected, and the data cleaned, go to the survey, and click on "Data & Analysis" at the top menu. On that page, select "Cross Tabs V1". In the next page, click the "+ Create a new Cross Tabulation" button or the link "Click here to create one."

The new page shows an ability to select the questions (variables) which are usable for cross tabulation data in either the banner (column) or the stub (row). (Figure 5) Once the selected boxes are checked, go to the bottom right to "Create Cross Tabulation." (This example is using real-world data.)

What results is a fully spelled out cross-tabulation analysis table at the top and item by item comparisons at the bottom by the respective row stubs. The calculations for chi square, degrees of freedom, and p-values are available to help identify potential associations and areas of interest. Data options for the main table are available in the dropdown at the top right: frequencies, expected frequencies, actual-expected, row percents, column percents, banner means, stub means, t-tests (if relevant), and others. In a highly zoomed-out view, a partial view could look like this. (For this particular data, nothing of statistical significance was found.) Figure 6 is offered not really for readability but to give a general sense of what the cross tabulation analysis table looks like in Qualtrics. There are tools for manual highlighting of selected cells by color, if those are needed.

An effect analysis would involve multiple exploratory setups of various cross tabulation tables. The tables are exportable in various PDF and digital visual formats

Figure 5. The landing page to create a cross tabulation analysis in qualtrics

Figure 6. A sample cross tabulation table with data pullouts at the bottom

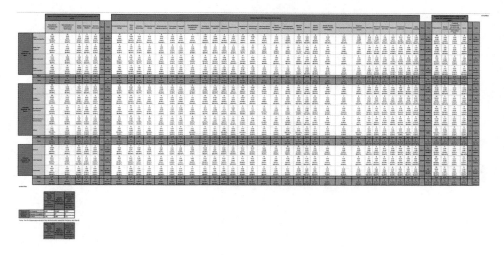

Section 2
In–Depth Data Elicitations

Chapter 3
Designing, Deploying, and Evaluating Open–Access Online Delphi Studies (OAODS)

ABSTRACT

This chapter describes the work of creating multimodal open-access online Delphi studies (OAODS). These are electronic Delphi studies that do not begin with an invited group of identified experts to seat a Delphi panel but rather with self-identified domain-specific authorities active on the Social Web, with post-data-collection vetting of the participants (when knowable) and their responses. This chapter explores how to design such instruments with efficacy and nuance, and built-in tests of respondent expertise, and fraud detection, and further, how to test such instruments for efficacy, reliability, and validity, while using some of the latest features available in online survey research platforms. The platform used in this work is the Qualtrics Research Suite.

INTRODUCTION

Classic Delphi studies involve obtaining forecasts about the future by seating selected certified domain experts to go through one or more rounds of questions. Rounds, or iterations, generally continue until the expert group arrives at a consensus or stability. Initial topics engaged were those dealing with sensitive military research. In general, Delphi Methods (DM) [also referred to as "Delphi Exercises" (Turoff & Hiltz, 1996, p. 2)] are applied to complex problems that are "not compatible to linear

DOI: 10.4018/978-1-5225-8563-3.ch003

or precise analytical techniques, and where subjective judgement on a collective basis could illuminate new perspectives" (Donohoe, Stellefson, & Tennant, 2012, p. 40). Ill-structured problems are those with "unclear goals and incomplete information" (Voss & Post, 1988). These challenges may be so nascent and new that there may be no defined paths forward, as-yet. The Delphi process enables experts to consider "what could/should be" (Miller 2006), so imagination combined with expertise can be relevant.

Early versions of Delphi studies in the late 1940s and 1950s apparently occurred in face-to-face contexts, and over time, online methods (electronic Delphi methods) have been harnessed as well. This work introduces a particular type of electronic Delphi study, dubbed the Open-Access Online Delphi Studies (OAODS). OAODS instruments may be created on and delivered through online survey platforms, dedicated specifically designed platforms for e-Delphi studies, and even learning management systems (LMSes), based on functionalities. A variety of technologies that may be harnessed for this process (Aengenheyster, et al., 2015), and over the years, a number of Internet-based research tools have gained traction. There has been work on building dedicated technology systems to enable some of these processes (Gomez-Sanz & Fernandez, 2015). Of interest, various types of socio-technical systems have been derived from Delphi methods and "emerged under names such as prediction markets, collaborative tagging, recommender systems…and social networks that usually serve a commercial objective" (Linstone & Turoff, 2011, p. 1713). Other areas that use ideas from the Delphi method include "Decision Support Systems (GDSS), Collaborative Systems, and Collective Intelligence, and CMC" (computer mediated communications) (Linstone & Turoff, 2011, p. 1713). Delphi methods have been used for non-research purposes as well, such as to "scaffold complex CMC (author note: computer-mediated communications) discussions by large groups of students learning together online" (Turoff, Hiltz, Yao, Li, Wang, & Cho, 2006, p. 76). A Delphi approach was used to create a multi-attribute decision analysis model, with weighting of the utility factors (Chan, Yung, Lam, Tam, & Cheung, 2001).

Based on integrations with social media platforms (social networking sites, microblogging sites, blogging sites, news-sharing sites, video sharing platforms, image sharing platforms, publication platforms, and others), open calls may be made seamlessly to a broad potential audience. [For example, Qualtrics has integrations with publishing platforms like WordPress® (Benton, Pappas, & Pappas, 2011) as well as social media ties with Twitter®, Facebook®, Reddit®, LinkedIn®, Google Plus®, Pinterest®, and others.] Micro-payment work platforms enable the seating of panels to respond to designed surveys, as do online research platforms. Open-links themselves may be broadcast via electronic mailing lists, websites, person-to-person emails, text messages, and other methods; they may be conveyed as texts, images, two-dimensional bar codes/Quick Response (QR) codes, and other forms.

There can be broad or narrow populations of invited individuals to serve as e-Delphi expert panel members. The panels should be kept anonymous from each other (but not necessarily from the researcher), with identities either not captured, partially captured, or kept confidential in a multi-blind way (with technologies potentially holding the key to re-identification, if that). The open-access means that anyone can respond. Others have argued for using online (human respondent) panels in coordination with online survey systems (Lowry, D'Arcy, Hammer, & Moody, 2016) and crowd-sourcing data collection, with the added capability of pre-screening respondents to some degree on the crowd-sourcing platforms (Lowry, D'Arcy, Hammer, & Moody, 2016, p. 236). Micropayment work sites may be used to find panel respondents, with micropayments of $1 to respond to a 15-minute survey (Christenson & Glick, Spring 2013, p. 27). Through platforms that provide access to paid participants, it is possible "to recruit participants for customized and flexible panel studies"…and to "recontact respondents" to "limit panel attrition" for multi-round Delphi studies (Christenson & Glick, Spring 2013, p. 27). [This does bring up the question of who is willing to be paid $4 an hour for thinking work, given that that "wage" is well below the federal minimum wage per hour in the U.S.]

Theoretically and technologically, it would be possible to create an OAODS instrument, launch it, and leave it live continuously over time for responses from any number of potential self-identified experts—as long as it possible to filter out feedback from subpar self-identified experts (without skewing the findings). These survey types may be one-round or multiple-rounds, and these may be deployed based on branching logic and other scripted logics (which stand in for the role of a "discussion leader" or facilitator in a Delphi study). A core feature, though, is the need for vetting of the expert status of respondents and the ability to clean data of suspect responses.

This work is based on prior published research using e-Delphi studies, first-hand work on an electronic Delphi study (Hai-Jew, 2014; Hai-Jew, June 20, 2014), and an analysis of the Qualtrics™ Research Suite, the leading global research platform out of Provo, Utah. This tool, whose name is a blended word from "quality" and "metrics" (Robinson, 2018, personal email), enables rich methods for eliciting questions, including some non-verbal ones. It has a language translation integration that enables the deployment of surveys in multiple languages (expressed cleanly in UTF-8 character sets). Its setup enables the deployment of "hidden questions" to better understand users' technologies (used to access the online surveys). It enables scripting for branching logic and specialized features. Its collaboration features enable distributed teams to work on a shared survey and to co-analyze data. The platform itself enables integrations of various types of digital multimedia, animations, simulations, video, slideshows, and interactive learning objects. A deployed OAODS instrument may be updated at any time on-the-fly, even after it has been deployed, and any of its scripts may be reworked based on research needs. Qualtrics has a commercial human panel-populating feature to enable reaching out to particular demographic slices of broad user populations. It also offers a basic self-explicated conjoint analysis approach. This platform enables a powerful cross-tabulation analysis (which treats questions as variables) and multi-variable "weighting" of constructs (factors). The platform has recently enabled text analysis for early topic modeling. Certainly, the platform enables downloads of data in a variety of file types [.csv, .tsv, .xml, and SPSS (.sav), among others]. With the power of third-party add-ons and tools, the functional enablements of Qualtrics for various types of e-Delphi studies may be powerful. (Some common integrations include Google Maps, WordPress, Zoom, and others.)

In terms of electronic Delphi methodologies, its features enable the deployment of "rounds" and the connections of invited respondents from closed lists to respond to follow-on rounds through re-identification of data…or security settings that enable continuance of a longer multi-round survey (from the same Internet Protocol or IP address)…and other methods. Tools to help respondents to be aware of each other may include automated data sharing and uses of real-time web conferencing software (through light integrations).

REVIEW OF THE LITERATURE

In the late 1940s or early 1950s, Norman Dalkey and Olaf Helmer of the RAND Corporation originated the so-called Delphi research method to harness the insights of experts in the field in order to better understand and plan for military risks. [Some published accounts include others who apparently contributed to the method, including Theodore J. Gordon (Linstone & Turoff, 2011, p. 1712) and Nicholas Rescher (Gordon, 2009, p. 3), and potentially others.] This qualitative research method was used to "forecast" and anticipate risks in an environment of uncertainty. There was also the sense that experts could provide more timely information than could be gleaned from "extant literature," particularly in the face of fast-changing events (Patton, 1990, as cited in Franklin & Hart, 2007, p. 237). This method is considered "well suited as a research instrument when there is incomplete knowledge about a problem or phenomenon" (Skulmoski, Hartman, & Krahn, 2007, p. 1). It was seen as an "alternative research technique" (Hallowell & Gambatese, 2010, p. 99).

The research design involved the defining of particular research questions and then the seating of expert "panels" with subject matter expertise. The experts' identities were kept anonymous to protect them and their points-of-view, and the questions were managed by a "discussion leader." In early work, findings by Delphi panels were restricted access. Different iterations of questions by "interview or questionnaire" (Dalkey & Helmer, July 1962, p. 11) would be handled based on insights obtained in the earlier "rounds," and the research would continue until some level of consensus (agreement) was obtained from the particular expert panels. As described by the originators, the research objective was to "obtain the most reliable consensus of opinion of a group of experts" through "a series of intensive questionnaires interspersed with controlled opinion feedback" (Dalkey & Helmer, July 1962, p. 11; Dalkey & Helmer, 1963, p. 458). The thinking work by the expert panelists involved their engagement in some "intuitive probability estimates" (Dalkey & Helmer, 1963, p. 459), for their projections. In terms of the general trajectory, the research begins with a "primary question" and then progresses to more specifics and other topics (Dalkey & Helmer, 1963, p. 461). Refinements are made to the follow-on questions with each iteration. These elicitations happen in "rounds" or "iterations," which change depending on the information collected in the prior session. Structured elicitations are used to attain better understandings of "a complex topic with little historical context that requires expert opinion to fully understand underlying issues" (Franklin & Hart, 2007, p. 237). The researcher or "discussion leader" or facilitator has a central role in controlling the process. [A research team suggests that measuring agreement is not about driving towards consensus or compromise but rather about "quickly identifying agreement and disagreement in order to focus attention" for the expert panelists (Turoff & Hiltz, 1996, p. 2)].

Apparently, the name "Project Delphi" was applied at the RAND Corporation "as a joke" to the research process because of the forecasting aspects of the research (Turoff & Hiltz, 1996, p. 1). Apparently, the originators of the method did not particularly care for the name, but it was memorable and catchy and so remained. The Delphi reference was to the Delphic oracle (who channeled Apollo and was consulted for decision making) ("Delphi," Sept. 19, 2018). The Oracle of Delphi in Ancient Greece, the seat of democracy, focused on "public policy to personal affairs" (Steurer, 2011, p. 959).

The Delphi method assumes two basic ideas, one, that "group decisions are usually more valid than decisions made by a single person" (and more valid "if the group is comprised of experts in the field") and that "anonymous group participation" may mitigate some of the challenges with face-to-face group meetings (with problems from "domineering group members, group bias, and group think") (Murry & Hammons, Summer 1995, p. 426).

VARIOUS EVOLVED TYPES OF DELPHI STUDIES

Changes to this methodology have come about because of local research needs and other practical considerations. Rapid DM originated because of a need to speed up the process "in tactical situations where rapid decisions are called for" (Gordon & Pease, 2006, p. 322).

If core elements of Classical Delphi focused on particular (research topics/"central problems") related to nuclear warfare and the future, with (certified experts), and (discussion leaders/facilitators) working with research participants in (real space), over a number of (rounds), depending on the level of (expert consensus) and other (data analytics), each of the elements has been revised in different types of follow-on variations on Delphi methods. The changes in DM also cover different purposes, processes, technologies, data analytics methods, and theoretical frameworks.

Research Topics

In the research literature, in the 80-some years since the Delphi Method (DM) was published to the world, a wide range of topics have been explored well beyond the military realm. The focus on forecasting the future also seems to have somewhat muted. In healthcare, the Delphi method has been applied to better understand general practitioners' information requirements (Green, Jones, Hughes, & Williams, 1999); dementia ((Ferri, et al., 2005); co-designing a quality framework for patient decision aids (Elwyn, et al., Aug. 2006); the redeveloping of "mental health first aid guidelines" for interventions for suicidal ideation and behavior (Ross, Kelly, & Jorm, 2014, p. 241); addiction recovery (Neale, et al., 2014); patient engagement (Oostendorp, Durand, Lloyd, & Elwyn, 2015), and others; it has been used to develop a "Chinese medicine assessment measure" (Schnyer, 2005). This research approach has been harnessed to study an early warning method for societal trends (van de Linde & van der Duin, 2011). The Delphi method has been used to define "characteristics of wisdom" definition (Jeste, et al, 2010) and operationalize terminology in a field (Rodríguez-Mañas, et al., 2013). It has been used to select quality indicators in a field (Boulkedid, et al., June 2011). In the public security space, it has been used for strategic management in law enforcement organizations (Loo, 2002). In workplace research, DM has been used to define competencies for those in particular professional roles (Brill, Bishop & Walker, 2006), the definition of "organizational social media risk" (with findings compared against an in-depth analysis of curated organizational policies to mitigate such risks) (Di Gangi, Johnston, Worrell, & Thompson, 2016, p. 1), and others. It has been harnessed for graduate research (Skulmoski, Hartman, & Krahn, 2007). In another case, it has been used to enhance scenario design (Nowack,

Endrikat, & Guenther, 2011). In education, the DM has been used to "improve idea generation" and "reduce information overload problems for large classes" (Turoff, Hiltz, Yao, Li, Wang, & Cho, 2006, p. 67); identify barriers to using ICT-supported collaborative project-based learning in the teaching classroom (Kramer, Walker, & Brill, 2007, p. 527); the creation of educational reporting guidelines (Phillips, et al., 2014), and others.

In the policy realm, researchers have explored policy experts' "propensity to change their opinion along Delphi rounds" based on background features and also along individual propensities (Makkonen, Hujala, & Uusivuori, 2016, p. 61). The Policy Delphi method works as a "hybrid research design" (Franklin & Hart, 2007, p. 238). In general, the objectives "of a policy Delphi are 'to ensure that all possible options have been put on the table for consideration, to estimate impact and consequences of any particular option, and to examine and estimate the acceptability of any particular option' (Turoff, 1997, p, 87, as cited in Franklin & Hart, 2007, p. 238). An important value is to find consensus around policies for different stakeholders with differing interests. As a "systematic, intuitive forecasting procedure used to obtain, exchange, and develop informed opinion on a particular topic," the Public Delphi method is conceptualized as occurring in stages:

First-stage policy Delphi questions typically include four categories of items: forecast, issue, goal, and options (Dunn, 1994). Forecast items provide the participant with a statistic or estimate of a future event. Participants are asked to judge the reliability of the information presented. For issue items, respondents rank issues in terms of their importance relative to others. Goal items elicit opinions about the desirability of certain policy goals. For options (sic) items, respondents identify the likelihood that specific options might be feasible policy goals. Because policy Delphi questions are designed to elicit conflict and disagreement as well as to clarify opinions, the response categories do not typically permit neutral answers. The response choices are often rated on a 4-point Likert-type scale. The response choices for forecast items range from certainly reliable to unreliable. For issue items, response categories range from very important to unimportant. The response choices for goal items range from very desirable to very undesirable. For option items, the range is from definitely feasible to definitely unfeasible. (Rayens & Hahn, 2000, p. 309)

Certified Experts

Sampling has always been a challenge in human subjects research because of the risks that recruitment may lead to biases and blindspots. There are risks in "small differences in personality…documented between participants recruited in different ways" leading to differences in findings (Buchanan, 2018, p. 235). One study found that one of the so-called Big Five character traits (openness, conscientiousness, extraversion, agreeableness, and neuroticism), "Openness to Experience," had an outsized effect on a studied phenomenon using "internet samples," with the warning that personality biases may be at play (Buchanan, 2018, p. 235).

The gold standard has been "random" selection of participants and the sufficient number of participants for statistical power. In a Delphi study, these calculations may be somewhat different, since in the classical version, experts are reviewed, vetted, selected, and invited to engage. The selection criteria for experts vary between the types of studies, and there is no sense that there has to be type-diversity or type-inclusiveness in published studies.

The individuals seated on particular expert panels need to be validated experts. In real-space with solid ways to validate expertise—professional roles, professional achievements ("production"), formal education, and others—it is somewhat easier to assess domain-based knowhow and capabilities (and even some aspects of personality). Sometimes, a "snowball method" is used to seat the expert panel but risk selection bias (Steurer, 2011, p. 960), given that people often cluster homophilously (the sense that "like attracts like"), and there may be an over-emphasis of people of a certain type or approach or belief or background or training.

It would seem reasonable to assume that expertise is "stratified," with experts with differing numbers of years of experience (and depths of expertise) and different areas of focus. Also, depending on the Delphi method applied, the seating of the certified experts may differ; for example, single-panel multi-round methods may involve different requirements than multi-panel multi-round methods. The types of research questions asked may also have an impact because the experts are thought to be able to speak to different aspects of an ill-structured problem.

In the research, one approach involves how well the available online panels from micropayment work sites and from other commercial survey-respondent empaneling services represent the overall population at a macro level. The idea is that crowd-sourcing survey responses should represent the general population so their responses are somewhat representative of the larger population. This is so if research questions relate to general populations, but what about close-in research based on expertise? Is it possible to find a "representative" cross-section of experts on a topic, and is that even desirable for the particular research focus? Is it better just to measure particular biases and to offset these by weighting responses? Are there ways to recruit or "sample" expert respondents responsibly and ethically? To the initial question of how well online panels represent the larger population, one research team found an "average discrepancy rate of 5 to 10% between the particular demographic characteristics of online respondents and their known distribution in the U.S. population" (Heen, Lieberman, & Miethe, Sept. 2014, p. 1), by comparing panel respondents on three platforms: Survey Monkey, Qualtrics, and Amazon's Mechanical Turk.

There is also the issue of numbers. There is not a sense that there is an upper limit to panel size (but the lower bound requires at least 10 members) (Parentè and Anderson-Parentè, 1987, as cited in Murry & Hammons, Summer 1995, p. 428). Also, in the literature, there is the idea that as the number of respondents increases, the more reliable the findings and the lessening of error (Cochran, 1983, as cited in Murry & Hammons, Summer 1995, p. 428).

And there is the issue of retention. Delphi panel "mortality" (De Leeuw, 2001) or panel attrition (Snow & Tebes, 1992) have been challenges. In some studies, like an online real-time Delphi approach, "the majority of panelists did not return to the web application to respond to other panelists' ratings and comments" (Geist, 2010, p. 152). In another study, the types of information feedback that participants in an online Delphi study, whether it was "statistics and rationales" or "rationales" alone made a difference in retention for follow-on rounds (Meijering & Tobi, 2016, p. 166).

Discussion Leaders/Facilitators

As with researchers using any number of other research methods and approaches, discussion leaders in Delphi studies bear a lot of responsibility for the effectiveness of the research and the insights from the work. Delphi experimenters (to use a classic term) have to exercise "considerable discretion" in interacting with experts so as not to accidentally influence their responses in a certain direction (Dalkey & Helmer, July 1962, p. 3). They have critical inputs in terms of how to pose questions at each round, and they decide when the Delphi experiment is done and no more rounds are needed. They also analyze the data for meaning.

Real Space

Early versions of Delphi studies apparently occurred in face-to-face (F2F) and real-physical venues. In ensuing years, various mixes of "space" have been engaged for Delphi rounds: wholly F2F, blended, or online, or some combination. Virtual space has come to the fore in e-Delphi studies. Some processes begin with a F2F stage and transition to a "non face-to-face stage" (Landeta, Barrutia, & Lertxundi, 2011, p. 1632). Even with online affordances, though, researchers suggest that there are "hard-to-involve Internet users" for electronic survey methodologies (Andrews, Nonnecke, & Preece, 2010).

Rounds

In terms of iterations of questions and elicitations, different types of Delphi processes range from "roundless" (single iteration) to multiple rounds (or "waves"), and from discrete phased rounds to continuous ones. Round-less real-time Delphi methods were introduced for more efficient research because of the fewer iterations (Gordon & Pease, 2006). What does "information efficiency" look like? Two researchers write:

Information is efficient if the obtained research data are relevant, the remarks and reactions really contribute to achieving the research objective, and hardly any information is unnecessary (Groenland 2002). The discussion leader thus has a crucial role, because he or she can control the flow of the discussion and interfere if respondents provide irrelevant information. Thus, we expect more efficient information than does the asynchronous e-Delphi method (Brüggen & Willems, 2009, p. 369).

In traditional approaches, expert panel consensus was a standard at which point the research would complete, and achieving consensus could take various numbers of rounds, generally between two and about eight, in the published research. An important goal is to capture "reliable group opinion from a set of experts" (Landeta, Barrutia, & Lertxundi, 2011, p. 1630).

Defining an agreement threshold *a priori* seems to be important, and certainly researchers do not want an arbitrary or subjective cut-off for when the Delphi study achieves completion but only when a certain level of "steady state" has been achieved with the feedback (Gordon & Pease, 2006, p. 324) or a level of "consensus or stability" have been met (Murry & Hammons, Summer 1995, p. 429) based on statistical analyses (Holey, Feeley, Dixon, & Whittaker, 2007, p. 1).

Expert consensus is formalized through statistical methods (Pankratova & Malafeeva, Sept. 2012). Consensus measures include the following: chi square test (for independence); McNemar change test; Wilcoxian matched-pairs signed-ranks test; intra-class correlation coefficient, kappa statistics; Spearman's rank-order correlation coefficient; Kendall's W coefficient of concordance; (and) t-statistics, F-tests" based on a review of the literature of consensus measurements by inferential statistics (von der Gracht, 2012, p. 1532). Certainly, there may be a point of "diminishing returns" at which point the rounds may end (Keeney, Hasson, & McKenna, 2006, p. 207). One research team found that "percent agreement" was often achieved often with "75% being the median threshold to define consensus" (Diamond et al, 2014, p. 401). Generally, "definitions of consensus vary widely and are poorly reported" in a number of assessed studies (Diamond et al, 2014, p. 401). Still, there is a practical angle at play, too, to wait until "target consensus" has been achieved before ending the research (Hallowell & Gambatese, 2010, p. 102). There is a cost to bringing experts together again to engage issues.

Expert Consensus

How experts dealt with thorny or contested issues have been an important part of classical Delphi studies. Delphi studies have been applied to hot topics where "disagreements among individuals are so severe or politically unpalatable that the communication process must be refereed and/or anonymity assured" (Murry & Hammons, Summer 1995, p. 428).

What expert consensus is was historically calculated as simple descriptive statistics: measures of central tendency (mean, median, and mode), dispersion (standard deviation, min-max ranges, variance), position (rankings), and frequency (counts). In many cases, "thresholds" were set above which consensus has been achieved and below which consensus has not. Whether consensus was achieved or not, expert insights still have value. If done well, Delphi Method studies may inform a domain space with new insights and potentially enable some more clarity in a context of complexity and uncertainty.

While early DMs focused on consensus and some level of agreement, or settled on a steady state of equilibrium, other methods now consider the value of dissensus or disagreement, with a focus on the "tenth man" arguments, in order to elicit a diversity of understandings. In other words, in each round, there may be divergence of points-of-view instead of convergence to some consensus. Over time, and over events (rounds), expert panelists may diverge instead of converge, and that state of the world may be desirable.

From early days, the Delphi Method focused on trying to mitigate social dynamics in the feedback from respective experts on the panels. Solomon Asch's studies in the 1950s "showed people changing their judgments in order to fit in with the majority, even though the correct response to the judgment task…was clear and unambiguous" (Bolger & Wright, 2011, p. 1501). People were found to also be susceptible to the sense of another's expertise and authority. This tradition of mitigating for social effects has continued with more contemporary research because of the importance of the independence of the experts on the panel:

We identify residual normative and informational pressures towards consensus that potentially reduce process gain that might otherwise be achieved. For instance, panelist confidence may act as a signal of status rather than be a valid cue to expertise, whereas consensus appears to have a strong influence on the final outcome that can reduce its accuracy when there are valid minority opinions. We argue that process gain in Delphi must occur through those further from the 'truth' changing their opinion more than those closer to the truth, with the general direction of opinion change being towards the truth. For such virtuous opinion change to occur we suggest the need to both facilitate opinion change and provide good cues as to where the truth lies. Research on Judge Advisor Systems shows that people usually do not change their opinion as much as they should, giving too much weight to their own opinion and too little to the views of others—this bias can be reduced by increasing involvement and motivation. In addition, we propose that the best way to provide good cues as to the direction of the truth is to elicit rich reasoning from panelists about the judgment or choice in question, then use this as feedback. We suggest practical ways of focusing and deepening panelists' consideration and evaluation of such reasoning—such that all proffered opinions are well-evaluated." (Bolger & Wright, 2011, p. 1500)

Research using "judge advisor systems" (JAS) in social psychology studies the amount of opinion change in "dyads and small groups." Recent findings suggest that there is a reluctance to change an initial position even in the face of new information. The co-researchers write: "In our view, of most interest here is the work on advice utilization—which has produced perhaps the most important finding of JAS research—that judges' final judgments are usually closer to their own initial opinion than they are to the advice given—which means, if the advice is good, as is usually the case, then the final judgment is not as good as it could have been…" in a process known as "egocentric discounting," which has been attributed to "information asymmetry, anchoring-and-adjustment, and egocentric bias" (Bolger & Wright, 2011, p. 1504). In the case of Delphi studies, the respective experts may well engage in egocentric discounting. One thread of research involves how much expert panel members change from round-to-round from original positions.

Data Analytics

"…some critics claim that many Delphi studies result in low-quality findings limited by the facilitator's survey instruments, poor choice of experts, lack of effort to reduce bias, unreliable analyses, and limited feedback during the study (Gupta and Clarke, 1996, as cited in Hallowell & Gambatese, 2010, p. 99). In this light, processes matter, and the quality of data analysis matters.

Generally, Delphi methods are considered qualitative research (Murry & Hammons, Summer 1995) because the elicitations are conceptual and analytical, without a main focus around numbers (although these are important for DM research as well). As a "generative" research method, the DM experiment is designed to surface new ideas. In some cases, DM is supported by evidence review explicitly, and in other cases, available research is included more on background (such as to inform the design of the questions). How the collected data is handled depends on informed weighting of the responses from the various experts. There are various identified pitfalls in the Delphi Method, particularly in the balance between qualitative and quantitative methods and data. This challenge requires researchers to engage the following work:

1) balancing between qualitative and quantitative, 2) balancing between formal structure and questions raised in the process, 3) framing questions to discover alternative future states, 4) paying attention to panellists' (sic) style, 5) dealing with lack of data for comprehensive cluster analysis, 6) considering scenario consistency, 7) understanding manager's responsibility and, 8) understanding the epistemological aspects of Delphi data (Tapio, Paloniemi, Varho, & Vinnari, 2011, p. 1616).

Others suggested that mixed methods approaches can be combined not in an "unholy marriage" of qualitative and quantitative methods in a Delphi study but actually be "a worthy adventure" and result in insightful research (Tapio, Paloniemi, Varho, & Vinnari, 2011, p. 1616). Qualitative and quantitative methods may be used to establish rigor in Delphi studies, based on "the methodological trinity of reliability, validity and trustworthiness" (Hasson & Keeney, 2011, p. 1696). These authors suggest various methods such as "test-retest measures, inter-observer reliability, parallel-form measures, content validity, construct validity, and criterion-related validity" (Hasson & Keeney, 2011, pp. 1698 - 1790).

DIFFERENT TYPES OF DELPHI STUDIES

With the popularization of the Delphi Method in the 1950s, its adoption apparently took some decades. By about 2007, there were only three types of general Delphi methods, according to one research team: "classical, decision-making, and policy Delphi" (Franklin & Hart, 2007, p. 238). The newer types seem to be based on different contexts in which the method was applied. Over the years, a number of different types of Delphi studies have been originated. Based on a review of the literature, two researchers have listed the different types, broadly speaking, as the following: "classical, modified, decision, policy, real time / consensus conference, e-Delphi, technological, online, argument, and disaggregative policy". These each have different research aims, target panelists, administration approaches, numbers of rounds, and designs of Round 1 (Hasson & Keeney, 2011, p. 1697). "Fuzzy" Delphi methods enable different ways to express uncertainty, in panel memberships (as sets) and in expert opinions and consensus (Chang, Huang, & Lin, 2000), based on fuzzy statistics and ultimately fuzzy set theory. Another spinoff, the "hybrid Delphi," combines aspects of "Focus Group, Nominal Group Technique and Delphi method" (Landeta, Barrutia, & Lertxundi, 2011, p. 1629), an in effort to harmonize "their potentialities" and reduce "their limitations." A Public Delphi involves citizen participation around policy-making (Di Zio, Rosas, & Lamelza, 2017, p. 143). A Mini Delphi or Estimate-Talk-Estimate (ETE) approach "speeds up the procedure" (Gustafson, et al.; Van de Ven and Delbecq, 1974, as cited in Di Zio, Rosas, & Lamelza, 2017, p. 143).

Others include Markov-Delphi, the Shang method, Nominal Group Technique, Abacus-Delphi, and others (Di Zio, Rosas, & Lamelza, 2017, p. 143), based on different approaches. Other variations may involve changes to the original DM and / or augmentations to the process.

A few of the new types are highlighted below in terms of their novel value. One new approach is in response to the perceived slowness of classical Delphis. One researcher writes:

But conventional Delphi studies have always taken a long time to complete (on the order of months) and have been expensive: a single round can easily require three weeks; a three-round Delphi is at least a three- to four-month affair, including preparation and analysis time. Real Time Delphi is a faster, less expensive system based on the Delphi principles of feedback of prior responses of the participating group and guarantees of anonymity of the respondents (Gordon, 2009, p. 3).

A Real-Time Delphi (RTD) may be single-round research that is deployed over online or offline electronic survey systems, in synchronous or asynchronous ways (Gordon & Pease, 2006, p. 323). Similarly to traditional Delphis, participants are "chosen for their expertise in some aspect of the problem under study" (Gordon & Pease, 2006, p. 322). For efficiency's sake, there is only one round, and "each respondent views their own earlier response when they return to the study. As they continue to watch their input form (or later on a return visit) they also see the new averages, medians, distributions, and reasons given by other panelists for their positions. This information appears whenever new inputs are received from other participants." (Gordon & Pease, 2006, p. 324) Theodore J. Gordon and Adam Pease originated this computerized Delphi approach without subsequent rounds (Gordon 2009; Gordon and Pease, 2006, as cited in Di Zio, Rosas, & Lamelza, 2017, p. 144). A Real-Time Delphi has to be able to ask various types of questions asked in other forms of Delphi studies, including those listed related to "individual competence/ expertise; estimating time intervals; estimating numerical data; evaluating tendencies, developments, scenarios; evaluating the same issue through different questions; personal data; (open questions and comments); (complex questions)" (Häder, 2009, p. 125, as cited in Aengenheyster, et al., 2015, p. 16). In addition, there should be enablements of "visualization, symbolic design and layout" of the questionnaire (Aengenheyster, et al., 2015, p. 16). For all their efficiencies, RTDs were critiqued because of the loss of participants between rounds, with fewer returning.

The central weakness of Real Time Delphi is its failure to attract most of its respondents back for re-estimation. The rate of returns in Real Time Delphi revisits has run about 25 – 50%. Depending on the design and the amount of cajoling, ordinary Delphi studies run higher than this, although differences among studies make it difficult to arrive at some standard panel persistence number. The low revisit rate of Real Time Delphi participants tempts one to say that the feedback principle of Delphi is being violated, but even first timers see the averages and reasons of those who have preceded them in the study, so the carrying of group response to all is still maintained. However, it would certainly be preferable if all participants revisited the study to update their inputs in view of what others have said. To overcome this weakness, at least partially, administrators have sent out reminder emails during the study and these have been found to be at least partially successful. (Gordon, 2009, p. 10)

One study of a real-time Delphi approach as compared to the conventional DM found no significant differences in terms of the research findings and data quality (Gnatzy, Warth, von der Gracht, & Darkow, 2011, p. 1681).

A Real Time *Spatial* Delphi (RTSD) is conducted online and often with the purpose of identifying locations that are optimal for particular target purposes (Di Zio & Pacinelli, 2011). Researchers explain that this new approach is a combination of Real-Time Delphi and Spatial Delphi:

This new technique, called Real Time Spatial Delphi, preserves most of the advantages of both methods, minimizes the disadvantages, and develops new potential. A panel of experts, suitably chosen according to the application, answers a geo-questionnaire by placing points on an online interactive map and presenting written arguments. The system automatically calculates and displays a circle representing the convergence of the opinions, which shrinks and moves in real-time. The final result is the delimitation of an area most suitable for a given action or for the occurrence of a future event and is immediately usable for decision support and /or spatial scenario building without any processing (Di Zio, Rosas, & Lamelza, 2017, p. 143).

This approach melds Real Time Delphi (Gordon & Pease, 2006) and Spatial Shang (Di Zio & Staniscia, 2014) to create Spatial Delphi "when consultations and consequent decisions concern matters of geographical location" but in a roundless way (Di Zio, Rosas, & Lamelza, 2017, p. 144).

On Computers and Online

Computers, of course, have been around since the 1930s. It turns out that the "first Delphi application was the replacement of a computer simulation by a process of subjective estimations by large groups of experts" (Dalkey & Helmer, 1951, as cited in Turoff, Hiltz, Yao, Li, Wang, & Cho, 2004, p. 2). That said, computers have returned to the fore again in this space, with Delphi research being practiced computationally as well.

While the classic Delphi started as a paper and pencil process, computer-assisted Delphi methods and e-Delphi methods have come to the fore and been around for some decades. One of the earlier versions was compared to "email discussions": "The e-Delphi method is comparable to email discussions, but the discussion leader aggregates and analyses the initial responses and returns a summary of the results to those respondents who initially reacted, thereby creating interaction between respondents" (Bröggen & Willems, 2009, p. 364). The advent of e-Delphi also brought along different ways of understanding expert panel contributions, such as by counting the highest numbers of words per respondent with the e-Delphi method and noting the most "substantive arguments per respondent" in the online focus groups (Bröggen & Willems, 2009, p. 373).

Described as a looped algorithmic process, the Delphi method's essential process is in the "round." Each round begins in the "organizational stage." From there, questionnaires are prepared. Panels of experts are formed. The "expert evaluation" occurs, and their responses are analyzed for consistency. A "representation of the results of the round" are made, and then comes a critical decision juncture: "Is the next round necessary?" If so, a revision is made of the expert judgments, and a new round is set up with the same prior steps. If not, the process ends. (Pankratova & Malafeeva, Sept. 2012, p. 712)

Researchers have worked to translate Delphi research approaches from physical spaces to online technological ones (Turoff & Hiltz, 1996). Some goals of computer-based Delphi processes include the following:

- "Improve the understanding of the participants through analysis of subjective judgements to produce a clear presentation of the range of views and considerations.
- Detect hidden disagreements and judgmental biases that should be exposed for further clarification.
- Detect missing information or cases of ambiguity in interpretation by different participants.
- Allow the examination of very complex situations that can only be summarized by analysis procedures.
- Detect patterns of information and of sub-group positions.
- Detect critical items that need to be focused on." (Turoff & Hiltz, 1996, p. 12)

These researchers conceptualize a "continuous Delphi process" outside of the traditional rounds (Turoff & Hiltz, 1996, p. 4).

The features of the harnessed technologies are of concern. "Before selecting e-survey software or service provider (e.g., Qualtrics, SurveyMonkey), several operational factors should be considered, such as: design features and interface (i.e., ease of use, accessibility, etc.), level of respondent access and technological support, and options for data management and analysis" (Donohoe, Stellefson, & Tennant, 2012, p. 43). A "friendly interface" is also necessary to allow "panel members to input data" (Chou, 2002, pp. 233 - 234). The "project leader" has to be able to monitor the study through the technology as well (Chou, 2002, pp. 233 - 234).

Based on limitations to traditional Delphi approaches, researchers have made recommendations for how e-Delphi may more effectively address limitations such as the following: "design sensitivity, recruitment (of expert panels), time commitment, attrition, and consensus" (Donohoe, Stellefson, & Tennant, 2012, p. 44). For this method, researchers suggest selecting those with "high interest in the research problem and / or results" and notifying them about "the process and goals at the outset" (Donohoe, Stellefson, & Tennant, 2012, p. 44).

With the advent of dedicated electronic research systems and online survey research suites, electronic Delphi studies (known as e-Delphi studies) have been harnessed. The broad geographical reach of these systems enable eliciting expert opinions without the need for physical co-location. Then, online panels with thin-sliced demographic features (down to individuals) became available through micropayment work platforms (like Amazon's Mechanical Turk) and as integrations with online survey platforms. Delphi experts suggest that the systems used will ensure that Delphi studies "are continuous, dispersed, and asynchronous" (Linstone & Turoff, 2011, p. 1718).

Some changes to the classic DM have been to shore up the process. The originators of the method suggest that this experimental procedure had some limitations, including the observation that expert responses were "not strictly independent," that there may be "leading" by experimenters, some vagueness in questions that produced "literary outpourings of little value for the analysis," and the lack of "firmer theoretical foundation(s)" for codifying "final responses" even if plausible (Dalkey & Helmer, 1963, p. 467). There are strengths and weaknesses of e-Delphi methods (Donohoe, Stellefson, & Tennant, 2012).

The topics that are addressed in contemporary Delphi studies may make it somewhat harder to conclusively support some findings with other data:

In contemporary research, the Delphi method is particularly useful when objective data are unattainable, there is a lack of empirical evidence, experimental research is unrealistic or unethical, or when the heterogeneity of the participants must be preserved to assure validity of the results (Hallowell & Gambatese, 2010, p. 99).

To shore up the rigor of such studies, researchers have conducted studies on the optimal number of rounds to achieve stability. In one study, convergence to stability occurred at four rounds, aligning with research by Martino (1983), with then-ranges from two to five (Erffmeyer, Erffmeyer, & Lane, March-June 1986, pp. 125 - 126). Some research has focused on ways to enrich the feedback of panelists, in some cases involving the reconciling of contradictory data. Some research has focused on the amount of opinion change in the expert panel members over each round. Researchers have been defining "expert consensus" in statistically validated ways and testing the actual predictivity of the method and other actions. Still, there is the sense that "any process to establish rigour (sic) in Delphi studies can be criticized (sic)" (Hasson & Keeney, 2011, p. 1701).

The articles in the literature review were selected based on relevance to this study, particularly to establish the history of the Delphi method and to understand electronic Delphi methods. A visual summary of these works may be seen in Figure 1.

Figure 1. A word cloud of the published articles from the review of the literature

OPEN-ACCESS ONLINE DELPHI STUDIES (OAODS)

The Open-Access Online Delphi Studies (OAODS) method is conceptualized as a five-step approach for planning, designing, developing, deploying a unique OAODS instrument, harnessing the resulting data, and then revising the original instrument (as necessary). The open-access feature is a critical defining one, which has broad

Figure 2. A conceptualized process for open-access online Delphi studies (OAODS)

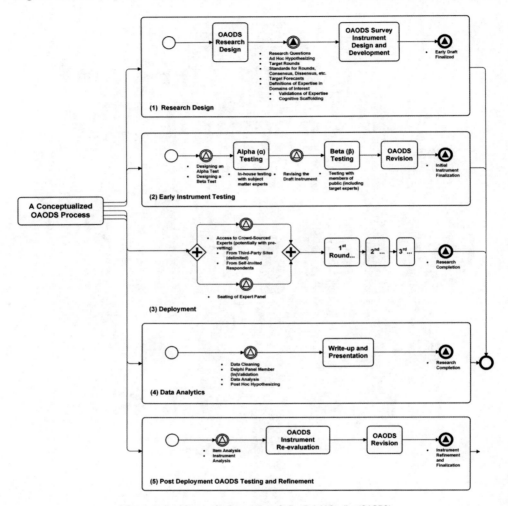

A Conceptualized Process for Open-Access Online Delphi Studies (OAODS)

implications for the work. The five steps are represented in Figure 2, a Business Process Model and Notation (BPMN) diagram.

1. Research Design
2. Early Instrument Testing
3. Deployment
4. Data Analytics
5. Post Deployment OAODS Testing and Refinement

1. Research Design

The research design has to include definitions of some elements fundamental to Delphi studies. For example, what is the focus of the research? The topic has to be something that members of the panels can address with some insights. The topic has to have relevance in the respective field. It generally should be something involving ill-structured problems and potentially the future (in a forecasting way). What research questions are being answered? Who are the target experts, and what are their areas of expertise? What are ways to motivate their participation? What questions and prompts and elicitation methods should be used to elicit information from the respective experts? What sorts of elicitations may be used to both elicit a sense of identity (personality, ego) and to establish bona fides for expertise? How should each of the rounds start, and when should each of the rounds end? What criteria should be used to decide whether the research goes to the next round? And when the research completes? In terms of analytics, when is "consensus" arrived at, and/or when is "dissensus" arrived at in a stable state equilibrium? Are there ways to falsify or disprove findings (to meet the requirement in science that hypotheses have to be testable and theoretically and practically falsifiable to be valid)? Are there other types of data that may be harnessed to enhance the design?

2. Early Instrument Testing

The general (experienced) parts to Open-Access Online Delphi Studies (OAODS) instruments may be seen in Figure 3. The parts are the following: (1) setup, (2) elicitations (including branching), (3) debriefing, and (4) next round(s) [or "completion" if roundless]. In the callouts (to the right of the steps), the contents of the respective segments are explained in more depth.

The research instrument may be tested in some straightforward ways. An "alpha" (α) study focuses on technological functionalities, all the branches of the branching logic, the writing, the multimedia, and other elements. Experts may be invited to review the instrument to ensure that it is as comprehensive as possible and represents the constructs of interest. The question writing may be analyzed to ensure that there are no mismatches between question stems and response options, or risk poorer data quality (Smyth & Olson, 2019). A complete walk-through should involve the collection of data to see how well the findings may be analyzed. Item analyses, with focuses on item non-response and response times, may be conducted on the elicitations, prompts, and questions.

A next step involves pilot testing. A "beta" (β) test focuses on how potential respondents to the e-Delphi study may experience it and what adjustments may

Figure 3. General sequential (experienced) parts of open-access online Delphi studies (OAODS) instruments

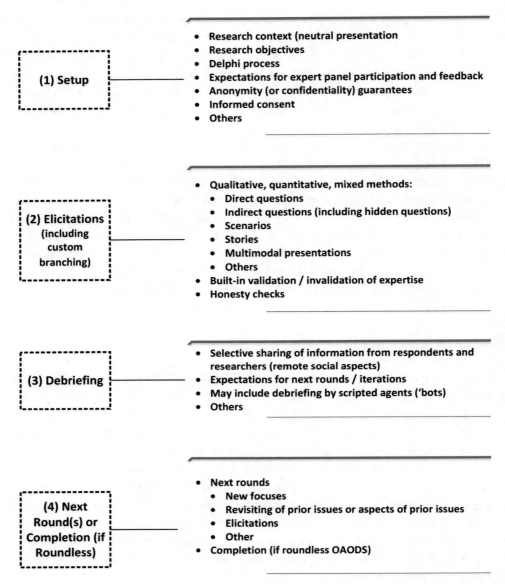

General Sequential (Experienced) Parts of
Open-Access Online Delphi Studies (OAODS) Instruments

need to be made to ensure that there is clear understanding of the study at every phase. The directions and elicitations should be clear. The settings for the survey data collection should align with the research design. The online survey settings should not introduce survey bias or any misleading outcomes.

There are formalized ways to conduct "item analyses" of the instrument. There are ways to run factor analyses to understand what the respective questions are actually capturing in terms of response data. (This would be from both alpha and beta testing.)

3. Deployment

One of the challenges of the Delphi method is to identify certified experts and to seat them on the respective panels to address particular hard problems. Early Delphi methods apparently drew domain experts from particular fields that were thought to be able to speak to particular topics. Some panels were apparently homogeneous, and others heterogeneous (with members from different domains or interdisciplinary ones). Certainly, sampling for heterogeneous individuals is standard in some Delphi studies (Steinert, 2009). In an online context, expert respondents may be drawn from closed lists, crowd-sourcing, micro-payment platforms, and other venues. The challenge will be to motivate the respective experts and to have an instrument that elicits the information properly.

Another approach is to build ways to measure expertise into the instrument. In the same way that "tells" may be built into a survey about actual beliefs, with ways to measure respondent honesty and ways to measure cognitive dissonance around particular topics, it I s possible to elicit expertise. Open-ended questions may be used to invite problem solving, to understand knowledge bases, methods, intelligence, and memory. (Hidden questions may be applied to understand the amount of time for the responses. Also, hidden questions may be applied to understand geographical location of the respondent, to aid in identify validation—in some cases.) Those responses may be tested against plagiarism, which is an indicator of honesty. Or thought experiment prompts may be offered. Or ethical cases may be offered. These may be fairly bald approaches to elicit understandings of the respondent and of expertise, but in the absence of other ways to vet, these may suffice. (Another method to vet may be to acquire lists of professional experts who recently took a regulatory exam…and did well…and to use that as a pre-vetted list of experts. Or participants in contests for ill-structured problems may be invited to participate. Indeed, there are many additional creative ways to approach this.)

That said, if people are determined to participate, there are a number of counter-measures that may be taken against the measures to establish expertise. Non-experts may study up on one small aspect of a field and use that to establish bona fides. Or they may pre-create contents to respond to elicitations. They may make claims about affiliations, which are inaccurate. Various fraudulent assertions exist in the real as well, on a not irregular basis.

Also, this expertise requirement should also be caveated. Some of the major advancements in a field are discovered by those who are new entrants to the field, working with experts and peers. This suggests that there may be powerful ideas elicited from new experts, who have basic knowledge of the field but who are also very flexible in thinking. Some discoveries have come from accidents and new experiences. Even if a respondent is not found to be a full-fledged expert, their ideas may have potency and insight and value.

Another issue has to do with the sociality aspect for the participants in an e-Delphi study. For example, how aware should the participants be of others' responses (even as other participants are anonymized)? If there is actual facilitation, how can that be arranged for synchronous interaction? What sequencing of participant experiences is most effective for the proper level of rumination and feedback, in order to capture the most insightful data, albeit without leading the participants in one direction or another?

How can the research be protected and secured against a "bad actor" who may be interested in harming the research or skewing the data or sharing the data in mid-stream?

4. Data Analytics

Classical Delphi methods require ways of understanding expert "agreement" or "disagreement," often through correlational analyses, Cohen's Kappa analysis, text analysis, ranking scores, and other approaches. The analytics may be both explicit and implicit (and latent).

In OAODS research, the data analytics phase should include an in-depth data cleaning approach that removes (but does not erase) what may be manipulated or fraudulent data. While vetting for experts is often done on the front end in classical Delphi studies, and is partially done with online ones (in some cases), a wholly open-access one may mean that those who are "wanna-be's" or aspirants to expertise, trolls, and others, may access the OAODS instrument and provide feedback. For the data to be as clean as possible, these should be removed from the analysis. Also, if biases (perceptions, attitudes, beliefs, and others) are detected in each data row, it is possible to weight particular responses for different consideration. Depending on the size of the studies, which may well be much larger than initial Delphi studies, given the access to online respondents, the "law of small numbers" may apply less.

Another form of assessment may require more time. Riggs (1983) suggested that testing the actual predictivity of the forecasts from Delphi studies should be compared against real-world events (as compared to forecasts from other forecasting methods). Similarly, if the OAODS test is used in a foreshadowing or predictive way, then it can be asked whether the predictions occurred as predicted and within the time span expected. This form of external validity may be the hardest to capture. Triangulation, though, is seen as a way to "balance validity with innovation"; further,"… the greater the departure from classical Delphi, the more likely it is that the researcher will want to validate the results, by triangulation, with another research approach" (Skulmoski, Hartman, & Krahn, 2007, p. 12).

There is also the question of how the participants will be informed about findings after the research. Researchers may conduct an informal release of the initial findings, albeit without broadcasting any sensitive data. One downside to this early reportage is that the analyses may be tentative; another challenge is that the information may not yet be ready for prime time or for others' awareness. Another option is to just share access to the published research once everything has been polished and finalized.

5. Post Deployment OAODS Testing and Refinement

After a deployment of an OAODS instrument, the learning from that deployment may be applied to a refinement of the instrument, for more efficacious applications later on. Participants may also be debriefed about their experiences with the online Delphi study to improve on its usability. The data may be analyzed to see how efficacious the instrument was in deployment.

Mitigating for the Open-Access Availability of the OAODS Approach

One of the signature features of this OAODS approach is the open-access link. To mitigate the easy access to this type of e-Delphi study, it is important to consider interventions at various phases of this five-step process.

- Panel vetting (recruitment)
- Elicited panel member information (instrumentation)
- Elicited panel member performance (instrumentation)
- Online survey security settings (deployment)
- Fraud detection (deployment)
- Data cleaning (analysis)

- Data analysis (analysis)
- Instrument design and refinement (instrument)

These mitigations may be seen in (Figure 4)

DISCUSSION

This work proposes a unique type of electronic Delphi study, with open-access features and crowd-sourcing expert respondent panels. This approach has been dubbed the Open-Access Online Delphi Studies (OAODS), and this method is built conceptually around the Qualtrics Research Suite. These types of research may be maintained "in the wild" for single- or multi-round or continuous data collection, with scripted rounds to elicit further data as needed and with the harnessing of automation. This work also introduced four general parts to such instruments, defined in general terms.

A core feature of this work is thinking about how to motivate respondents from online spaces and how to verify the expertise of the respondents, through panel vetting, elicited panelist information, elicited panel member performance, online survey security settings, fraud detection, data cleaning, data analysis, and evolving instrument design and refinement. These efforts touch on a number of work phases: recruitment, instrumentation, deployment, analysis, and instrument revision and refinement.

Figure 4. Validating expert panelists in open-access online delphi studies (OAODS)

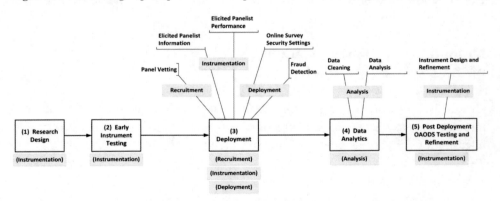

Validating Expert Panelists in Open-Access Online Delphi Studies (OAODS)

FUTURE RESEARCH DIRECTIONS

It may help to begin with some general research directions, such as: What are some other variations on both e-Delphi studies in general and OAODS approaches in particular? What are some challenges with this process? What are some ways to address inefficiencies or "process loss" in this method? What are ways to ensure that information is not missed or loss during the process?

There may be practical applied research, such as: How does OAODS work on a different experimental platform than Qualtrics?

In terms of future research, certainly, each step of the OAODS process may be further researched and refined: Research Design, Early Instrument Testing, Deployment, Data Analytics, and Post Deployment OAODS Testing and Refinement. Some sample questions follow:

Research Design

- Are there ways to optimize the combination of qualitative, quantitative, and mixed methods research?
- What are ways to create powerful instruments with high validity and reliability for a particular context?

Early Instrument Testing

- What are ways to effectively design OAODS instruments?
- What are relevant ways to test OAODS instruments?
- What are ways to harness cutting-edge multimedia for OAODS research?

Deployment

- What are ways to engage in expertise-hunting in a global environment to seat the optimal panels?
- Are there was to improve recruitment of experts with open links? With finite lists of experts?
- How can modern experts of all stripes be properly incentivized to engage… through the respective rounds…and with powerful insights?
- What are powerful ways to incentivize respondents from micropayment platforms, in ethical and professional ways?

- What are ways to benefit from the knowledge of experts with cross-domain skills?
- What standards should be applied to the selection of technologies used for OAODS studies? What functionalities are requisite, and which are desirable but less critical?
- Are there some risks of skewing results with certain tool features? Certain user bases of particular tools? How can these be mitigated for?
- What are fraud detection methods that can help identify non-experts or trolls during the survey phases and post-research when cleaning data?

Data Analytics

- What are powerful ways to clean data and identify "sketchy" responses from OAODS surveys? How may these data be managed without lossiness of authentic responses?
- How can outlier data be used and appreciated (and not automatically treated as problematic)?
- What are some computational analytics approaches that can optimize analysis of the data?

Post Deployment OAODS Testing and Refinement

- What are some ways to apply rigorous testing to OAODS instruments—for classic issues of validity and reliability? For accuracy, for efficacy, or for predictivity?
- What are some ways to conduct "alpha" and "beta" tests of OAODS instruments, and why?

CONCLUSION

The future, as a target, is a difficult one to understand because the future unfolds in non-linear ways, at punctuated equilibrium speeds, and is near impossible to predict with any level of accuracy. There are so many moving parts that even very simple computational simulations are rendered moot with more than a few elements because of combinatorial complexity, and forecasting can be a tough challenge. Capturing insights about ill-structured challenges, while somewhat less daunting than predicting the mid- and far-future, involves plenty of challenges as well given complexity and given dynamic simultaneous changes over time.

Open-Access Online Delphi Studies (OAODS) is a proposed approach to enable single-round, multi-round, and / or continuous ("roundless") e-Delphi studies online, with automated sequences (to stand in for the "discussion leader") and built-in ways to detect expertise through recruitment (panel vetting), instrumentation (elicited panel member information, elicited panel member performance), deployment (online survey security settings, fraud detection), analysis (data cleaning, data analysis), and additional instrumentation (instrument design and refinement).

REFERENCES

Aengenheyster, S., Cuhls, K., Gerhold, L., Heiskanen-Schöttler, M., Huck, J., & Muszynska, M. (2017). Real-Time Delphi in practice—A comparative analysis of existing software-based tools. *Technological Forecasting and Social Change, 118,* 15–27. doi:10.1016/j.techfore.2017.01.023

Andrews, D., Nonnecke, B., & Preece, J. (2010). Electronic survey methodology: A case study in reaching hard-to-involve Internet users. *International Journal of Human-Computer Interaction, 16,* 2.

Benton, M. C., Pappas, J., & Pappas, E. (2011). WordPress+Qualtrics: A plugin supporting research and new pedagogy to develop personal sustainability via 360° evaluation. In *Proceedings of 17ᵗʰ Americas Conference on Information Systems (AMCIS 2011).* Association for Information Systems AIS Electronic Library. Retrieved from https://aisel.aisnet.org/cgi/viewcontent.cgi?referer=https://www.google.com/&httpsredir=1&article=1129&context=amcis2011_submissions

Bolger, F., & Wright, G. (2011). Improving the Delphi process: Lessons from social psychological research. *Technological Forecasting and Social Change, 78*(9), 1500–1513. doi:10.1016/j.techfore.2011.07.007

Boulkedid, R., Abdoul, H., Loustau, M., Sibony, O., & Alberti, C. (2011, June). Using and reporting the Delphi Method for selecting healthcare quality indicators: A systematic review. *PLoS One, 6*(6), e20476. doi:10.1371/journal.pone.0020476 PMID:21694759

Bröggen, E., & Willems, P. (2009). A critical comparison of offline focus groups, online focus groups and e-Delphi. *International Journal of Market Research, 51*(3), 363–381. doi:10.2501/S1470785309200608

Brill, J.M., Bishop, M.J., & Walker, A.E. (2006). The competencies and characteristics required of an effective project manager: A web-based Delphi study. *Educational Technology Research and Development (ETR&D), 54*(2), 115 – 140.

Buchanan, T. (2018). Personality biases in different types of 'internet samples' can influence research outcomes. *Computers in Human Behavior, 86*, 235–244. doi:10.1016/j.chb.2018.05.002

Chan, A. P. C., Yung, E. H. K., Lam, P. T. I., Tam, C. M., & Cheung, S. O. (2001). Application of Delphi method in selection of procurement systems for construction projects. *Construction Management and Economics, 19*(7), 699–718. doi:10.1080/01446190110066128

Chang, P.-T., Huang, L.-C., & Lin, H.-J. (2000). The fuzzy Delphi method via fuzzy statistics and membership function fitting and an application to the human resources. *Fuzzy Sets and Systems, 112*(3), 511–520. doi:10.1016/S0165-0114(98)00067-0

Chou, C. (2002). Developing the e-Delphi system: A web-based forecasting tool for educational research. *British Journal of Educational Technology, 33*(2), 233–236. doi:10.1111/1467-8535.00257

Christenson, D. P., & Glick, D. M. (2013). Crowdsourcing panel studies and real-time experiments in MTurk. *The Political Methodologist, 20*(2), 27 – 32. Retrieved from https://thepoliticalmethodologist.files.wordpress.com/2013/09/tpm_v20_n21.pdf

Dalkey, N., & Helmer, O. (1962, July). *An experimental application of the Delphi Method to the use of experts. Memorandum.* RM-727/1-Abridged. Prepared for United States Air Force Project Rand. Retrieved on Sept. 26, 2018, from https://www.rand.org/pubs/research_memoranda/RM727z1.html

Dalkey, N., & Helmer, O. (1963, April). An experimental application of the Delphi Method to the use of experts. *Management Science, 9*(3), 458–467. doi:10.1287/mnsc.9.3.458

Delphi. (2018, Sept. 19). In *Wikipedia*. Retrieved from https://en.wikipedia.org/wiki/Delphi#Oracle_of_Delphi

Di Gangi, P.M., Johnston, A.C., Worrell, J.L., & Thompson, S.C. (2016). What could possibly go wrong? A multi-panel Delphi study of organizational social media risk. *Information Systems Frontiers*, 1 - 20. DOI: . doi:10.100710796-016-9714-2

Di Zio, S., & Pacinelli, A. (2011). Opinion convergence in location: A spatial version of the Delphi method. *Technological Forecasting and Social Change, 78*(9), 1565–1578. doi:10.1016/j.techfore.2010.09.010

Di Zio, S., Rosas, J. D. C., & Lamelza, L. (2017). Real Time Spatial Delphi: Fast convergence of experts' opinions on the territory. *Technological Forecasting and Social Change, 115,* 143–154. doi:10.1016/j.techfore.2016.09.029

Diamond, I. R., Grant, R. C., Feldman, B. M., Pencharz, P. B., Ling, S. C., Moore, A. M., & Wales, P. W. (2014). Defining consensus: A systematic review recommends methodologic criteria for reporting of Delphi studies. *Journal of Clinical Epidemiology, 67*(4), 401–409. doi:10.1016/j.jclinepi.2013.12.002 PMID:24581294

Donohoe, H., Stellefson, M., & Tennant, B. (2012). Advantages and limitations of the e-Delphi technique: Implications for health education researchers. *American Journal of Health Education, 43*(1), 38–46. doi:10.1080/19325037.2012.10599216

Elwyn, G., O'Connor, A., Stacey, D., Volk, R., Edwards, A., Coulter, A., ... Whelan, T. (2006). Developing a quality criteria framework for patient decision aids: Online international Delphi consensus process. *BMJ (Clinical Research Ed.),* 1–15. PMID:16908462

Erffmeyer, R. C., Erffmeyer, E. S., & Lane, I. M. (1986). The Delphi technique: An empirical evaluation of the optimal number of rounds. *Group & Organization Studies, 11*(1-2), 120–128. doi:10.1177/105960118601100110

Ferri, C. P., Prince, M., Brayne, C., Brodaty, H., Fratiglioni, L., Ganguli, M., ... Scazufca, M. (2005). Global prevalence of dementia: A Delphi consensus study. *Lancet, 366*(9503), 2112–2117. doi:10.1016/S0140-6736(05)67889-0 PMID:16360788

Franklin, K. K., & Hart, J. K. (2007). Idea generation and exploration: Benefits and limitations of the Policy Delphi Research Method. *Innovative Higher Education, 31*(4), 237–246. doi:10.100710755-006-9022-8

Geist, M. R. (2010). Using the Delphi method to engage stakeholders: A comparison of two studies. *Evaluation and Program Planning, 33*(2), 147–154. doi:10.1016/j.evalprogplan.2009.06.006 PMID:19581002

Gnatzy, T., Warth, J., von der Gracht, H., & Darkow, I.-L. (2011). Validating an innovative real-time Delphi approach – A methodological comparison between real-time and conventional Delphi studies. *Technological Forecasting and Social Change, 78*(9), 1681–1694. doi:10.1016/j.techfore.2011.04.006

Gomez-Sanz, J. J., & Fernandez, R. F. (2015). Revisiting the Delphi Method for agents. In J. Bajo (Eds.), PAAMS 2015 Workshops, CCIS 524. Academic Press. doi:10.1007/978-3-319-19033-4_32

Gordon, T., & Pease, A. (2006). RT Delphi: An efficient, 'round-less' almost real time Delphi method. *Technological Forecasting and Social Change, 73*(4), 321–333. doi:10.1016/j.techfore.2005.09.005

Gordon, T. J. (2009). The Real-Time Delphi Method. In J.C. Glenn & T.J. Gordon (Eds.), *Futures Research Methodology Version 3.0.* The Millennium Project, American Council for the United Nations University. Retrieved from http://107.22.164.43/millennium/RTD-method.pdf

Green, B., Jones, M., Hughes, D., & Williams, A. (1999). Applying the Delphi technique in a study of GPs' information requirements. *Health & Social Care in the Community, 7*(3), 198–205. doi:10.1046/j.1365-2524.1999.00176.x PMID:11560634

Hai-Jew, S. (2014). Iff and Other Conditionals: Expert perceptions of the feasibility of Massive Open Online Courses (MOOCs) – A modified E-Delphi study. In S. Hai-Jew (Eds.), Remote Workforce Training: Effective Technologies and Strategies. Hershey, PA: IGI Global.

Hai-Jew, S. (2014, June 20). Expert perceptions of the feasibility of MOOCs. *SlideShare.* Retrieved Sept. 26, 2018, from https://www.slideshare.net/ShalinHaiJew/feasibilityof-moo-cs

Hallowell, M. R., & Gambatese, J. A. (2010). Qualitative research: Application of the Delphi Method to CEM Research. *Journal of Construction Engineering and Management, 136*(1), 99–107. doi:10.1061/(ASCE)CO.1943-7862.0000137

Hasson, F., & Keeney, S. (2011). Enhancing rigour in the Delphi technique research. *Technological Forecasting and Social Change, 78*(9), 1695–1704. doi:10.1016/j.techfore.2011.04.005

Heen, M.S.J., Lieberman, J.D., & Miethe, T.D. (2014, Sept.). *A comparison of different online sampling approaches for generating national samples.* Research in Brief. Center for Crime and Justice Policy. University of Nevada, Las Vegas.

Holey, E. A., Feeley, J. L., Dixon, J., & Whittaker, V. J. (2007). An exploration of the use of simple statistics to measure consensus and stability in Delphi studies. *BMC Medical Research Methodology, 7*(52), 1–10. PMID:18045508

Jeste, D. V., Ardelt, M., Blazer, D., Kraemer, H. C., Vaillan, G., & Meeks, T. W. (2010). Expert consensus on characteristics of wisdom: A Delphi Method study. *The Gerontologist, 50*(5), 668–680. doi:10.1093/geront/gnq022 PMID:20233730

Keeney, S., Hasson, F., & McKenna, H. (2006). Consulting the oracle: Ten lessons from using the Delphi technique in nursing research. *Methodological Issues in Nursing Research,* 205 – 212.

Kramer, B. S., Walker, A. E., & Brill, J. M. (2007). The underutilization of information and communication technology-assisted collaborative project-based learning among international educators: A Delphi study. *Educational Technology Research and Development, 55*(5), 527–543. doi:10.100711423-007-9048-3

Landeta, J., Barrutia, J., & Lertxundi, A. (2011). Hybrid Delphi: A methodology to facilitate contribution from experts in professional contexts. *Technological Forecasting and Social Change, 78*(9), 1629–1641. doi:10.1016/j.techfore.2011.03.009

Linstone, H. A., & Turoff, M. (2011). Delphi: A brief look backward and forward. *Technological Forecasting and Social Change, 78*(9), 1712–1719. doi:10.1016/j.techfore.2010.09.011

Loo, R. (2002). The Delphi method: A powerful tool for strategic management. *Policing: An International Journal of Police Strategies & Management, 25*(4), 762–769. doi:10.1108/13639510210450677

Lowry, P. B., D'Arcy, J., Hammer, B., & Moody, G. D. (2016). 'Cargo Cult' science in traditional organization and information systems survey research: A case for using nontraditional systems of data collection, including Mechanical Turk and online panels. *The Journal of Strategic Information Systems, 25*(3), 232–240. doi:10.1016/j.jsis.2016.06.002

Makkonen, M., Hujala, T., & Uusivuori, J. (2016). Policy experts' propensity to change their opinion along Delphi rounds. *Technological Forecasting and Social Change, 109*, 61–68. doi:10.1016/j.techfore.2016.05.020

Meijering, J. V., & Tobi, H. (2016). The effect of controlled opinion feedback on Delphi features: Mixed messages from a real-world Delphi experiment. *Technological Forecasting and Social Change, 103*, 166–173. doi:10.1016/j.techfore.2015.11.008

Miller, L. E. (2006, Oct.). *Determining what could/should be: The Delphi technique and its application.* In The 2006 annual meeting of the Mid-Western Educational Research Association, Columbus, OH.

Murry, J.W., Jr., & Hammons, J.O. (1995). Delphi: A versatile methodology for conducting qualitative research. *The Review of Higher Education, 18*(4), 423 – 436. DOI: doi:10.1353/rhe.1995.0008

Neale, J., Finch, E., Marsden, J., Mitcheson, L., Rose, D., Strang, J., ... Wykes, T. (2014, August). How should we measure addiction recovery? Analysis of service provider perspectives using online Delphi groups. *Drugs Education Prevention & Policy*, *21*(4), 310–323. doi:10.3109/09687637.2014.918089

Nowack, M., Endrikat, J., & Guenther, E. (2011). Review of Delphi-based scenario studies: Quality and design considerations. *Technological Forecasting and Social Change*, *78*(9), 1603–1615. doi:10.1016/j.techfore.2011.03.006

Oostendorp, L. J. M., Durand, M.-A., Lloyd, A., & Elwyn, G. (2015). Measuring organizational readiness for patient engagement (MORE): An international online Delphi consensus study. *BMC Health Services Research*, *15*(61), 1–13. PMID:25879457

Pankratova, N. D., & Malafeeva, L. Y. (2012, September). Formalizing the consistency of experts' judgments in the Delphi method. *Cybernetics and Systems Analysis*, *48*(5), 711–721. doi:10.100710559-012-9451-6

Phillips, A. C., Lewis, L. K., McEvoy, M. P., Galipeau, J., Glasziou, P., Hammick, M., ... Williams, M. T. (2014). A Delphi survey to determine how educational interventions for evidence-based practice should be reported: Stage 2 of the development of a reporting guideline. *BMC Medical Education*, *14*(1), 159–170. doi:10.1186/1472-6920-14-159 PMID:25081371

Rayens, M. K., & Hahn, E. J. (2000). Building consensus using the Policy Delphi Method. *Policy, Politics & Nursing Practice*, *1*(4), 308–315. doi:10.1177/152715440000100409

Riggs, W. E. (1983). The Delphi technique: An experiment evaluation. *Technological Forecasting and Social Change*, *23*(1), 89–94. doi:10.1016/0040-1625(83)90073-2

Rodríguez-Mañas, L., Féart, C., Mann, G., Viña, J., Chatterji, S., Chodzko-Zajko, W., ... Vega, E. (2013, January). Searching for an operational definition of frailty: A Delphi Method based consensus statement, The Frailty Operative Definition-Consensus Conference Project. *The Journals of Gerontology. Series A, Biological Sciences and Medical Sciences*, *68*(1), 62–67. doi:10.1093/gerona/gls119 PMID:22511289

Ross, A. M., Kelly, C. M., & Jorm, A. F. (2014). Re-development of mental health first aid guidelines for suicidal ideation and behaviour (sic): A Delphi study. *BMC Psychiatry*, *14*(1), 241–252. doi:10.118612888-014-0241-8 PMID:25213799

Schnyer, R. N., Conboy, L. A., Jacobson, E., McKnight, P., Goddard, T., Moscatelli, F., ... Wayne, P. M. (2005). Development of a Chinese medicine assessment measure: An interdisciplinary approach using the Delphi method. *Journal of Alternative and Complementary Medicine (New York, N.Y.)*, *11*(6), 1005–1013. doi:10.1089/acm.2005.11.1005 PMID:16398591

Skulmoski, G. J., Hartman, F. T., & Krahn, J. (2007). The Delphi Method for graduate research. *Journal of Information Technology Education*, *6*, 1–21. doi:10.28945/199

Smyth, J. D., & Olson, K. (2019). The effects of mismatches between survey question stems and response options on data quality and responses. *Journal of Survey Statistics and Methodology*, *7*(1), 34–65. doi:10.1093/jssammy005

Steurer, J. (2011). The Delphi method: An efficient procedure to generate knowledge. *Skeletal Radiology*, *40*(8), 959–961. doi:10.100700256-011-1145-z PMID:21667147

Tapio, P., Paloniemi, R., Varho, V., & Vinnari, M. (2011). The unholy marriage? Integrating qualitative and quantitative information in Delphi processes. *Technological Forecasting and Social Change*, *78*(9), 1616–1628. doi:10.1016/j.techfore.2011.03.016

Turoff, M., & Hiltz, R. (1996). Computer based Delphi processes. In M. Adler & E. Ziglio (Eds.), *Gazing into the Oracle: The Delhi Method and its Application to Social Policy and Public Health*. London: Kingsley Publishers. Retrieved from https://web.njit.edu/~turoff/Papers/delphi3.html

Turoff, M., Hiltz, S. R., Yao, X., Li, Z., Wang, Y., & Cho, H.-K. (2006). Online collaborative learning enhancement through the Delphi Method. *Turkish Online Journal of Distance Education*, *7*(2), 66–79.

Van de Linde, E., & van der Duin, P. (2011). The Delphi method as early warning: Linking global societal trends to future radicalization and terrorism in The Netherlands. *Technological Forecasting and Social Change*, *78*(9), 1557–1564. doi:10.1016/j.techfore.2011.07.014

von der Gracht, H. A. (2012). Consensus measurement in Delphi studies: Review and implications for future quality assurance. *Technological Forecasting and Social Change*, *79*(8), 1525–1536. doi:10.1016/j.techfore.2012.04.013

Voss, J. F., & Post, T. A. (1988). On the solving of ill-structured problems. In M. T. H. Chi, R. Glaser, & M. J. Farr (Eds.), *The nature of expertise* (pp. 261–285). Hillsdale, NJ: Lawrence Erlbaum Associates, Inc.

ADDITIONAL READING

Linstone, H. A., & Turoff, M. (2002). *The Delphi Method: Techniques and Applications.* Retrieved from https://web.njit.edu/~turoff/pubs/delphibook/delphibook.pdf

KEY TERMS AND DEFINITIONS

Consensus: Consent, agreement.

Debriefing: An elicitation of information to better understand a phenomenon or event.

Delphi Study: A type of research involving experts, who engage in single- or multi-stage rounds of questions and other elicitations, in order to understand elusive future events or other topics.

Discussion Leader: Facilitator of a Delphi study.

Dissensus: Dissent, disagreement.

E-Delphi Study: An electronic Delphi study deployed off of a socio-technical platform, such as a dedicated platform, an online survey platform, or social media platform.

Expert Panel: The individuals who have varying levels of expertise in a particular domain, mixed-domain, or peripheral domain.

Open-Access Online Delphi Studies (OAODS): Often-continuous online (electronic) Delphi studies that involve open links that self-professed experts may access and respond to (requiring validation of expertise).

Real-Time Delphi Study: An online Delphi study with potentially only one round.

Round: An iteration or "wave" of a Delphi study.

Chapter 4

Conducting a Basic Self-Explicated Conjoint Analysis Online With Qualtrics®

ABSTRACT

A recent feature in the Qualtrics® Research Core Platform 2018 (or Qualtrics Research Suite) is a basic self-explicated conjoint analysis, which is a research method to understand respondent preferences in a real-world context with limited available features and selection tradeoffs at respective price points. This chapter will introduce the basic self-explicated conjoint analysis tool and how to design questions for this, how to deploy the conjoint analysis (as either part of a larger survey or as a stand-alone survey), and how to analyze and use the resulting data. This chapter will describe the assertability of the findings based on the back-end factorial statistical analysis and suggest ways to explore beyond the initial conjoint analysis.

INTRODUCTION

On a typical day, a person may make hundreds of decisions based on his or her conscious, subconscious and unconscious preferences. These decisions may be mundane, but they may also be surprisingly persistent; taken together, individual decisions may have personal impacts, including larger-scale emergent ones. Individuals and organizations have an interest in eliciting client preferences, so they may provide the products and services that others want. There are a certain class

DOI: 10.4018/978-1-5225-8563-3.ch004

of survey instruments that enable choice experiments, through "choice modeling," a term of art that collectively refers to "choice experiments, contingent ranking, contingent rating, (and) paired comparisons" (Hanley, Mourato, & Wright, 2001, p. 438), among others. "Choice experiments" require respondents to "choose between two or more alternatives (where one is the status quo)"; "contingent ranking" research requires respondents to "rank a series of alternatives"; "contingent rating" research requires respondents to "score alternative scenarios on a scale of 1 – 10"; "paired comparisons" require respondents to "score pairs of scenarios on similar scale" (Hanley, Mourato, & Wright, 2001, p. 438).

One basic and popular form of choice experiments research is the "conjoint analysis" (CA), in which respondents make selections of particular attributes or packages of attributes based on their own preferences about a particular product, service, or decision space (in real-world and practical contexts and sometimes in theorized ones). "Conjoint analysis" is a collective term, "covering both the theory and methods of a variety of different paradigms that can be used to design, implement and analyse (sic) *judgment data* experiments" …or "evaluative rankings or ratings of a set of multi-attribute alternatives" (Louviere, 1988, pp. 94 – 95). The sets of multi-attribute alternatives may be constructed using experimental or quasi-experimental design techniques.

Conjoint analyses come in various types. These variants are…

… based on the way preference scores are elicited (e.g., ratings, rankings, self-explicated, constant sum, choice), the type of designs used (e.g., full factorial, fractional factorial, adaptive), the type of models estimated (e.g., regression, logit, probit, hierarchical Bayes), and the estimation procedures employed to make inferneces (e.g., maximum likelihood, Markov Chain Monte Carlo) (Ding, Grewal, & Liechty, 2004, p. 1).

One classification of types is by those in a conjoint analysis suite in Qualtrics, which include the following: self-explicated conjoint analysis, choice-based / discrete choice, adaptive choice-based, menu-based, and MaxDiff ("What is a conjoint…?" 2018). Other types differentiate between classic conjoint analyses and adaptive ones, which are computerized and adapt to the feedback from the survey participants. "Conjointedness" refers to the "combining of all (factors) involved," so preferences in a constrained practical environment become clearer.

A basic self-explicated conjoint analysis in Qualtrics enables the building of a conjoint module that presents various specific attributes (features, dimensions) of a product, service, or choice space; the attributes are optimally "orthogonal," with no overlap with other features (so the analysis may be discriminative between attributes and features) and sufficiently sensitive), and survey respondents select their best-worst options among the subsets, and their in-between preferences (between their defined best-worst preferences) in a stepwise approach. This research method helps explicitly decompose the respective variables that affect people's decision-making in selecting particular products, services, or policies. One research team describes conjoint analysis as a decompositional method:

CA is a decompositional method which asks for general judgments on alternatives (stimuli, products) which are decomposed into part-worths for single attribute levels. In any version of CA, the DM (note: decompositional method) has to evaluate tradeoffs between different levels of several attributes in order to decide whether an alternative A is better, equivalent or worse than another alternative B and sometimes additionally how strong this preference is. (Scholl, Manthey, Helm, & Steiner, 2005, p. 766)

The resulting data is reported out as user preferences captured as part-worths, measures of respondent utility in relation to particular attributes (factors or dimensions) of a target product, service, or other choice-space. Part-worths are also known as attribute importance scores, level values, utility scores, and others. The idea was to apply "an attribute-based theory of value" in the research (Hanley, Mourato, & Wright, 2001, p. 435). A range of part-worth estimation methods emerged from the 1960s – 1980s, with various feature mixes of profiles (full or part), variable types, and variable features (Carroll & Green, Nov. 1995, p. 386), described in a light classification. How part-worth measures are calculated may be fairly complex:

Consequently, most practical and academic researchers who analyse ranking judgments assume that individuals' rankings are generated by a strictly additive (no non-additivities or interactions) function of the unknown part-worth utility measures. Part-worth utilities are estimated by least-squares procedures (for example, MONANOVA) that optimise the fit between observed and predicted rankings, assuming that an additive utility specification is correct. "Badness-of fit" statistics known as "stress" measures are used as an index of how well additive or other specifications fit the observed rankings. Unfortunately, "stress" measures are closely related (Louviere, 1988, p. 95).

In the research literature, conjoint analyses have been applied to estimate or forecast human preferences in business, marketing, political science, healthcare, economics, transportation, and the environment, among others. The acceptance of this method has resulted in the availability of a quality checklist for how to run such studies in the domain, in this case, healthcare (Bridges, et al., 2011 p. 406). Stated-preference methods are a class of evaluation techniques to study the interests of stakeholders (Johnson, et al, 2013, p. 6).

Setting up conjoint analyses require various steps. One older work suggests that six steps are required: "selection of a model of preference, data collection method, stimulus set construction for the full-profile method, stimulus presentation, measurement scale for the dependent variable, (and) estimation method" (Green & Srinivasan, Sept. 1978, p. 105), to set up these "alternate models of preference" (p. 106).

The stages of setting up a choice modeling exercise include the following: "selection of attributes, assignment of levels, choice of experimental design, construction of choice sets, measurement of preferences, and estimation procedure" (Hanley, Mourato, & Wright, 2001, p. 437). This sequence is even simpler viewed from the side of setting up a software version of a conjoint analysis, in four steps: "configure, review, distribute, (and) analyze" (*12 business decisions…*, 2018, p. 9), aided by a software conjoint configuration wizard.

This chapter provides an overview of how to create a research design and set up a self-explicated conjoint analysis on the cloud-based Qualtrics® Research Core Platform 2018. The makers of the Qualtrics® Research Core Platform 2018 with a basic conjoint analysis integration calls this "the foremost methodology for getting customer insights on product development, pricing, packaging, benefits decision, and so much more" in their e-book *12 business decisions you can optimize with conjoint analysis* (2018, p. 3). The business case for such studies is to better understand consumers in the market, and to segment them based on purchasing power and preferences in combination. This information may help avoid suboptimal combinations of products and services to consumers but to get as close to consumer preferences as possible, given the limits of the prices that consumers are willing to pay. [Shortly after this work was completed, Qualtrics retracted this feature from the Qualtrics Research Core Platform 2018, and they moved it to a conjoint analysis suite available at a different licensure level. This means that those who may want this feature either have to add a full conjoint analysis suite (with a wide range of additional conjoint analyses), or create their own using the online survey tool and then analytics outside of the tool to capture the fractional factorial insights.] Qualtrics, a blended and disambiguated term from "quality" and "metrics" (Robinson, Sept. 24, 2018), is one of the foremost companies in the world enabling online research.

REVIEW OF THE LITERATURE

The core work credited with introducing conjoint analysis into the customer preference space stems from 1971, with efforts at "quantifying judgmental data" and turning "rank-ordered input, yet yield(ing) interval-scaled output" (Green and Rao, 1971, p. 355). The co-authors write, "As the name suggests, conjoint measurement is concerned with the joint effect of two or more independent variables on the *ordering* of a dependent variable" (Green and Rao, 1971, p. 355). Conjoint measurement "has psychometric origins as a theory to decompose an ordinal scale of holistic judgment into interval scales for each component attributes (sic) (Hauser & Rao, 2002, p. 1). The "conjoint measurement" originated as "a new development in mathematical psychology" (Green and Rao, 1971, p. 355). Some argue that from a more purely mathematical standpoint, conjoint analysis (CA) may be the wrong tool to use: conjoint analysis "evolved out of the theory of "conjoint measurement" (CM), which is purely mathematical and concerned with the behavior of number systems, not the behavior of humans or human preferences" (Louviere, Flynn, & Carson, 2010, p. 59); these authors suggest that "discrete choice experiments" may be more applicable in economic demand research. Others suggest other theoretical approaches informing the CA process: "Theoretical justification for the multiattribute modeling of consumer preferences was provided in the growing literature on the Fishbein-Rosenberg class of expectancy-value models and the new economic theory of consumer choice" (Lancaster 1971; Ratchford 1975, as cited Green & Srinivasan, 1975, p. 104). Going back further, the Von Neumann-Morgenstern utility theory (1947), which suggests that people make decisions based on the expected value of a function or action, also informs this work. The respective measures of "utils," or units of satisfaction, are measured in part by CA (as "utility coefficients").

"Discrete Choice Experiments," dating back to Thurstone (1927), offers selections as pairs of options (Louviere, Pihlens, & Carson, 2010, p. 2). More modern "choice experiments" were first introduced in 1983 based on "simulated choice situations" (Louviere & Woodworth, Nov. 1983). Early applications were for product and service design, but over the years, have been applied to public goods like the environment (Hanley, Wright, & Adamowicz, 1998). Preference studies differentiate between revealed preferences, which address latent preferences, as compared to explicitly stated preferences. Broadly speaking, the various attributes of products, services, and choice-spaces may be composed into packages of tightly-coupled goods, or they may be decomposed into lightly-coupled attributes that together make up a high-level feature of a product, service, or choice-space.

Attributes are variables that together comprise top-level features of products and services. "Attributes" are "the entire set of product/service variables that will be tested within the conjoint study. The attributes will be the entire structure of factors for the respondent to consider when evaluating bundles. The attributes will be architected in a nested-hierarchy with multiple variables that can range from 2 to N units" (*12 business decisions…*, 2018, p. 8). And "levels" are "the units found within each of the features" and "the base item of the conjoint study and will be interchanged in the bundles presented to the respondent" (*12 business decisions…*, 2018, p. 8). Simpler forms of conjoint analyses may not necessarily include levels. For example, in terms of preferences for "instructional design" services, perhaps not all services may be desirable, and only some will be preferred over others. In this case, what is being selected will be attributes, not levels of particular attributes. Table 1 shows some ways to conceptualize the general elements of a conjoint analysis (with the caveat that attribution levels may or may not be used, and that there will be varying numbers of high-level features and attributes (the choices that respondents will engage).

Table 2 shows the delivery of a training service.

Some filled tables follow below to show how these elements may work. Table 3 shows a combined product (the food) and service (the presentations) in a high-end tasting menu performance.

Table 4 shows a conceptualized choice space.

In theory, there are large numbers of possible choices with just a few features and a few attributes and related levels; however, not all the available combinations will be offered for respondents. Rather, given real-world trade-offs, the attributes and

Table 1. Basic compositional elements of a generic self-explicated conjoint analysis

(Target) Product / Service / Choice-Space					
High-Level Feature A		**High-Level Feature B**		**High-Level Feature C**	
Attribution A1		Attribution B1		Attribution C1	
	A1 Attribution Levels		B1 Attribution Levels		C1 Attribution Levels
Attribution A2		Attribution B2		Attribution C2	
	A2 Attribution Levels		B2 Attribution Levels		C2 Attribution Levels
Attribution A3		Attribution B3		Attribution C3	
	A3 Attribution Levels		B3 Attribution Levels		C3 Attribution Levels

Table 2. A basic training as a self-explicated conjoint analysis

A Requested Training					
Professional Trainer(s)		**Target Topic Coverage**		**Learning Practice**	
In-person and face-to-face		**Minimal**		**Basic practice**	
	Room sizes, Room amenities,		Basic introductory topics		Usage of paper and pencil practices, Basic hands-on practices
Virtual trainer(s)		**Intermediate**		**Intermediate practice**	
	In-person rooms, Room amenities, Virtual option (live or pre-recorded)		Intermediate topics		Usage of high-end and loaded laptops, Access to digital downloadables, Medium range of trained skills
Attribution A3		**Extensive**		**Advanced practice**	
	A3 Attribution Levels		Advanced topics		Usage of high-end and loaded laptops, Access to downloadables, Customized supports, Wide range of trained skills

Table 3. A high-end tasting menu and performance as a self-explicated conjoint analysis

A High-end Tasting Menu and "Performance"					
Menu		**High-Level Feature B**		**Server Performances**	
Menu Option A with Dessert		Chef's Appearance with Basic Story		Food Service by Team	
	Regional Selections		Story A, Photos		Basic Presentations and Interactions
Menu Option B with Two Desserts		Chef's Appearance with Extended Story		Food Service by Team and Musical Performance / Accompaniment	
	Deluxe Regional Selections, with Seasonal Specialties, Dessert Types		Story B, Photos		Song Lists
Menu Option C with Two Desserts and Wine Options		Chef's Appearance with Demo		Food Service by Team and Musical Performance / Accompaniment and Dramatic Performances	
	Luxury Regional Selections, with Seasonal Specialties, Chef's Choice of Special Sides, Dessert Types, Wine Options		Story C, Photos, Cooking Demo Types		Music Performance Selections, Dramatic Performance Types

Table 4. A voting choice-space as a self-explicated conjoint analysis

A Voting Ballot						
Position A		Position B		Policy Option		
Candidate A		Candidate A		Yes		
	Candidate features, Policy stances		Candidate features, Policy stances			Attributes
Candidate B		Candidate B		No		
	Candidate features, Policy stances		Candidate features, Policy stances			Status Quo
Candidate C		Write-in				
	Candidate features, Policy stances		Candidate features, Policy stances			

levels offered will be depicted in ways that reflect what is feasible. An underlying assumption is a "can't have everything" approach and one of trade-offs (more of one variable will mean less of another, in a somewhat zero sum way). Qualtrics documentation suggests adding "at least three features, but no more than eight" (*12 business decisions…*, 2018, p. 12), and within each of these features are a certain number of attributes and under those particular levels. Other considerations include the limits of respondent motivation, mental focus, and fatigue, with recommendations for such assessments to run two to 10 minutes only.

Presentation Order

Once attributes have been identified, how they may be presented (and in what order) is also relevant because prior research has identified variations in respondent responses based on the order of the presented attributes: "The order in which attributes appear within the conjoint profiles and the order of the conjoint task in the overall survey can both affect subjects' responses enough to influence resulting conjoint models significantly (Johnson, 1989; Huber et al., 1991, as cited in Chrzan 1994, p. 165).

Precision Data?

The precision in results from conjoint analyses depends on various factors in addition to presentation order. Sample sizes may be a factor: "For all studies, precision increases rapidly at sample sizes less than 150 and then flattens out at around 300 observations" (Johnson, et al, 2013, p. 6). In other words, sample sizes smaller than 150 benefit from more numbers of respondents, but at around 300, the marginal benefits of each new respondent may decline. There is the sense that out-of-sample prediction needs to be strengthened. For others, the lack of actual consequences has meant a move to using small amounts of money to incentivize a stronger sense of consequence and realism and "true" preferences (for compensatory decision making).

There are controls for how many choices a participant is asked to make to avoid respondent fatigue. One team suggests "ten to 15 choices in a conjoint analysis study, with each choice task involving three to five different competitive alternatives" (Garver, Williams, Taylor, & Wynmne, 2011, p. 130).

Once the data are collected, a number of different statistical modeling approaches (e.g. logit, latent class, counting analysis, etc.) can be used to calculate quantitative importance scores for each attribute as well as preference scores for the different levels of performance on that attribute (Orme, 2009). Hierarchical Bayes (HB) estimation may be the best estimation method for conjoint models, particularly because results are at the individual level for both importance and preference scores (Gilbride and Allenby, 2004). Note that both of these metrics are essential in the formation of actual customer choices and for need-based segmentation" (Garver, Williams, Taylor, & Wynmne, 2011, p. 133).

This analytical method also enables relating preferences to demographic factors, to understand market segmentation and to inform business and marketing strategies.

There are a range of statistical methods to strengthen the analysis of data quality for online conjoint analyses (Melles, Laumann, & Holling, 2000, pp. 34 - 35). Researchers suggest the importance of taking reasonable steps to shore up the value of online conjoint analyses in terms of validity and reliability, including using "as many criteria as possible to test the reliability and validity of the conjoint analysis," incentivizing respondents to give "reliable responses (e.g. giving a feedback of goodness-of-fit)," encouraging respondents to provide feedback and to "use as much feedback as possible," to prevent multiple responses from individuals, and sorting out bad data (Melles, Laumann, & Holling, 2000, p. 37). It is important to minimize participant dropouts from the research by using effective web design, incentivizing, the time brevity of the online conjoint analysis, and emphasizing "the importance of completely filled in questionnaires" (Melles, Laumann, & Holling, 2000, p. 34), which is often handled technologically using forced-responses.

Another design angle requires an optimal number of profiles that respondents may engage:

The specific set of these profiles must meet some critical requirements to produce optimal results. The minimal advisable number of profiles that participants need to evaluate is typically a multiple of the difference between the total number of levels and the number of attributes used. The set of profiles should be relatively balanced (each level of an attribute should appear an equal number of times) and orthogonal (each level of an attribute should appear together with each level of every other attribute approximately the same number of times). The researcher can choose to exclude the pairing of some levels and attributes to increase the realism of the test... (Caruso, Rahnev & Banaji, 2009, p. 130)

Other efforts to strengthen CAs include multiple factors related to research design and sampling:

The results of the study suggest that the measurement scale and the size of the holdout sample can have a significant impact on conjoint analysis results. In general, rating scales tend to be more reliable than ranking scales. However, rank order data were better predictors of product moment correlations and the percentage of correct hits than were self-explicated data, and rating tasks were better for predicting the correct first choice (Loveland, Dec. 1995, p. ix).

Another way to test the efficacy of conjoint analyses in a particular case is to see how well the participant preferences line up with in-world behaviors and "observed behavior" data. If a conjoint analysis is capturing actual preferences, there may be convergent validity based on findings from other research methods... potential alignment with in-world behaviors (external validity), and theorized validity (based on relevant theory, models, and theoretical frameworks, and follow-on theorizing). "Consumer utility functions" should have evidence in the world for external validity (McKenna 1985).

Part-worths are usually scaled to sum to zero for each attribute, with negative and positive values for each level of an attribute (or if levels are not used, each attribute of a high level feature). A high positive number indicates higher desirability, and a negative number indicates undesirability, and 0 is neutral. (These values may also be represented as percentages or decimal-based values). From these utility measures, it is possible to calculate the relative importance of the attribute within the feature space. Likewise, it is possible to calculate the importance of each feature within the product, service, or choice-space. Various quantitative data types may be created from conjoint analyses, including nominal or categorical data, ordinal or ranking data, interval data (based on equal increments), and ratio data. One work explains how the data are captured and analyzed:

Those stimuli are selected by systematically deriving a fractional factorial design. Such a set of stimuli can be represented as a plan which contains stimuli as rows and attributes and their levels, respectively, as columns. The (note: multi-attribute) design has to fulfill certain conditions such that the further steps of CA can be performed properly. In particular, the levels of different attributes must be independent from each other, i.e., the corresponding columns of the array have to be uncorrelated. Arrays which meet this elementary requirement are called orthogonal. (Scholl, Manthey, Helm, & Steiner, 2005, p. 767)

Part-worths may be expressed in multiple ways, such as linear preferences (on a line graph, with increasing preferences as compared to decreasing preferences), idea-point preferences (the highest preference in a curve), and discrete (part-worth) preferences (as points of highest preference, next highest preference, lowest preference) (Green, Krieger, & Wind, May-Jun., 2001, p. S60).

Some researchers have observed risks to online conjoint analyses and suggest that there is "lower reliability" as compared to computational conjoint analyses:

The results show that data drawn from an Internet conjoint analysis seem to be somewhat lower in reliability (internal consistency) compared to traditional computerized conjoint analysis. Nevertheless, the reliability seems to be sufficient even in the case of its online form. Regarding predictive validity, both data collection methods lead to comparable results. There is no evidence that the number of thirty paired comparisons might be too high in the case of Internet conjoint analysis. More paired comparisons seem to be favorable taking the moderate internal consistency of responses into account and the additional possibilities of reliability testing (Melles, Laumann, & Holling, 2000, p. 31).

Some red flags may be collinearity between explanatory variables (Freeman, 1993), which may result in coefficients with wrong signs (+, -) or implausible magnitudes (Greene, 1993), so these should be controlled for (Earnhart, 1998, p. 5). Attribute data is often orthogonal (with other attributes fixed while the level of another attribute changes) to avoid collinearity, where a predictor variable can be linearly predicted from others (so indicated an association and a relationship), which may suggest that the attributes themselves are representing some shared construct potentially. When researchers may choose from the numerous possible combinations of features and attributes and levels, many select more "orthogonal arrays" of respective attributes (Green, Krieger, & Wind, May-Jun., 2001, p. S57).

In general, respondent utility for a particular product, service, or other decision-space is calculated as an additive part-worth function, with the overall evaluation of collective features decomposed to relative part-worth utils related to the respective attributes. Multiple attributes collectively define features, and features themselves collectively define a product, service, or choice-space. The understandings from conjoint analyses may inform how to select features and attributes for particular products and services; they may be suggestive of people's preferences in policies and other choice-spaces. This work is informed by multi-attribute value theory.

Recently popularized research suggests that people tend to make decisions in environments of uncertainty based on a number of cognitive biases. Respondent surveys are limited by various response biases, including the social influence of others and people's need to be liked and to belong socially and to please others. The assumption that people act on their preferences may not be an accurate one, and there may be gaps between stated intentionality and actual actions. A self-explicated conjoint analysis deals with stated respondent preferences, albeit with these limitations and others. Some have applied conjoint analyses to understand people's latent or "covert preferences" vs. overt ones by using indirect or implicit measures (Caruso, Rahnev & Banaji, 2009). One compelling study found a distinct preference for thinner prospective teammates and a willingness to accept lower IQ in a partner in order to have one with less weight (Caruso, Rahnev & Banaji, 2009), a bias that people may not be aware of or which would be too difficult to admit socially due to social costs.

SETTING UP A CONJOINT ANALYSIS ONLINE

The details in Table 1 help inform the research design. The prompts to the respective CA respondents may be text-based, or imagery, audio, video, and simulation elements may also be brought into play to enrich the respondent experience and elicit particular information. The conjoint analysis may be designed for face-to-face usage, blended usage, or fully online usage.

Once the research design has been completed, the next step is to set this up in Qualtrics. This tool is a cloud-based one created by the leading company in online research currently. The conjoint analysis may be part of a survey with other question types and features, or it may be a stand-alone work. It is necessary to set up a "project" first. Once, that is done, from the Tools dropdown, select "Conjoint Analysis" (Figure 1).

A window with all existing created conjoint analyses will open. In the same way that saved surveys and saved blocks and saved questions may be re-used, conjoint analyses themselves may be reused across projects. They may also be shared with others for co-editing and co-use.

Figure 1. "Conjoint analyses…" in dropdown menu

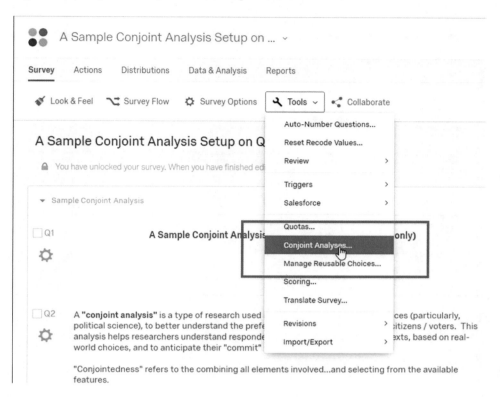

Click the "Add Another Conjoint" link. The conjoint configuration wizard will open. An explanation of this tool (context-sensitive help) may be accessed here for the basic self-explicated conjoint analysis. (Figure 2)

The user adds a title for the conjoint analysis in the next window. This should be an informational title, so users can be clear of what the content entails. (If this is named incorrectly the first time, renaming later is a simple procedure.) Below is an auto-created data export tag to be used in the data column headers to label the related data from the conjoint analysis. (Figure 3) The data label differentiates conjoint data from the other data in a survey when a conjoint is part of a survey sequence.

In the next window, users may define the core of the conjoint analysis, based on four tabs: Features and Attributes, Question Text – 1, Question Text – 2, and Conjoint Options. To add a Feature, type in the text field and click "Add" (Figure 4). A Feature is a high-level category that is part of the target product/service/ choice-space.

Figure 2. Built-in context-sensitive explanation of a conjoint analysis in "add conjoint analysis"

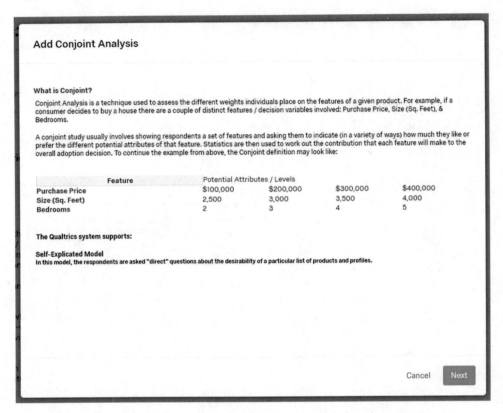

The attributes of the respective Feature may be added by highlighting the target feature in the left text box, and typing the attributes in the right text box. After each attribute, press "Enter" or the return key.

In the Question Text – 1 and Question Text – 2, there is already default text in the spaces, and these may be changed. (It helps to do a walk-through to see how the questions align with how you set up the other parts of your question later on.)

Finally, in the "Conjoint Options" tab, you have a choice of selecting one of two conjoint display options: (1) Feature Importance Constant Sum and (2) Desirability Upgrade Constant Sum. The first explores the most desired and least desired features in a space. The second enables respondents to indicate their level of desirability with added-on features to a basic service. (Hai-Jew, Spring-Summer 2018)

Figure 3. Naming the conjoint analysis

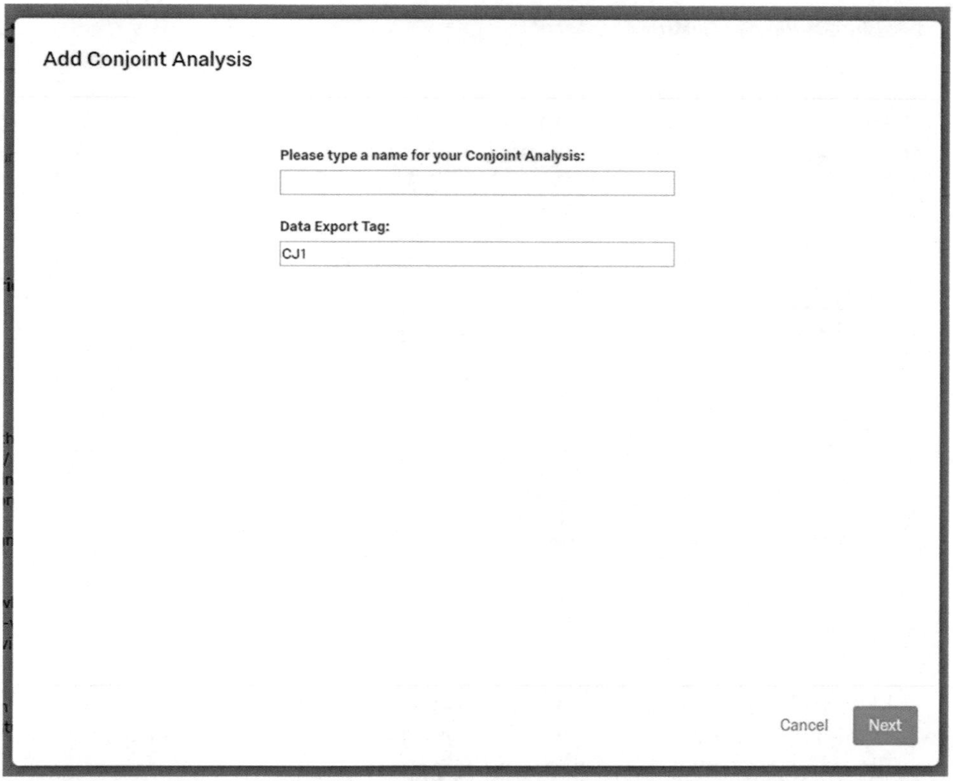

In the documentation by the software maker, they explain the conjoint analysis tool:

Self-explicated conjoint analysis does not require the statistical analysis or the heuristic logic required in many other conjoint approaches. This approach has been shown to provide results equal or superior to full-profile approaches, and places fewer demands on the respondents. There are some limitations to self-explicated conjoint analysis, including an inability to trade off price with other attribute bundles. ("What is a conjoint analysis?" 2018)

The documentation then suggests that other methods of conjoint analysis might then be more preferable. (The simple version of the conjoint may have been released to customers for a period to "tease" the availability of the fuller conjoint analysis suite by the software maker.)

Figure 4. Adding features and related attributes / levels

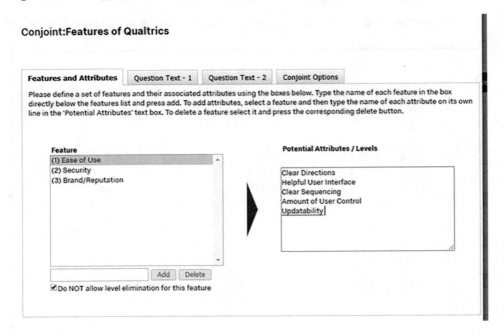

Once "Save" is clicked, the conjoint analysis is available for use, but it still needs to be added into the target survey's sequence. This is done in the "Survey Flow" area (Figure 5). The conjoint analysis should be placed in a logical part of the sequence, and order does matter in terms of affecting response outcomes. Next, remember that the conjoint analysis is a stepwise process, and even if the "Back Button" is enabled, respondents will not be able to reverse through a conjoint to an earlier part of the survey. Some people deal with this by placing the conjoint near the end of the extant survey, so respondents can go forwards and backwards through a survey without any challenges until they come to the conjoint analysis. If respondents are expected to move backwards and forwards throughout a survey, it makes sense to put in some light "forced response" features or indicators of incomplete responding to encourage fuller responses. Note that the conjoint analysis' appearance is different from other survey blocks in the Survey Flow. Also, from the user side, the conjoint analysis has its own page breaks as they move through the selections, and these are part of the conjoint analysis function. An early part of this sequence also involves a MaxDiff feature which asks respondents to bracket the attributes by selecting the "best" and the "worst" of the feature set, before labeling their responses to the rest of the available attributes. One of the research works describes a general best-worst approach:

Figure 5. Adding a conjoint analysis to a survey flow

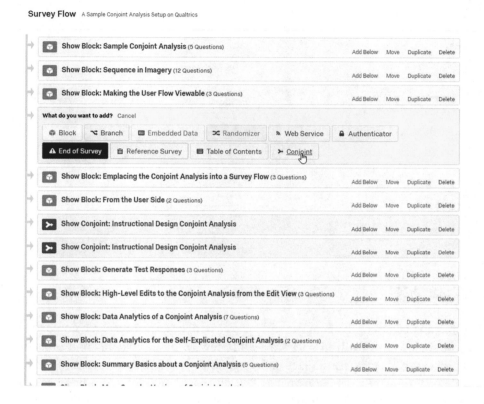

'Best-worst' choices can be applied in a sequential fashion in order to obtain a full raking (sic) of all alternatives by asking respondents to choose their preferred option, then to choose the worst option, then the best of the remaining options, etc. While imposing a higher cognitive burden on the respondent than 'pick-one', the tasks are easier to deal with than traditional ranking methods (Marley and Louviere, 2005). Compared with 'pick-one', a sequential best-worst response format greatly reduces the number of choice tasks required to obtain the same number of observations (Lancsar et al., 2013). Best-worst scaling has been found to be superior when dealing with qualitative data such as the different conservation requirements and different monitoring arrangements explored in this choice experiment (Flynn et al., 2007; Goodman et al., 2005). (Greiner, Bliemer, & Ballweg, 2014, p. 36)

A close-in of what the conjoint analysis looks like on the back end in the "Survey Flow" follows (Figure 6). The data label is highlighted at the top left.

Figure 6. Conjoint services and attributes example in instructional design

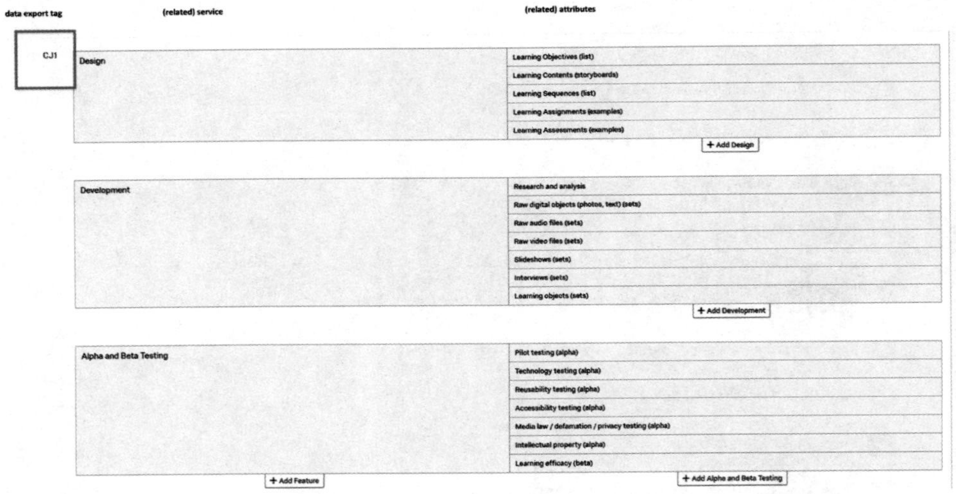

DISCUSSION

Conjoint analyses have been in use for decades in a variety of research contexts. Its methodologies have evolved over time with new resultant insights and practices. This process of research formalizes understandings of offered products and services as well as options in a decision-space. The self-explicated form is a basic one but also seen as effective even though there may have been a sense that "self-explicated procedures would manifest significantly lower predictive validity than the conjoint analysis procedures, particularly the full-profile and hybrid variations of conjoint analysis" (McKenna 1985, p. 106). In its released ebook, Qualtrics shares the following observations:

Self-explicated conjoint analysis offers a simple but surprisingly robust approach that is easy to implement and does not require the development of full-profile concepts. Self-explicated conjoint analysis is a hybrid approach that focuses on the evaluation of various attributes of a product. This conjoint analysis model asks explicitly about the preference for each feature level rather than the preference for a bundle of features. ("What is a conjoint analysis?" 2018)

The experience of a conjoint informs a decision maker of his / her sensibilities regarding a product, a service, or a choice-space, and this may enhance their decision making in contexts of multiple attributes and other complexities. More complex

CA methods enable various combinations of attributes in more complex ways to enable preference modeling with different mixes and combinations. The different versions of CA all harness decompositional methods to judge "a restricted number of complete or partially described alternatives, which are generated systematically, on a specified (verbal) scale" (Scholl, Manthey, Helm, & Steiner, 2005, p. 763).

FUTURE RESEARCH DIRECTIONS

One future direction for research may be for users to design conjoint analyses outside of the Qualtrics Research Suite, based on the rich question types in the online survey tool and the data analytics statistical packages. In other words, are there ways to create custom online conjoint analyses so as to go beyond the pre-baked types of conjoint analyses—especially given the flexibility of the tool? However, emulating a specialized data collection methodology is no small feat, and there may be a hard cost in developer time.

The academic research fields would benefit from the sharing of different applied cases of online conjoint analyses, using Qualtrics and / or other survey platforms. One dimension may be the different types of elicitations and stimuli, potentially using multimedia, for example. Multi-attribute judgments may be more accurately elicited using multimedia and multimodal means.

Interestingly, on the user side of the online conjoint analysis, a designed conjoint which is a part of a longer survey or is stand-alone does not look or feel much different than a typical survey. The one major difference is that for surveys with the "back button" option, a respondent cannot back up to prior to the stepwise sequence because the conjoint is not designed to allow that back-and-forth (and it may be because the dependencies of stepwise sequences may not be made reversible in the software tool). Another aspect of research may be how to make online conjoint analyses more user-friendly.

CONCLUSION

Conjoint analyses are a popular form of research, with "thousands of applications of conjoint analysis have been carried out over the past three decades" (Green, Krieger, & Wind, May-Jun., 2001, p. S60). Conjoint analysis modeling has been made much more accessible with the ease of use of software that enable these "multi-attribute utility models" (Green, Krieger, & Wind, May-Jun., 2001, p. S60). Many may be deployed without engaging the complex maths, and most tools are sufficiently well documented to enable wide applications. As one exemplar, the Qualtrics® self-explicated conjoint analysis tool is easy-to-use, and the complex calculations occur in an encapsulated way on the back end.

REFERENCES

Bridges, J. F. P., Hauber, A. B., Marshall, D., Lloyd, A., Prosser, L. A., Regier, D. A., ... Mauskopf, J. (2011). Conjoint analysis applications in health—a checklist: A report of the ISPOR Good Research Practices for Conjoint Analysis Task Force. *Value in Health, 14*(4), 403–413. doi:10.1016/j.jval.2010.11.013 PMID:21669364

12 . business decisions you can optimize with conjoint analysis. (2018). *Qualtrics.* Retrieved Sept. 29, 2018, from https://www.qualtrics.com/ebooks-guides/optimize-business-decisions-with-conjoint-analysis/

Carroll, J. D., & Green, P. E. (1995). Guest editorial: Psychometric methods in marketing research: Part 1, Conjoint Analysis. *JMR, Journal of Marketing Research, 32*(4), 385–391.

Caruso, E. M., Rahnev, D. A., & Banaji, M. R. (2009). Using conjoint analysis to detect discrimination: Revealing covert preferences from overt choices. *Social Cognition, 27*(1), 128–137. doi:10.1521oco.2009.27.1.128

Chrzan, K. (1994). Three kinds of order effects in choice-based conjoint analysis. *Marketing Letters, 5*(2), 165–172. doi:10.1007/BF00994106

Ding, M., Grewal, R., & Liechty, J. (2004, May). *Incentive-aligned conjoint analysis.* Pre-publication draft.

Earnhart, D. (1998). *Combining revealed and stated data to examine decisions of housing location: discrete-choice hedonic and conjoint analysis.* University of Kansas. Retrieved from http://www2.ku.edu/~kuwpaper/Archive/papers/Pre1999/wp1998_2.htm

Garver, M. S., Williams, Z., Taylor, G. S., & Wynne, W. R. (2011). Modelling choice in logistics: A managerial guide and application. *International Journal of Physical Distribution & Logistics Management, 42*(2), 128–151. doi:10.1108/09600031211219654

Green, P. E., Krieger, A. M., & Wind, Y. J. (2001, May-June). Thirty years of conjoint analysis: Reflections and prospects. *Interfaces, 31*(3), S56–S73. doi:10.1287/inte.31.3s.56.9676

Green, P. E., & Rao, V. R. (1971). Conjoint measurement for quantifying judgmental data. *JMR, Journal of Marketing Research, 8*(2), 3, 355–363.

Green, P. E., & Srinivasan, V. (1978, September). Conjoint analysis in consumer research: Issues and outlook. *The Journal of Consumer Research, 3*(2), 103–123. doi:10.1086/208721

Greiner, R., Bliemer, M., & Ballweg, J. (2014). Design considerations of a choice experiment to estimate likely participation by north Australian pastoralists in contractual biodiversity conservation. *The Journal of Choice Modelling, 10*, 34–45. doi:10.1016/j.jocm.2014.01.002

Hai-Jew, S. (2018). Exploring people's preferences in defined contexts with conjoint analysis in Qualtrics. *C2C Digital Magazine, 1*(9).

Hanley, N., Mourato, S., & Wright, R. E. (2001). Choice modelling approaches: A superior alternative for environmental valuation. *Journal of Economic Surveys, 15*(3), 435–462. doi:10.1111/1467-6419.00145

Hanley, N., Wright, R. E., & Adamowicz, V. (1998). Using choice experiments to value the environment: Design issues, current experience and future prospects. *Environmental and Resource Economics, 11*(3-4), 413–428. doi:10.1023/A:1008287310583

Hauser, J. R., & Rao, V. R. (2002). *Conjoint analysis, related modeling, and applications*. Draft.

Johnson, F. R., Lancsar, E., Marshall, D., Kilambi, V., Möhlbacher, A., Regier, D. A., ... Bridges, J. F. P. (2013). Article. *Value in Health, 16*, 3–13. doi:10.1016/j.jval.2012.08.2223 PMID:23337210

Louviere, J. J. (1988). Conjoint analysis modelling of stated preferences: A review of theory, methods, recent developments and external validity. *Journal of Transport Economics and Policy, 22*(1), 93–119. Retrieved from http://www.jstor.org/stable/20052837

Louviere, J. J., Flynn, T. N., & Carson, R. T. (2010). Discrete choice experiments are not conjoint analysis. *Journal of Choice Modeling, 3*(3), 57–72. doi:10.1016/S1755-5345(13)70014-9

Louviere, J. J., Pihlens, D., & Carson, R. (2010). Design of discrete choice experiments: A discussion of issues that matter in future applied research. *Journal of Choice Modeling*, *4*(1), 1–8.

Louviere, J. J., & Woodworth, G. (1983, November). Design and analysis of simulated consumer choice or allocation experiments: An approach based on aggregate data. *JMR, Journal of Marketing Research*, *20*(4), 350–367. doi:10.1177/002224378302000403

Loveland, K. A. (1995, Dec.). *Conjoint analysis reliability and validity: The impact of self-efficacy, self-assessments, and selected methodological choices* (Dissertation). New Mexico State University.

McKenna, W. F. (1985, Jan.). *An empirical study of the comparative external validity of alternative approaches to the measurement of consumer utility functions* (Dissertation). Temple University.

Melles, T., Laumann, R., & Holling, H. (2000). Validity and reliability of online conjoint analysis. *Proceedings of the 2000 Sawtooth Software Conference*, 31 – 40.

Scholl, A., Manthey, L., Helm, R., & Steiner, M. (2005). Solving multiattribute design problems with analytic hierarchy process and conjoint analysis: An empirical comparison. *European Journal of Operational Research*, *164*(3), 760–777. doi:10.1016/j.ejor.2004.01.026

What is a conjoint analysis? Conjoint types & when to use them. (2018). *Qualtrics*. Retrieved Sept. 29, 2018, from https://www.qualtrics.com/experience-management/research/types-of-conjoint/

KEY TERMS AND DEFINITIONS

Attribute: A feature.

Conjoint Analysis: A type of choice-based experiment in which respondents indicate their preferences among a selection of attributes related to a particular choice-space (product, service, or other real-world and/or theoretical decision space).

Conjointedness: The combination of all factors involved.

MaxDiff (Maximum Difference Scaling, Best-Worst Scaling): A paired comparison method in which respondents identify their best and worst attributes among a set, which reveals a number of other ranked preferences among paired sets.

Part-Worth (Attribute Importance Scores, Level Values, Utility Score, Part Utility): A utility measurement ("util") that shows a weighted preference for a particular attribute (or factor or dimension) in a product, service, or choice-space.

Self-Explicated Conjoint Analysis: A basic form of choice experiment in which respondents explicitly define their preferences from lists of attributes that comprise a particular product or service or real-world and/or theoretical choice-space.

Chapter 5

Setting Up Education–Based "Crosswalk Analyses" on an Online Survey Platform

ABSTRACT

Practically, crosswalk analyses in education may be used to identify gaps for decision making and program planning, enable cross-system comparisons, promote cross-disciplinary work, and others. Often, crosswalk analyses require the expertise of a cross-disciplinary and/or distributed team. Setting up a crosswalk analysis on an online survey platform stands to benefit this collaborative work in ways that are more powerful than a co-edited shared online file. This chapter describes some ways to set up education-based crosswalk analyses on an online survey platform and highlights some online survey features that can enhance this work.

INTRODUCTION

"Crosswalk analyses" are a fairly modern analytics approach which maps the granular elements of one system with those of another. One common approach is to map one database schema to that of another, so the data from both databases can be melded and somewhat interchanged. Outside of database administration, though, crosswalk analyses are used in a more loosely coupled way to map one system to another laterally (in one direction), and these may include schemas, ontologies, taxonomies, frameworks, standards, compliance criteria, performance criteria, datasets (including structured and semi-structured data), and others.

DOI: 10.4018/978-1-5225-8563-3.ch005

A "crosswalk analysis" bridges between at least two systems to identify commonalities and differences (comparisons and contrasts) between them, in order to enable integration of datasets, programmatic gaps analyses, cross-disciplinary work, and other applications. The systems compared include a range of content types, including schemas, ontologies, taxonomies, frameworks, standards, compliance criteria, performance criteria, datasets, and others. Crosswalk analyses are considered efficient because they maintain the integrity of the compared systems—by keeping the terminology and phrasing verbatim—by showing connectivity at a basic unit level of analysis for each respective system. As such, they do not break down silos but connect "content silos" (Johnston, June 22, 2015). [Note: Such crosswalk analysis bridging can also occur more abstractly or at a higher level of abstraction, but for usability, the precision at the most granular units of analysis seem to be preferable. These have also been referred to as "equivalent elements" ("Schema crosswalk," Sept. 28, 2018).] The innovation of this analytic technique is in the crosswalk, and the overlap between the systems is somewhat interpretive (and defined by the objectives of the crosswalk analysis). The crosswalk itself is partial and selective and does not include all potential overlaps between the two disparate systems. (Figure 1) Or, not all overlaps between two systems will likely be seen as relevant. This is not to suggest that some crosswalks may not be comprehensive, and in some cases, that level of detail may be required and often depicted in a crosswalk analysis matrix.

Figure 1. A Venn diagram analogy to the crosswalk analysis

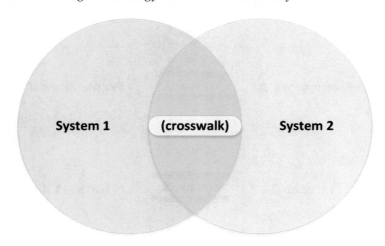

A Venn Diagram Analogy to the Crosswalk Analysis

(The essential structure of this is to have one system represented in the row headers down the leftmost column, and the other system represented in the column headers across the top row.)

In Figure 2, the bridging or connective function is depicted. The systems that are being studied are on each side of the crosswalk, but the main focus is to see how the left system crosswalks to the one on the right, with the main focus on the original system (shown to the left). How does Metadata Schema B map to Metadata Schema A? How do professional competencies map to the professional standards? How does Framework B map to Framework A? How does Dataset B map to Dataset A? The question is how the second system maps to the first. The idea of a focal

Figure 2. A crosswalk analysis (with bridging or connective functions)

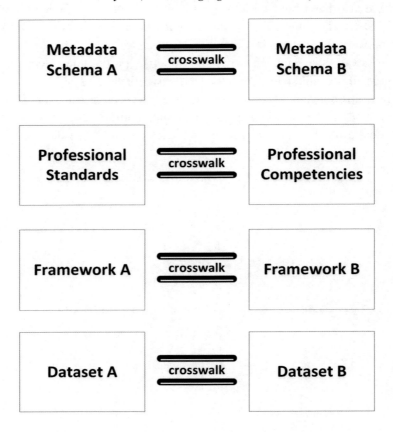

**A Crosswalk Analysis
(with bridging or connective functions)**

system matters because of the "lateral" or one-directional nature of crosswalks in many cases. (Figure 2) More on how crosswalk analyses work will be presented in the body of the paper.

Since crosswalks are usually built by subject matter experts or content experts with expertise in particular disciplines, it is important to be able to access expertise across geographical distances. While there are benefits to using co-edited documents hosted online (whether as first-party or third-party platforms), online survey systems offer a range of benefits to creating crosswalk analyses. This work describes some basics about building such an instrument on a modern-day online survey platform.

REVIEW OF THE LITERATURE

One of the more common uses of crosswalk analyses are to bridge metadata schemas. A "schema crosswalk" connects data fields to enable the sharing of information between datasets and for "data harvesters (to) create catalog" and to enable federated searches by search engines ("Schema crosswalk," Sept. 28, 2018). These analyses help define data relationships by "merging" or "crosswalking" data (Walker, Dec. 2, 2015). The identification of shared "data elements" between data products enables comparisons (Ponzio, 2004, p. 350) to resolve the "semantic heterogeneity" from "multiple data source providers" by the creation of a "crosswalk analysis matrix" (Ponzio, 2004, p. 349). Crosswalks have been used in the library sciences for data management (El-Sherbini, 2001). Crosswalks have been applied to "harmonize" data (Dodge, et al., Jan. 2017, p. 3). Crosswalk analysis is the "most popular method for comparison" of metadata schemes "property-by-property" (Chan & Zeng, 2006, as cited in Willis, Greenberg, & White, 2012, p. 1508).

In the research literature, crosswalks have been used in a variety of other applications: to understand risks to public health from cybersecurity threats (Bamett, Sell, Lord, Jenkins, Terbush, & Burke, 2013); to capture ideas for curriculum planning by comparing two documents—one related to K12 social studies standards and the other a state's standard course of study to look for "similarities and differences" related to "content coverage and cognitive process" ("2010 NC Social Studies K-12 Essential Standards," Feb. 25, 2011); to help military personnel close gaps in skills with the civilian world by mapping military skills to civilian ones in a Military Occupational Codes (MOC) Crosswalk ("Military Occupational Codes Crosswalk: Translating Your Training and Experiences," 2016); by defining professional roles and the related necessary skills to fulfill those (Uriarte, 2015, p. 9); by identifying alignments between Deeper Learning Skills (DLS) and Common Core State

Standards (CCSS) (Conley, July 13, 2011); to link articles on a global convention on the rights of persons with disabilities and survey questions on an instrument (Tichá, Qian, Stancliffe, Larson, & Bonardi, Sept. 2018); to identify similarities between professional expectations (Boyd, June 2012), and others. Online, there are some examples of courses and the formal student learning objectives mapped to each course.

Some crosswalk matrices involve coding to make them less textually expansive and unwieldy. Some crosswalks are achieved through computational methods and not human manual coding. While many crosswalks are created on a granular level of detail, others are mapped based on higher levels of abstractions. One study involved a large dataset. Here, computational methods were used to arrive at "intermediate" alignments but with the finding of "a strong inverse relationship between recall and precision when both intermediates where (sic) involved in the crosswalking" (Reitsma, Marshall, & Chart, 2012, p. 1). (Ideally, both recall and precision should be high for an effective crosswalk. Low recall suggests that relevant bridges or similarities go unidentified, and low precision means that many non-relevant elements were mistakenly identified as false positives.)

Crosswalks generally take a few basic forms. One is a side-by-side (Table 1). Here, System 1 is represented in one column and System 2 in the other. The alignment of elements in each row shows some sort of association between the elements. If there are blanks, that means that there is no association for the element from either System 1 or System 2.

Another structure has a middle column in which the bridging is captured, often in the researchers' own words. Or there can be multiple middle columns focused on different aspects of the crosswalk—such as phases or other specifics. These can be more nuanced. System 1 and System 2 elements are kept verbatim. In this structure, it is possible to have additional middle columns to indicate level of agreement, and other details of the crosswalk or bridge. (Table 2).

Table 1. A side-by-side crosswalk analysis (in a two-columned table)

System 1	System 2

Table 2. A middle-column crosswalk analysis (in a multi-columned table)

System 1	Own Words / Own Coding	System 2

One of the more complex forms of a crosswalk analysis is a matrix. It is described in one research work as the following:

A crosswalk, as used in this study, is a means to examine relationships by arraying two sets of statements orthogonally in a matrix format and then examining the intersection of each element of each statement...in a unique cell. (Conley, July 13, 2011, p. 1)

A basic matrix structure has one system's elements represented in the row headers and the other systems' elements in the column headers. The respective intersecting cells contain the crosswalk. (Table 3) If multiple systems are being compared, it is possible to push the matrix into three dimensions (y-axis) and more.

No matter how essentially similar or disparate the initial systems being compared in a crosswalk, a crosswalk focuses on similarities. It takes a comparison approach

Table 3. A crosswalk analysis matrix (in a matrix structure)

to find overlaps and compatibilities. Also, the crosswalks may connect the compared systems in a tightly coupled way or a loosely coupled way. A tightly coupled approach would be to identify a dense number of linkages (if available) in close synchrony; a loosely coupled approach would be to connect the systems on an abstract level with light overlaps and loose matching.

What is compared in a crosswalk analysis does not have to be of a similar type. A framework may be compared to a database schema. A taxonomy may be compared to a dataset. Crosswalks based on metadata schemas are often lateral (one-directional or one-way) (Caplan, 2003, p. 39), so this requires mapping from A -> B and B -> A for full understandings. When the type of system is the same, this backwards and forwards mapping is required for fuller understandings. When there is contrast to the underlying data, though, the mapping seems more reflexive because of the foundational differences in the underlying data types (Figure 3).

Also, the research suggests that such crosswalks may be indicative of transitivity between systems (Figure 4). This would suggest that preliminary work bridging systems may have broader applications beyond the directly compared systems.

Figure 3. "Lateral" and "multilateral" crosswalk analysis mappings depending on system-system type alignment or (non-)/disalignment

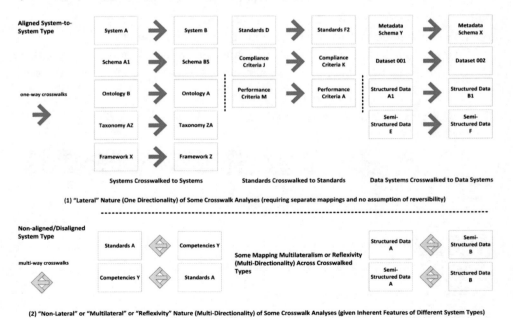

(1) "Lateral" Nature (One Directionality) of Some Crosswalk Analyses (requiring separate mappings and no assumption of reversibility)

(2) "Non-Lateral" or "Multilateral" or "Reflexivity" Nature (Multi-Directionality) of Some Crosswalk Analyses (given Inherent Features of Different System Types)

"Lateral" and "Multilateral" Crosswalk Analysis Mappings Depending on System-System Type Alignment or (Non-)/Disalignment

Figure 4. Potential crosswalk analysis transitivity

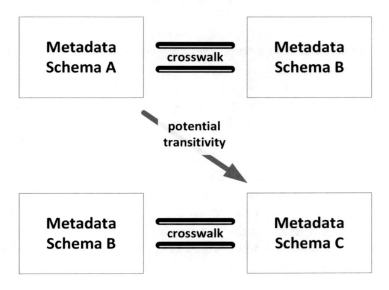

Potential Crosswalk Analysis Transitivity

SETTING UP AN EDUCATION-BASED CROSSWALK ANALYSES ON ONLINE SURVEY SYSTEMS

How crosswalk analyses are set up will vary. Some comparisons are based on theory, formal research, experimentation, and practice. In a review of the literature, the most common types seem to be based on practical questions and practical decision making and planning needs.

In higher education, crosswalk analyses have been applied in various ways in the service of improved teaching and learning and research:

- Cross-disciplinary learning objectives matched between learning domains;
- Degree programs mapped to course sequences, portfolio projects mapped to learning competencies, learning assignments mapped to learning outcomes,
- And others.

Elicitations for crosswalk analysis work may be achieved in an online survey platform to achieve a number of aims. For example, in an online survey, the following functionalities may be achieved:

Survey Construction

- Full access to both system documents may be made available to the respondents, to enable them to get into the proper mindset for the crosswalk analysis work.
- If the documents are sectioned, these may be represented in different blocks.
- It may be possible to set up drag-and-drop responses to codify particular elements into categories across systems.
- The work of crosswalk analyses may be sequenced, with particular steps achieved and analyzed…and follow-on work done on the platform. For example, an initial iteration may be more abstract, and then follow-on ones may be more detailed and granular. There is room to evolve the work. (Part of the sequence may involve face-to-face work, for a blended experience.)
- It is possible to elicit further information based on a respondent's unique responses through tools like Loop & Merge or defined conditionals.
- It is possible to customize the experience through the use of custom piped text {a}.
- Updates to the crosswalk analysis survey may be made at any time, as new information comes in.
- Partially filled data tables may be emplaced (as part of a "default answer") in a text-based survey question to set up more complex elicitations, like side-by-side crosswalk analyses, or multi-column crosswalk analyses.
- Online survey systems may be scripted to enforce particular response rules, such as whether a particular granular unit can be single-use or multi-use in a category, for example, and others. There can be automated approaches to scoring. There can be values assigned to various responses. These capabilities may be applied to the instrument for automated supports of human data collection.

Survey Respondents

- Depending on the expertise of the survey respondents, they may be branched off to particular pieces of the crosswalk analysis.
- Control over survey respondent elicitation may enable the running of an online Delphi study with particular invited experts to respond.

Data Capture

- In the online survey systems, it is possible to use inline frames to enable access to PDF forms or online hosted documents…to collect data through multiple means.
- A file upload question type may enable the capturing of any type of digital file (within size limits and digital file types), for richer data elicitations. The crosswalk analyses explored in a review of the literature show the centrality of language and symbolic processing. However, there is nothing to say that imagery, audio, video, and multimedia cannot be bridged, or that these digital contents cannot be part of digital elicitations.
- The collected data may be captured and downloaded for analyses in other data analytics packages (such as qualitative crosstabulation analyses). One important measure, for example, would be similarity analyses to either validate or invalidate particular pieces of the respective granular crosswalks. The percentage agreements may be calculated by cells in an "item analysis" approach using external technologies.

Data Analytics

- Built-in analytics to the online survey platform—like text analysis of open-ended question text responses and quantitative crosstabulation analyses—offer abilities to analyze the survey respondent responses. Also, findings from the online analytics may enable validation / invalidation of the crosswalks.
- It is possible to conduct preliminary analytical work and simplify the crosswalk analysis work for respondents.

The above are all construction methods that have been applied in the building of online elicitations.

DISCUSSION

This work introduced the practice of crosswalk analysis and reframed it as a distributed method of data capture to bridge two (or more) disparate systems. This work suggests the importance of online survey systems to capture insights related to this work.

FUTURE RESEARCH DIRECTIONS

The approach described here suggests the importance of eliciting insights from domain content experts, but there may be some types of crosswalk analyses that would benefit from the wisdom of crowds. It is possible that non-experts may offer some insights that the respective experts may miss. Some crowd-sourcing micropayment work sites may offer some ways to reach a broad public audience for some of these endeavors.

This particular work was built on the capabilities of the Qualtrics Research Suite, but there are other online survey systems that may offer additional or different capabilities for building online crosswalk analyses.

Other technologies may be explored. In an applied sense, there are software tools for qualitative data analysis that enable qualitative crosstabulation analyses that may offer a computational means of extracting overlaps by word use (synonyms). One such software tool is NVivo 12 Plus. Also, this particular software also enables ways to calculate statistical similarity coefficients, which may advance the work of testing for the reliability of a crosswalk analysis.

How the respective crosswalks may be validated/invalidated may also be important to explore. These will differ based on the context and types of crosswalking.

CONCLUSION

Crosswalk analyses do not register as a common word used in scanned books on the Google Books Ngram Viewer. As a search term on Google Search, it also does not register as much of a common term in the U.S. on Google Correlate. In the research literature, a few dozen works were found. Still, as a method of linking disparate systems based on commonalities, this method offers insights that would not be attainable in other ways, and it does so efficiently given the building on existing knowledge structures instead of reconfiguring the respective systems. This qualitative content analysis and coding result in new understandings and new linking structures.

Using an online survey system to capture insights of bridges between systems may be one way to effectively create crosswalk analyses.

REFERENCES

2010 NC Social Studies K-12 Essential Standards. (2011, Feb. 25). *North Carolina Council for the Social Studies. 41ˢᵗ Annual Conference. Greensboro, North Carolina. Accountability and Curriculum Reform Effort in Response to A Framework For Change.* Public Schools of North Carolina.

Bamett, D. J., Sell, T. K., Lord, R. K., Jenkins, C. J., Terbush, J. W., & Burke, T. A. (2013). Cyber security threats to public health. *World Medical & Health Policy, 5*(1), 37–46. doi:10.1002/wmh3.19

Boyd, B. (2012, June). *Alignment of Washington State Core Competencies for Early Care and Education Professionals and the NAEYC Standards for Early Childhood Professional Preparation Programs.* Early Childhood Teacher Preparation Council.

Caplan, P. (2003). *Metadata fundamentals for all librarians.* Chicago: American Library Association.

Conley, D.T. (2011, July 13). *Crosswalk analysis of Deeper Learning Skills to Common Core State Standards.* Educational Policy Improvement Center (EPIC).

Dodge, H.H., Zhu, J., Hughes, T.F., Snitz, B.E., Chang, C.-C.H., Jacobsen, E.P., & Ganguli, M. (2017, Jan.) Cohort effects in verbal memory function and practice effects: A population-based study. *International Psychogeriatrics, 29*(1), 137–148.

El-Sherbini, M. (2001). Metadata and the future of cataloging. *Library Review, 50*(1), 16–27. doi:10.1108/00242530110363217

Hai-Jew, S. (2019). Creating an exploratory 'crosswalk analysis.' *C2C Digital Magazine.* Retrieved Jan. 5, 2019, from http://scalar.usc.edu/works/c2c-digital-magazine-spring--summer-2019/creating-an-exploratory-crosswalk-analysis

Johnston, M. R. (2015, June 22). *How do you connect content silos? Crosswalks!* Content Marketing Institute. Retrieved Jan. 5, 2019, from https://contentmarketinginstitute.com/2015/06/crosswalks-content-silos-ann-rockley/

Military Occupational Codes Crosswalk: Translating Your Training And Experiences. (2016, Dec.). Participant Guide.

Ponzio, F. J. (2004). Authoritative data source (ADS) framework and ADS maturity model (practice-oriented paper). *Proceedings of the Ninth International Conference on Information Quality (ICIQ-04),* 346–357.

Reitsma, R., Marshall, B., & Chart, T. (2012). Can intermediary-based science standards crosswalking work? Some evidence from mining the Standard Alignment Tool (SAT). *Journal of the American Society for Information Science and Technology*, *63*(9), 1843–1858. doi:10.1002/asi.22712

Schema crosswalk. (2018, Sept. 28). In *Wikipedia*. Retrieved Jan. 5, 2018, from https://en.wikipedia.org/wiki/Schema_crosswalk

Tichá, R., Qian, X., Stancliffe, R. J., Larson, S. A., & Bonardi, A. (2018, September). Alignment between the Convention on the Rights of Persons with Disabilities and the National Core Indicators Adult Consumer Survey. *Journal of Policy and Practice in Intellectual Disabilities*, *15*(3), 247–255. doi:10.1111/jppi.12260

Uriarte, J. (2015). *A snapshot of community health worker training in the United States* (Doctoral thesis). University of Texas School of Public Health.

Walker, D. (2015, Dec. 2). Crosswalking data relationships for analysis. *Development Gateway*. Retrieved Jan. 5, 2019, from https://www.developmentgateway.org/blog/crosswalking-data-relationships-analysis

Willis, C., Greenberg, J., & White, H. (2012). Analysis and synthesis of metadata goals for scientific data. *Journal of the American Society for Information Science and Technology*, *63*(8), 1505–1520. doi:10.1002/asi.22683

KEY TERMS AND DEFINITIONS

Crosswalk Analysis: A technique used to identify similarities and differences between two different systems (of a type or of different types) to aid in understandings, decision making, planning, and other applications; a bridging technique.

Online Survey: A structured information elicitation conducted online.

Chapter 6
Setting Up and Running a Q–Methodology Study in an Online Survey Research Suite

ABSTRACT

The q-method, as a graphic (visual) elicitation, has existed since the mid-1930s. Setting up a q-method, with q-sort capabilities, in an online survey platform, extends the reach of this method, even as data has to be processed in a quantitative data analytics suite. This chapter describes the setting up of a visual q-sort and the related debriefing on the Qualtrics Research Suite. The available data may be extracted and analyzed in a basic statistical analysis tool for factors and preference clusters.

INTRODUCTION

A q-methodology study (q-method, q-inquiry) elicits "operant subjectivity" through the presentation of various selected text and visual elements to a p-set (of respondents) to place into three general categories: agree strongly, neutral, or disagree strongly. The presented elements are selected from a "concourse" of elements from the particular relevant issue universe related to the particular research question. After select respondents (in the p-set) provide insights, they also are asked to debrief their responses for follow-on information. The q-method provides insights about general preferences around a particular issue but also individual human patterns of preferences, which may be studied as preference clusters.

DOI: 10.4018/978-1-5225-8563-3.ch006

Often, when researchers want to understand what people think of particular policies, practices, messaging, and in-world phenomena, among other things, they will conduct interviews, focus groups, surveys, and other research approaches. They will generalize from the findings and use their insights for awareness, decision making, policy making, policy implementation, marketing, and advertising. One lesser-known approach for understanding people's thinking is the q-methodology, a "card sorting" approach based on various topic-related statements that involves selected insider participants (in small groups) to represent diverse opinions (to saturation) and to map various stances around particularized topics. Q-methodology enables the exploring of "tastes, preferences, sentiments, motives and goals, the part of personality that is of great influence on behaviour but that often remains largely unexplored" (van Exel & de Graaf, 2005, p. 2). Here the sampling is "strategic" vs. "random" (Armatas, et al., 2014, as cited in Sy, et al., 2018, p. 4). One key feature is the convenience of the setup for analysis.

Q-methodology (q-method, q-inquiry, q-technique) was first introduced back in 1935 by British physicist and psychologist William Stephenson (1902 – 1989). This approach enables data collection through a card sorting activity (known as the q-sort) by a group of selected "insider" respondents (known as the p-set). Here, the data analysis is described as an "inverted factor analysis" with "persons as the variables rather than the tests, and the population (as)…the group of tests rather than the group of persons; i.e. the rows of the matrix are correlated" (Stephenson, 1936).

These individual rankings (or viewpoints) are then subject to factor analysis. Stephenson (1935) presented Q methodology as an inversion of conventional factor analysis in the sense that Q correlates persons instead of tests; "(w)hereas previously a large number of people were given a small number of tests, now we give a small number of people a large number of test-items". Correlation between personal profiles then indicates similar viewpoints, or segments of subjectivity which exist (Brown 1993). By correlating people, Q factor analysis gives information about similarities and differences in viewpoint on a particular subject. If each individual would have her/his own specific likes and dislikes, Stephenson (1935) argued, their profiles will not correlate; if, however, significant clusters of correlations exist, they could be factorised, described as common viewpoints (or tastes, preferences, dominant accounts, typologies, et cetera), and individuals could be measured with respect to them. (van Exel & de Graaf, 2005, p. 1)

A follow-on to the card sorting involves debriefing the respondents about their selections to better understand them. Q-methodology research and analysis enables

Table 1. Q-Methodology and sorting through topic-related cards to express subjective preferences

Disagree Strongly	Neutral	Agree Strongly

the study of selected people's subjective perceptions (viewpoints, beliefs, values, opinions, tastes, and preferences) around target issues to understand their "operant subjectivity," their unique points of view which may inform their public stances and behaviors. This method enables the mapping of people's individual response patterns around a topic (based on collections of granular opinion statements as the basic units of analysis) and group-based subjective patterns. The respective textual cards are sorted into three general categories: agreement, neutrality, and disagreement (Table 1). [Other variations are like "most like how I think," neutral," and "least like how I think," for example, to align with colloquial expressiveness. Some research studies only use two categories: agreement or disagreement. The "distinguishing statements" are those placed on the sorting grid "in a statistically significant different position compared with all other factors", and the "characterizing statements" are those "placed at the two polar ends of the sorting grid of each factor" and will affect how the research is understood (Paige, 2015a, p. 76).] Some q-methodology research involves the usage of imagery, audio, video, and a mix of other types of informational contents, beyond cards. This research approach is also referred to as "discourse analysis" (Baxter & Hacking, 2015, p. 3111), in part because of the aligning of the cards to be sorted with the level of knowledge of the respondents in relation to the focal research topic. (A q-methodology research targeting experts would differ from the research related to lay-persons.)

As compared to a factor analysis, a q-method describes "a population of viewpoints" vs. "a population of people." Its main question is to ask "what is the relationship between different peoples' viewpoints" as compared to "what is the inter-relationship among a large set of observed variables." In a q-method study, "opinion statements are the unit of analysis" as compared to people as the unit in conventional factor analyses. The statements of a Q-sort are "interactive" as compared to "statements in a survey…(which) are independent" (Brown, 1980; Newman & Ramlo, 2010, & Stephenson, 1953, as cited in Paige, 2014, p. 640). In q-methodology research, participants assign scores to their intensities and directions of evaluations of statements. They are assumed to be self-aware and accurate in their responses.

In traditional applications of this research, the researcher(s) engages with respondents to conduct the research. However, with the capabilities of online survey research suites, this graphic elicitation method (using the visual grid of the card sort to elicit feedback) of research may be achieved using an online tool—with a wide range of technological enablements (ability to control the question elicitations, data collection, data visualizations, and others), and broad geographical reach. This work explores the potential usage of a popular online survey platform for conducting an online q-methodology

REVIEW OF THE LITERATURE

In the research, q-methodology (or q-method) is achieved in five principal steps:

1. 'Concourse' or the 'Q-universe' definition
2. 'Q-set' or the 'Q samples' development
3. 'P-set' or 'person-sample' definition
4. 'Q-sort' gathering
5. Factorial analysis and interpretation (McKeown & Thomas, 2013, as cited in Iofrida, De Luca, Gulisano, & Strano, 2018, p. 47)

An earlier description of the five necessary steps add "conditions of instructions" in Step 3, which is important to the integrity of the research.

Subjectivity Concourse

A q-methodology study is a close-ended and ipsative (forced choice) one, in some ways, with select respondents asked to sort q-sort cards from a universe of statements a comprehensive domain-based topic-based concourse (or "subjectivity concourse"). A "concourse" is defined as a flow of communicability:

In Q, the flow of communicability surrounding any topic is referred to as a **concourse** *(from the Latin* **concursus***, meaning 'a running together,' as when ideas run together in thought), and it is from this concourse that a sample of statements is subsequently drawn for administration in a Q sort. (Brown, Apr./July 1993, pp. 94 - 95)*

The "level of discourse dictates the sophistication of the concourse..." (Brown, Apr./July 1993, p. 95). Interestingly, depending on the research and based on the available concourses in a review of the literature, the respective concourse statements are not necessarily single-barreled at all and may be fairly complex. Concourses comprise "the raw materials for Q methodology" (Brown, Apr./July 1993, p. 97). Another definition of a concourse may be "any subjective statement related to the topic" (Øverland, Thorsen, & Størksen, 2012, p. 314).

The contents of a concourse may be informed through formal sources like literature reviews, expert interviews, policy documents, news media, and so on, as well as informal sources like gray literature, social media contents, internet discussions, or some mix of the formal and informal. The criticality of the concourse is that it is the full set of contents from which select q-set statements are drawn for the "cards," which are sorted by participants. (Gaps in the concourse and then the derived q-set may mean blind spots in the research and gaps in knowledge.) While many q-methodologies are based on text-based q-sets, concourses may include "collections of paintings, pieces of art, photographs, and even musical selections... The idea of concourse incorporates virtually all manifestations of human life, as expressed in the lingua franca of shared culture" (Brown, Apr./July 1993, p. 95). [In digital q-methodologies, analogically, the "cards" may be multimodal, and may comprise of text and imagery, audio, video, and a mix of contents.]

Researchers describe different methods of finding elements for a concourse. They emphasize the importance of comprehensiveness or saturation in capturing contents for q-methodology concourses and then selecting the proper q-set materials for a wide range of distinctive "cards" for the q-sort activity. [Note: In some q-methodology designs that elicit responses for micropayments from crowd-sourced work sites, some add "attention traps" to validate/invalidate the level of attention paid by the online respondent. These may be simple statements that tell respondents to put a particular item into a particular category.]

Based on the research data, various statistical analyses (like scree tests) are run to extract underlying factors to understand differing clustering around points of view about the topic (Mandolesi, Nicholas, Naspetti, & Zanoli, 2015, p. 29).

Q-Set (or Q-Samples)

The q-set is comprised of a selection from the subjectivity concourse "universe" of possible contents. The contents of the q-set "must always be *broadly representative* of the opinion domain at issue" to help answer the particular research question(s) at issue (Watts & Stenner, 2005, p. 75). Capturing contents for the q-sort may come from literature reviews (Vizcaíno, García, Villar, Piattini, & Portillo, 2013) as well as a range of other less formal sources. The q-set is a form of "item sampling" and should be "heterogeneous" and conceptually distinctive to cover a range of topics (Watts & Stenner, 2005, p. 74).

The q-set "typically consists of 30 to 60 sentences, or a third of the entire concourse" and depends on the "researcher's discretion" (Iofrida, De Luca, Gulisano, & Strano, 2018, p. 47). The optimal size of a q-set is related to several factors: the amount of "cards" needed to represent the domain and research question space, the practical size of the q-sort grid, respondent knowledge, respondent fatigue, and other practical concerns. The composite q-set is generally thought to be somewhat larger than the p-set (number of invited participants). The heart of the q-methodology is the q-sort, where "a person is presented with a set of statements about some topic, and is asked to rank-order them (usually from 'agree' to 'disagree), an operation referred to as Q sorting." (Brown, Apr./July 1993, pp. 92 - 93)

One research team writes: "In Q-methodology, breadth and diversity of views are more important than proportionality in the selection of subjects (Brown, 1980, p. 260). Typically, it requires from 20 to 50 subjects (Q-set), and involves 30 to 50 statements (Q-sample). The small Q-set often raises concerns with the generalization of the findings beyond the studied group, as noted by Hermans et al. (2012: p. 87)," as cited in Pereira, Fairweather, Woodford, & Nuthall, 2016, p. 2).

P-Sets (or People Samples)

In q-method, the individuals invited to participate in the research are those "data rich" respondents who have access to the relevant information (possibly based on their roles in a field), such as stakeholders to particular in-world phenomena or experts (such as those brought into Delphi studies). Q-method research engages the sense of power in "insiders' views" (Pereira, Fairweather, Woodford, & Nuthall, 2016, p. 2). In q-method, the unit of measure involves the "psychological significance of each statement for each individual" (McKeown & Thomas, 1988, p. 48, as cited in Pereira, Fairweather, Woodford, & Nuthall, 2016, p. 2).

The number of members to a p-set are those generally supposed to be smaller than the q-set (Brewer, 1999, as cited in van Exel & de Graaf, 2005, p. 6). Ultimately, there should be a sufficient number to enable their segmentation into various typologies of respondent types (based on patterned mixes of shared perceptions and opinions). In the research literature, the ranges mentioned are 40 – 60 respondents in a typical p-set, with the idea that the right number enables stable findings with additional respondents not changing findings much (practically or ideally). The clusters of correlations from factorizing provide senses of "common viewpoints" (van Exel & de Graaf, 2005, p. 1) and points of "mutual coherence" for respondents (Brouwer, 1999, as cited in van Exel & de Graaf, 2005, p. 3). A q-methodology research approach does not require large numbers of participants as in R correlations "for it can reveal a characteristic independently of the distribution of that characteristic relative to others characteristics" (Smith, 2001, as cited in van Exel & de Graaf, 2005, p. 2).

The identification of possible respondents in the p-set stems from qualitative sampling methods, with smaller sets of select "informants". Q methodology is seen as a way to "subvert the assumptions of dominant objectivism that underlie the R-methods" to enable a post-positivist approach to data collection and analysis (Durning, 1999). Human subjectivities may be structured in more formalized ways. For a full range of opinions, the p-set should be as diverse as possible, reflecting different points of view and different population segments.

Demographic variety is likely important as well, and the related data is sometimes reported with the respective extracted factors and salient preferences (Ha, 2018, p. 127). Sociodemographic characteristics may be extracted and compared with factor weights for a p-sample (Park, Yeun, & Hwang, 2016, p. 146). Item analysis may be run against the statements in the q-set to understand convergences and divergences of agreements among particular q-methodology participants (Park, Yeun, & Hwang, 2016, p. 147). Respective statements from the q-set may be analyzed for respective values in factor arrays to understand how each item loads on particular factors (Iofrida, De Luca, Gulisano, & Strano, 2018, p. 51). Different stakeholder groups may be identified based on their similarities and differences in how they emplace the respective q-sort cards (Sy, et al., 2018, p. 7), and names or labels may be applied to these respective groups based on focuses. Q-factor analysis has been labeled "an early form of cluster analysis" (Brown, Apr./July 1993, p. 99). Particular mapping may be done to understand consenses around particular items and divergences around others at a macro level (Sy, et al., 2018, p. 8). Correlation matrices may be run to identify co-occurring items and associations between (Paige, 2015a, p. 75). Ultimately, a q-methodology analysis identifies correlations between respondents (subjective actors) across a sample of variables (sorted items). This enables the extraction of the main population stances around a particular topic as defined by respective weightings of particular items in combination. The respective participant groups may be identified based on their expressed card-sorting and their loading on different factors (Iofrida, De Luca, Gulisano, & Strano, 2018, p. 52); in other cases, respondents may be pre-identified and studied based on their preferences (with known group identities).

The Q-Sort and Follow-On Debriefing Research

This Q-methodology approach is a fairly straightforward one, as described, but the underlying assumptions seem somewhat revolutionary. People's opinions are seen as having powerful insights. Even one response can be powerful: "In principle as well as practice, single cases can be the focus of significant research" (Brown, Apr./July 1993, p. 94). Q-methodologies enable a range of askable questions:

- What are people's (stakeholders', experts', others') main perceptions and preferences from a q-set of cards or other informational contents (surrounding a particular issue or question)?
- What are some group patterns of preferences? How can these groups be named to understand segments of a population (by opinion)?
- What do the identified preference patterns suggest of follow-on actions? Expenditures? Behaviors (individual and group)?
- What are the implications of the identified preferences and the non-preferences? What do the findings suggest for decision making and design and other actions?

A q-methodology is considered including quantitative and qualitative means. Factor analyses are typically from quantitative research studies while selecting "q populations" or concourses, q-sets, and respondent p-sets of small groups of insiders is more from qualitative research practices (Ha, 2018, p. 125). In this method, there are both assumptions of objectivity and subjectivity in this mixed methods work. (Ha, 2018, p. 125) Another researcher observes that factor analysis is quantitative and factor interpretation is qualitative, and both are required in q-methodology (Paige, 2015a, p. 75).

A q-sort is a "ranking order" of information items in a "forced distribution using Q sort table" (Ha, 2018, p. 125). The card-sort grid, q-sort table, q-sort scoresheet is not only just the graphic elicitation for the card sort, but it also is used as a visual representation of frequency findings (as in an intensity matrix or table). In general, this q-grid is "bell shaped" (Baker, Feb. 28, 2013) and evokes a normal or "bell curve" shape, somewhat suggestive of a standard or "quasi-normal distribution" (Watts & Stenner, 2005, p. 77). That intuition is accurate in that the extremes tend to be somewhat less common than the more moderate opinions in the middle of the curve. In some cases, the card-sort grid may be set up as in Figure 1, or may be flipped with the curve vertical. The "most agreeable" items would be at the +4 column, and the "most disagreeable items" would be in the -4 column. (Watts &

Figure 1. A basic card-sort grid in Q-Methodology (as a graphic elicitation)

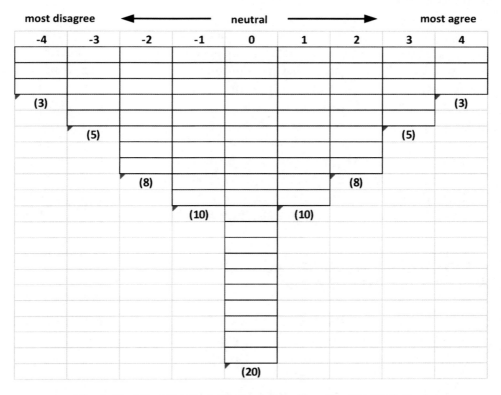

A Basic Card-Sort Grid in Q-Methodology (as a Graphic Elicitation)

Stenner, 2005, p. 79) The number of available cells for the cards should be exactly sufficient for the available numbers of cards. This q-sorting score sheet (or card-sort grid, or q-board) form is not only used to elicit responses from the p-set but also to showcase different patterned responses as intensity matrices. These may be used to provide spatial senses of the issues of highest interest and of preference patterning and subjectivities around the topic. (Figure 1)

A q-method research sequence is comprised of two parts. One involves the card-sorting, and the second part is an interview to explore the subjective actor's ideas more deeply (Brown, Apr./July 1993, p. 106). Replicability is an important value for this research (van Exel & de Graaf, 2005, p. 3).

Data Analytics

Within q-methodology, there are various practices to promote research quality. The concourse should be a full one, capturing the universe of expressed opinions in a particular space. The q-method may be pilot-tested for improvements. In terms of data analysis, there are standards for rigor in running factor analyses (in terms of eigenvalues, in terms of factor loading, in terms of rotations), principal components analyses, analyses of variances of factor scores, centroid factor analysis, computational clustering, numbers of items in q-sets, numbers of participants in p-sets, and in manual coding textual responses, interrater comparisons enable quality standards. There are various types of external validation methods. One research project involved validating through citizen validation to connect the research insights with the larger societal group (Forrester, Cook, Bracken, Cinderby, & Donaldson, 2015, p. 203).

A WIDE RANGE OF RESEARCH TOPICS IN Q-METHOD RESEARCH

Q-method research has a "long pedigree in psychological, political and sociological research" and has application for human geographers (Eden, Donaldson, & Walker, 2005, p. 413), among others. Q-method has been applied to a range of topics in psychology, healthcare, environmental policy and practice, food production, business and marketing, employment, consumer experiences, social advancement, education, ethics, leadership, assessment of test instruments, and other fields. The research method creates a sense of the local, of a close-in question, of particular thin-slicing of people groups, and of defined decision spaces reliant on human knowledge, actions, and cooperation.

In terms of "psychology" studies (Serfass & Sherman, 2013), q-methods have been applied to personality description (Block, 1961); attachment relationships (Waters & Deane, 1985); attachment behaviors of one-year-olds (Vaughn & Waters, Dec. 1990); infant-mother attachment (Pederson, Moran, Sitko, Campbell, Ghesqire, & Acton, Dec. 1990); affect regulation (Westen, Muderrisoglu, Fowler, Shedler, & Koren, 1997); children's emotion regulation (Shields & Cicchetti, 1997); emotional attachment patterns (van IJzendoorn, Vereijken, Bakermans-Kranenburg, & Riksen-Walraven, July/Aug. 2004); "wisdom in the Korean elderly" (Sung, 2011), and other topics.

In "healthcare," q-methods have been applied to those living with chronic pain (Risdon, Eccleston, Crombez, & McCracken, 2003); individual perspectives on "health-related quality of life" (Stenner, Cooper, & Skevington, 2003, p. 2161);

patient preferences for the management of hypertension (Morecroft, Cantrill, & Tully, 2006); elderly patients' attitudes towards death and dying (Yeun, 2005); lay understandings of Down's syndrome (Bryant, Green, & Hewison, 2006); informal caregivers' views of respite care (van Exel, de Graaf, & Brouwer, 2007); patients with chronic conditions and their care preferences (Jedeloo, van Staa, Latour, & van Exel, 2010); the perception of maternity services across different generational groups (Cross-Sudworth, Williams, & Herron-Marx, 2011); "informed choice in antenatal screening" in ethical healthcare (Ahmed, Bryant, Tizro, & Shickle, 2012, p. 997); motivating reasons for orthodontic treatment (Prabakaran, Seymour, Moles, & Cunningham, 2012); the promotion of healthy food environments (Kraak, Swinburn, Lawrence, & Harrison, 2014); self-management support for those with chronic conditions (van Hooft, Dwarswaard, Jedeloo, Bal, & van Staa, 2015); priority setting for health care in ten European countries (van Exel, Baker, Mason, Donaldson, Brouwer, and EuroVaQ Team, 2015); health beliefs (Stone, et al., 2016);"kidney transplant patients' attitudes towards self-management support" (Grijpma, et al., 2016); ways to reduce anxiety among adult orthodontic patients (Lin, et al., 2017); acceptance of health promoting hospitals (Mahmoodi, Sarbakhsh, & Shaghaghi, 2018); turnover intention in a clinical setting for male nurses (Kim & Shim, 2018); clinical nursing resilience experiences in a hospital setting (Shin, Kim, & Ji, 2018); laypersons' senses of smile aesthetics (Batra, Daing, Azam, Miglani, & Bhardwaj, 2018), and experiences with sensory relearning after hand surgery (Vikström, Carlsson, Rosén, & Björkman, 2018).

In terms of "environmental policy and practice," "Q" has been applied to the study of attitudes towards national forest management (Steelman & Maguire, 1999); environmental issues and sustainability (Barry & Proops, 1999); wind farms (Ellis, Barry, & Robinson, 2007); environmental sustainability (Doody, Kearney, Barry, Moles, & O'Regan, 2009); an environmental regime's effectiveness in a particular region (Frantzi, Carter, & Lovett, 2009); various conceptualizations of "rurality" (Duenckmann, 2010); "energy options from biomass" (Cuppen, Breukers, Hisschemöller, & Bergsma, 2010, p. 579); land-use changes in an indigenous community (Lansing, 2013); non-market valuations for natural resources for policymaking (Armatas, Venn, & Watson, 2014); the solving of energy problems on a developing continent (Matinga, Pinedo-Pascua, Vervaeke, Monforti-Ferrario, & Szabó, 2014); hydrogen production from waste studies (Baxter & Hacking, 2015); the exploration of stakeholder perceptions of "complex environmental problems" (Forrester, Cook, Bracken, Cinderby, & Donaldson, 2015, p. 199); the valuing of "non-market environmental goods and services" (Zanoli, Carlesi, Danovaro, Mandolesi, & Naspetti, 2015); community experiences with resource extraction and mining (Chapman, Tonts, & Plummer, 2015); the opinions of various stakeholders to a "payment for watershed services" approach to manage a forest watershed (Jaung, Putzel, Bull, Kozak, & Markum, 2016); socioeconomic impacts of mineral resources (Weldegiorgis & Ali, 2016); fair trade carbon projects (Howard, Tallontire, Stringer, & Marchant, 2016); the "impact of photovoltaic applications on the landscape" in a photo-based card-sort (Naspetti, Mandolesi, & Zanoli, 2016, p. 564); forest management (Hugé, et al., 2016); ecosystem services (Hermelingmeier & Nicholas, 2017); communities' primary motivations and barriers to achieving decarbonization (Byrne, Byrne, Ryan, & O'Regan, 2017); sustainability in business practices (Silvius, Kampinga, Paniagua, & Mooi, 2017); the recycling of potable water based on insights of water stewards (Ormerod, 2017); invasive alien species (Vaas, Driessen, Giezen, van Laerhoven, & Wassen, 2018); community perceptions of gold mining (Nguyen, Boruff, & Tonts, 2018); ecosystem services (Sy, et al., 2018); the policies and practices around environmentally protected areas (Niedziałkowski, Komar, Pietrzyk-Kaszyńska, A., Olszańska, A., & Grodzinńska-Jurczak, M., 2018); the study of expert decision making from "attitudinal divergences that exist and... patterns of shared assumptions forming attitude-related communities" around forest use decision making (Nijnik, Nijnik, Sarkki, Muñoz-Rojas, Miller, & Kopiy, 2018, p. 210); agri-ecology (Schall, Lansing, Leisnham, Shirmohammadi, Montas, & Hutson, 2018); farmers and their environmental behaviors (Walder & Kantelhardt, 2018); scale of fisherman enterprises and fisherman attitudes towards marine protections policies (Bueno & Schiavetti, 2019), and ecotourism planning (Lee, 2019).

Q-methods have been applied to "food production" research. For example, there have been studies on agri-environmental studies such as attitudes towards the use of agricultural water as a resource (Forouzani, Karami, Zamani, & Moghaddam, 2013); stakeholder views of marine fish farming (Bacher, Gordoa, & Mikkelssen, 2014); innovation in "low-input and organic dairy supply chains" (Mandolesi, Nicholas, Naspetti, & Zanoli, 2015, p. 25); beef farming (Pereira, Fairweather, Woodford, & Nuthall, 2016); money crop production (Iofrida, De Luca, Gulisano, & Strano, 2018), and food marketing (Brard & Lê, 2018).

In "business and marketing," researchers have explored perceptions of global software development or "GSD" (Vizcaíno, García, Villar, Piattini, & Portillo, 2013); e-commerce website design (Liu & Chen, 2013); tourism market segmentation (Mokry & Dufek, 2014); product development (Courcoux, Qannari, & Faye, 2015); and product placement in digital contents (Kim & Shin, 2017). In "employment" research, q-techniques were applied to the study of social work (Ellingsen, Størksen, & Stephens, Dec. 2010). "Consumer experiences" have been studied, including home owner experiences with domestic energy retrofits (Kerr, Gouldson, & Barrett, 2018) and non-professional consumer theories of healthy nutrition (Yarar & Orth, 2018).

In studies related to "social advancement," there have been q-methods studies related to "political subjectivity" in political science (Brown, 1980); transportation and "social inclusion" (Rajé, 2007); self-acceptance in the form of "ego-integrity" in "old adults" (Chang, et al., 2008, p. 246); energy infrastructure projects (Cuppen, Bosch-Rekveldt, Pikaar, & Mehos, 2016); concepts of global citizenship attitudes (Sklarwitz, 2017), and attitudes towards small hydroelectric plants (Pagnussatt, Petrini, dos Santos, & da Silveira, 2018).

Q-method-based studies of "education" address topics like health education and health promotion (Cross, Apr. 2005); practices in preschool classrooms (Bracken & Fischel, 2006); nursing research (Akhtar-Danesh, Baumann, & Cordingley, Oct. 2008); teacher ideas about "children of divorce" (Øverland, Thorsen, & Størksen, 2012); "the level of methodological skills of the prospective teachers" (Evelina & Nadia, 2014, p. 60); attitudes towards the video-assisted debriefing of a learning simulation for nursing students (Ha, 2014); methods by preschool teachers to promote peer relations (Gamelas & Aguiar, 2014); nursing education (Yeun, Bang, Ryoo, & Ha, 2014; Paige, 2015b); clinical practice by nursing students (Ha, 2015); senses of poverty among "midwestern nursing students" (Work, Hensel, & Decker, 2015, p. 328); priorities for early childhood education practices among different parental groups (Hu, Yang, & Ieong, 2016); library priorities for undergraduate learners (Kelly & Young, 2017); preschool teachers' views on linguistic diversity (Sung & Akhtar, 2017); the examination of learning among nursing students (Ha, 2018); the experiences of graduate students engaging in intercultural practices (Zhang, 2018), and undergraduate nursing students' senses of peer tutoring in a simulation laboratory (Li, Petrini, & Stone, 2018).

Q methods have been applied to elicit sexual ethics among undergraduate students (Park, Yeun, & Hwang, 2016). "Q" has been applied to the evaluation of collective leadership (Militello & Benham, 2010). Q-techniques have been applied to the assessment of questionnaire items (Nahm, Rao, Solis-Galvan, & Ragu-Nathan, Winter 2002) and other test instruments.

To summarize, Q-method research has been applied in various ways to suit local research purposes (Brard & Lê, 2018). Q-methodologies are not always used in stand-alone ways. Sometimes, there is a mix of both Q and R methodologies in one study (Kim & Lee, 2015). Q-methodology "has its origins in factor analysis, with the difference being the inversion of rows and columns" (Pereira, Fairweather, Woodford, & Nuthall, 2016, p. 2). In another case, q-method was combined with participatory mapping (Forrester, Cook, Bracken, Cinderby, & Donaldson, 2015). In another study, q-methods were combined with eye-tracking research (Kim & Shin, 2017). Also, q-analysis is not just applied as a one-off; it can be applied over time to understand changes in perspectives (Davies & Hodge, 2012).

SOME EXAMPLES OF DATA RELATED TO Q-METHODOLOGY

It is possible to understand the most salient "agreement" and "disagreement" items from the p-set of respondents through simple frequency counts. It is possible to see what is most non-salient, in terms of neutral items from the q-set (sample from the concourse). It is possible to acquire a respondent sense of what is "meaningful" (Watts & Stenner, 2005, p. 74). Factor theory, q-form not R, informs q-methodology (Stephenson, Oct. 1993/Jan. 1994, p. 13). The "centroid" extraction is often used "in conjunction with hand rotation" instead of the Varimax rotation method for q-methodology (Newman & Ramlo, 2010, p. 510).

A general data table may involve the item scores for each of the q-set items as in Table 2. This would show the min-max ranges of the respective positions of the q-set items in a min-max range across a number of positions (in this case, five positions). Such a table shows "comparative ranking" of the items generally and / or based around particular factors (Watts & Stenner, 2005, p. 83).

Another approach involves identifying the top "most like / most unlike statements" by creating a table like this Table 3.

Table 4 shows what the factor table may look like.

Table 5 shows what a pre-profiled grouping may be done in relation to the identified factors.

Table 2. Min-max ranges from Q-Sort grid positionality of Q-Set items

Unique Identifier	Q-set item (or statement) in original order	A Lowest Position in Q-sort Grid	B Intermediate	C Center-most	D Intermediate	E Highest Position in Q-sort Grid
	Item 1					
	Item 2					

Table 3. Q-Set items and their positionality in relation to other items

Unique Identifier (like a number)	Q-set item (or statement)	z-score	Grid position (like -6 to +6, depending on column position in the q-sort /card sort grid)

Table 4. Composite factor scores of the Q-Set

Q-set items	Factor 1	Factor 2	Factor 3	Factor 4
Item 1	(factor loadings)			
Item 2				
Item 3				

Table 5. Pre-Q-Method research profile groups and factor loadings

Role-based members of the p-set	Factor 1	Factor 2	Factor 3	Factor 4	Factor 5
Group 1					
Group 2					
Group 3					

To understand the segments of the population in terms of card sorts, cluster analyses are conducted:

Q-sorts from all respondents are correlated and factor analysed in order to yield groups of people who have ordered the statements similarly (i.e., have similar views). In this process, statements have little importance by themselves; more important is the relationship amongst statements, which is revealed by the way respondents sort them (Addams, 2000; Brown, 1980; McKeown and Thomas, 1988). The resulting factors represent major viewpoints: the higher the respondent's loading on a factor, the greater is that person's association with the viewpoint represented by that factor (McKeown and Thomas, 1988). Interpretation of factors occurs by consistently producing explanations for the factor arrays. Finally, labels are typically established for each factor to pinpoint its salient characteristics that summarise the viewpoints represented by the factor (Addams, 2000: p. 33). (Pereira, Fairweather, Woodford, & Nuthall, 2016, p. 2)

Understanding the opinion segmentation may be represented in Table 6.

Besides the simple frequency counts and factors and identification of groups from shared factor loadings, it is important to analyze the textual debriefing data as well. The text analyses may be linked to particular quantitative q-sort responses to see

Table 6. Factor loadings (or item patterns) and applied group identities based on Q-Set profiling

Role-based descriptions based on Factor Loadings	Named Group A	Named Group B	Named Group C	Named Group D	Other
Factor 1 / Item Pattern 1 (with item breakdowns)					
Factor 2 / Item Pattern 2 (with item breakdowns)					
Factor 3 / Item Pattern 3 (with item breakdowns)					

if there are patterns of interest. It is important to engage in "distant reading" of the responses to capture insights such as topic focus and sentiment analysis. Then, there is the "close reading" of the textual contents, too, for deeper understandings of the responses and the selection of quotations for "color" in reporting out of the findings.

RUNNING A Q-METHODOLOGY STUDY IN AN ONLINE SURVEY RESEARCH SUITE

Based on the research, it is possible to draft out a four-phase sequence of how to set up and deploy a q-methods study on an online survey research platform. (Figure 2)

A Universe Concourse to Q-Set Items

Arriving at a fully explicated concourse of objects or items is important to the setup of the cards for the sorting. Researchers point to a variety of ways to arrive at these, such as from reviews of the formal literature, the gray literature, expert interviews, and other efforts. From the concourse, the q-set cards are selected, and these should be highly differentiated from each other. Researchers suggest that q-sets should be "somewhere between 40 and 80 statements" (Curt, 1994; Stainton Rogers, 1995, as cited in Watts & Stenner, 2005, p. 75).

To actualize this early test of a q-methodology on Qualtrics, the author brainstormed a range of features of graduate student research, including practices related to research topic selection, literature reviews, faculty support for the research, cost management, time management, the roles of concepts, tactics, and other dimensions. The elicitation reads as follows:

In graduate-level higher education studies research related to educational technologies, the research project should...

Figure 2. A basic sequence for Q-Methodology setup and deployment on an online survey research suite

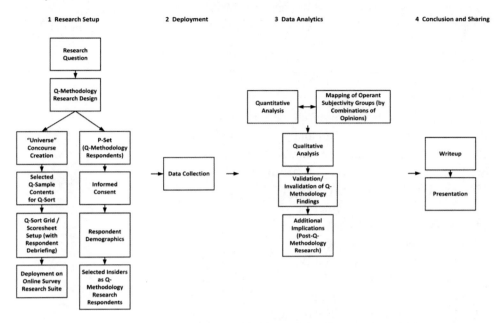

A Basic Sequence for Q-Methodology Setup and Deployment on an Online Survey Research Suite

1. Include full saturation in the literature review
2. Include partial review of the literature
3. Involve other co-researchers
4. Be a stand-alone research work
5. Be aligned with the graduate advisor's research
6. Involve multimodal informational resources
7. Include multiple educational technologies
8. Include well known educational technologies
9. Include open-source educational technologies
10. Be novel
11. Be publishable
12. Involve educational technology testing
13. Relate to the student researcher's biographical history
14. Be personally meaningful to the student researcher
15. Be low cost
16. Be high cost
17. Involve inherited (non-self-generated) datasets

Table 7. A Q-Sort grid with seven categories

Strongly Agree +3 (3)	Agree +2 (5)	Somewhat Agree +1 (8)	Neither Agree nor Disagree (neutral) 0 (20)	Somewhat Disagree -1 (8)	Disagree -2 (5)	Strongly Disagree -3 (3)

18. Involve established research methods
19. Involve established data analytics methods
20. Involve new research methods
21. Involve new data analytics methods
22. Be about a "hot" current issue
23. Be funded by government
24. Be funded by industry
25. Be secret and embargoed
26. Be achieved within deadline
27. Be closely supervised by the faculty advisory team
28. Be distantly supervised by the faculty advisory team
29. Be informed by a theory or theories
30. Be informed by a model or models
31. Be informed by a framework or frameworks
32. Be practically applicable
33. Involve data visualizations
34. Include diagrams and illustrations
35. Be based on graduate student researcher's ambition for a future career
36. Involve travel
37. Be related to the physical location of the university
38. Involve a second language
39. Be done in a first language
40. Include a byline with the masters or doctoral committee members when published
41. Include some crediting of the masters or doctoral committee members
42. Capture the student researcher's personality as a signature
43. Have the research costs borne by the university
44. Have the research costs borne by the student and the student's family
45. Be prosocial
46. Be revolutionary
47. Lead to social change

48. Protect the status quo
49. Include patent-able discoveries
50. Provide research instruments available at no charge to other researchers
51. Provide research instruments for pay to other researchers
52. Challenge an existing model

From these 52 cards (yes, like a card deck), respondents to the q-methodology study (members of the p-set) are asked to Pick, Group, & Rank those objects into a q-sorting score sheet. [While one researcher suggested using Qualtric's "Pick, Group, & Rank" question type for a q-methodology (Gaskin, Sept. 24, 2015), he suggested that the ranking within the categories could be used in the sort; however, for most practices, the categories on q-sort templates or score sheets themselves do not contain within category ranking but treat all objects within the templates as of equal value (Mandolesi, Nicholas, Naspetti, & Zanoli, 2015, p. 28).] The number of cells in each scoring sheet equals the number of cards to be sorted. There do not seem to be a "don't know" or "other" opt-out options. For this setup, seven categories were used instead of the three, and there were limits placed on the amounts of items in each category to create the q-sort grid. (Table 7)

Figure 3 shows what this graphic elicitation may look like in Qualtrics. The items are in a stack to the left, and the various categories are to the right. There did not seem to be a way to technologically limit the number of items in a particular category

Figure 3. An online Q-Sort on the Qualtrics research suite using a "pick, group, & rank" question type

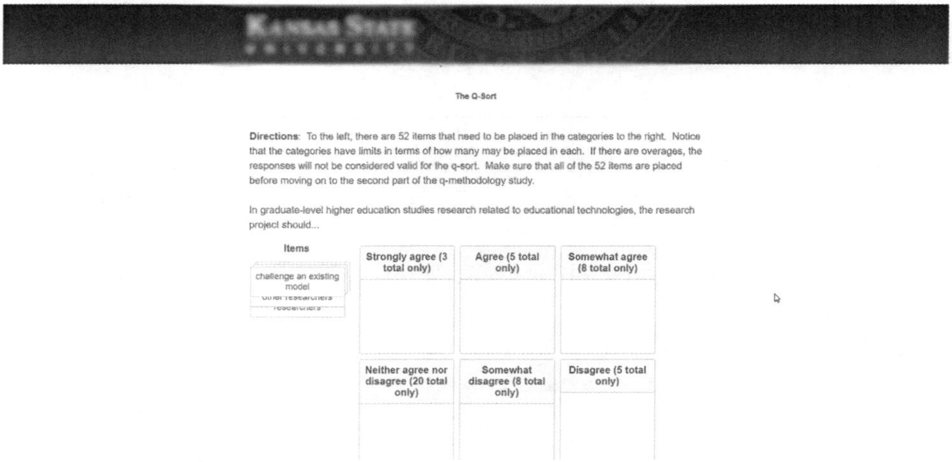

through validation or through other means, so those item limits were included in the labels for the respective categories.

Researchers suggest that randomizing the order of the elements in a q-sort may minimize order effects. Empirically, "items appearing near the end of the Q-Sort have less variance and more central placement" (Serfass & Sherman, 2013, p. p. 853). These higher levels of convergence and less variance in q-sorts have been attributed to item order effects. The co-researchers elaborate:

Carelessness, or a lack of proper incentive, is probably one of the mechanisms that cause these item order effects. This tendency may stem from the simple fact that raters do not reevaluate item placements that they have already made. Instead, they simply fill in the open spaces in the distribution toward the end of a Q-Sort. Personality, compensation, intrinsic interest, and experience with the measure may all be important factors influencing these order effects. (Serfass & Sherman, 2013, p. p. 857)

A walk-through of the draft q-methodology research in Qualtrics with 52 items suggests that the interface requires scrolling up and down to emplace the items. (In the mobile version, this would become tedious quickly.) The automated ranking by placement of the respective items in each category is not used for analysis per se by rank but may be useful to ensure that the total number of items in each category does not surpass the stated limits. (Figure 4) The ranking feature may be useful when the "cards" are not as numerous as in this case.

For the text-based debriefing, survey participants are asked to use the back button to see their responses, and the platform is sufficiently stable and reliable to enable this toggling (Figure 5). In some sources, this debriefing is described as an interview or a think-aloud exercise.

This research should result in two sets of data: the physical distribution of sorted "cards" and the text responses in the debriefing. (The modalities of the datasets may vary, with "cards" comprised of visuals, audio, video, or some combination of multimedia, and with the debriefing comprised of video, audio, uploaded files, or other data.)

It is possible to add more complex elicitations using Loop & Merge and piped text features in Qualtrics to customize the responses (along with Embedded Data to capture the dynamic information). More details about this trial q-methodology setup may be found in the Appendix, and the full online version may be found at https://kstate.qualtrics.com/jfe/form/SV_eFGyjy8agDFWtil.

Figure 4. Automatic application of ranking numbers per category, which may be used for totaling items per category

Figure 5. Debriefing the Q-Methodology by eliciting follow-on text responses from the p-set respondents

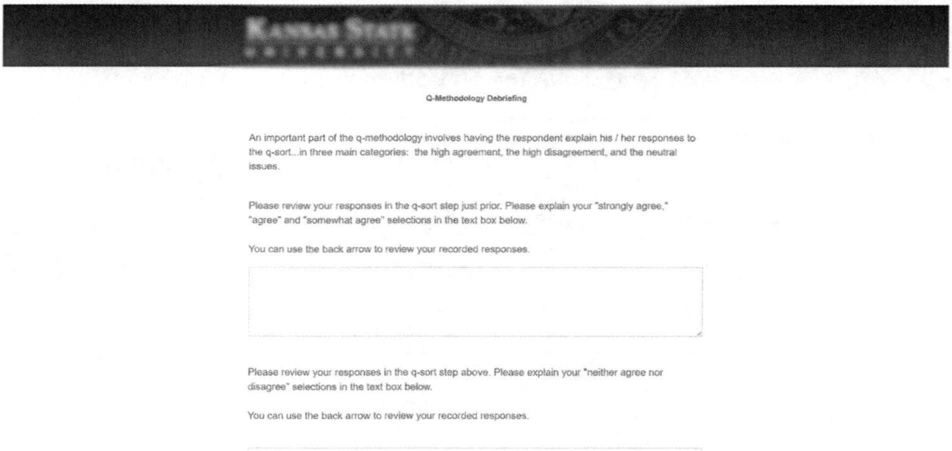

Finally, Figure 6 shows a Preview version of this test online q-methodology experience and what happens when a respondent tries to bypass the q-sort without any minimum response. A validation reaction occurs.

Finally, on Qualtrics, it is possible to view individual responses one-by-one using the "View Response" option in the "Data & Analysis" section. This approach enables a fuller by-individual-respondent view, including the demographic information, the q-sort, and the q-methodology debriefing (by text response). (Figure 7)

Certainly, this process is not deemed successful if the enablement is only to engage in graphic elicitation of responses. The Qualtrics platform enables full download of the data in .csv, .tsv, .sav, and other formats. The Reports feature enables more close-in downloads of summary statistical tables as well as basic table data for the particular q-sort question, which is the way to access data that is easiest to run on external quantitative data analytics software tools. (The automated data visualizations of the data are not as useful and not particularly coherent with complex data.)

DISCUSSION

An online survey research suite may seem like a natural fit to q-method research, with the richness of visual engagements for respondents and statistics-enabled back-ends. However, depending on the software, the prior assertion may have its limits.

Figure 6. The validation reaction in the Q-Methodology survey preview

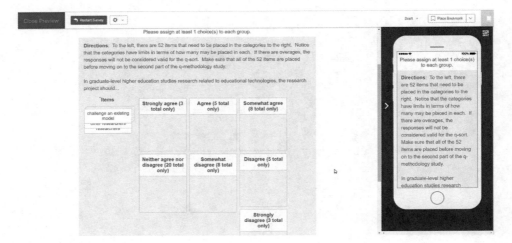

Figure 7. A scrollable individual response view online to view holistic respondent-by-respondent data

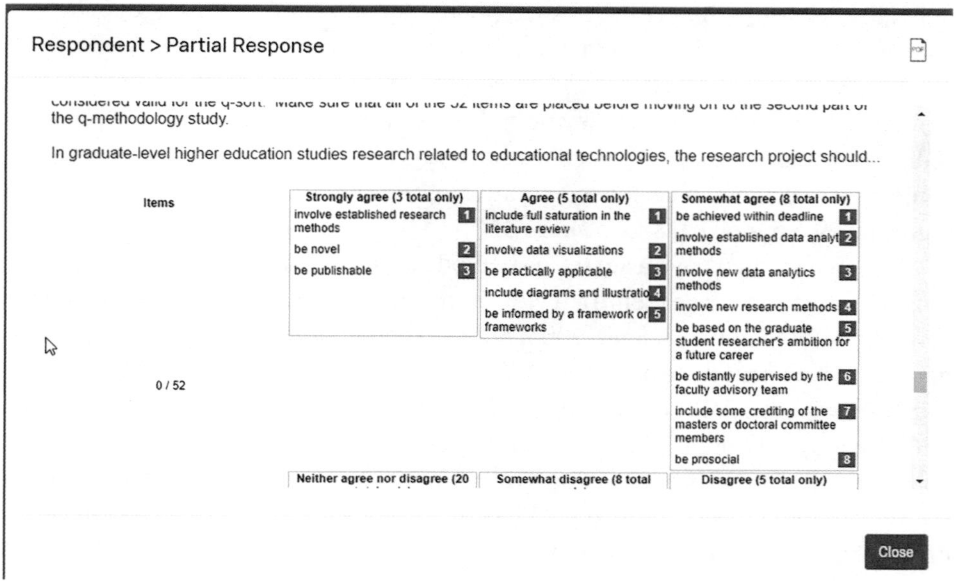

While the Pick, Group, & Rank question type fits the bill to some degree in terms of a graphic elicitation and the sense of placing "cards," there are some down sides. There is not a clear way of using images or video or multimedia elements for the content items. To test the online q-method study, it is not possible to autogenerate test results within the numerical limits of the test categories. (Or if scripting could be used to limit these, the method is non-obvious within the limits of the platform.) If a sequential card sort is set up, that is also possible and may enable limits through custom validation, but then, to make this look of a piece, there cannot be any page breaks between the elements…and there has to be scripting to restrict double-use or multi-use of any of the items. Ideally, there would be something closer to the bell-shaped distribution of the q-sort grid. Also, the Pick, Group, & Rank question requires the use of mouse-actions, and there is not a keyboard shortcut option. This means that accessibility is a challenge. The data on the back end will require some work to ensure that it can be analyzed for a factor analysis in a third-party quantitative analytics tool.

Some postings on Qualtrics discussion forums may suggest that there are ways to control the drag-and-drop box height based on possible amounts of choices available. It is quite possible that as the hosted Qualtrics research platform is updated that changes may make online q-methodologies more or less possible to deploy effectively.

As compared to other research methods, an advantage of q-methodology is perceived as the following: "Viewpoints do not represent the views of a particular individual; rather, they are a constructed aggregate that represents the shared subjectivity of those who loaded significantly on that factor" (Iofrida, De Luca, Gulisano, & Strano, 2018, p. 52).

Researchers who have used the q-method caveat it in several ways. One is that it "makes no claim to have identified viewpoints that are *consistent within individuals* across time." (Watts & Stenner, 2005, p. 85). Another downside is the forcing of the data "into a normal distribution grid (Iofrida, De Luca, Gulisano, & Strano, 2018, p. 52). There are additional weaknesses. If a q-set is incomplete, those weaknesses will affect the research findings. If a researcher does not know a field sufficiently, he / she / they may not know how to interpret the results effectively. Also, if a researcher does not have empathy with others, he or she will not be able to make use of the observed sets of opinion types and the resulting q-sort profiles. A researcher needs to see the internal consistencies among the differing profiles and to be able to understand respondent interests inherent in the data.

This work demands some sophistication in terms of quantitative and qualitative data analytics. There are limits from the p-set of respondents, in their low number, in self-reportage and the gaps between self-claims and actual actions. The lack of wider knowledge of this research method may also be a delimiter in terms of how receptive professional audiences may be to this method. Q-method does bring something unique to qualitative and mixed methods research (Watts & Stenner, 2005).

FUTURE RESEARCH DIRECTIONS

This work offers an early cobbled approach to deploying an online q-methodology research study. Certainly, there are ways to improve both the card-sorting and the post-sorting debriefing elicitations and data captures. This work may be built upon with more multimodal "cards" for the sorting. There can be follow-on work with a pilot q-methods study using Qualtrics and the carrying through of this approach with real-world data analyses and applied insights. Real-world validation of online q-methods findings would also provide rich ways to advance this work.

CONCLUSION

This work provides a first walk-through of using the Qualtrics Research Suite for a potential online q-methods study. In this case, only the author completed the initial walk-through of the q-sort. This initial effort is sufficiently promising though to suggest that others may advance this work further and use the platform for a full q-methods study deployed to a full p-set, for a pilot study and more.

REFERENCES

Ahmed, S., Bryant, L. D., Tizro, Z., & Shickle, D. (2012). Interpretations of informed choice in antenatal screening: A cross-cultural, Q-methodology study. *Social Science & Medicine*, *74*(7), 997–1004. doi:10.1016/j.socscimed.2011.12.021 PMID:22326381

Akhtar-Danesh, N., Baumann, A., & Cordingley, L. (2008, October). Q-methodology in nursing research: A promising method for the study of subjectivity. *Western Journal of Nursing Research*, *30*(6), 759–773. doi:10.1177/0193945907312979 PMID:18337548

Armatas, C. A., Venn, T. J., & Watson, A. E. (2014). Applying Q-methodology to select and define attributes for non-market valuation: A case study from Northwest Wyoming, United States. *Ecological Economics*, *107*, 447–456. doi:10.1016/j.ecolecon.2014.09.010

Bacher, K., Gordoa, A., & Mikkelsen, E. (2014). Stakeholders' perceptions of marine fish farming in Catalonia (Spain): A Q-methodology approach. *Aquaculture*, *424 – 425*, 78 – 85.

Baker, R. (2013, Feb. 28). Rachel Baker introduces Q Methodology. *YouTube*. Retrieved Jan. 27, 2019, from https://youtu.be/ZbZ2Kq-Fzxo

Barry, J., & Proops, J. (1999). Seeking sustainability discourses with Q methodology. *Ecological Economics*, *28*(3), 337–345. doi:10.1016/S0921-8009(98)00053-6

Batra, P., Daing, A., Azam, I., Migliani, R., & Bhardwaj, A. (2018). Impact of altered gingival characteristics on smile esthetics: Laypersons' perspectives by Q sort methodology. *American Journal of Orthodontics and Dentofacial Orthopedics*, *154*(1), 82–90. doi:10.1016/j.ajodo.2017.12.010 PMID:29957325

Baxter, J., & Hacking, N. (2015). Expert hydrogen perspectives for technological innovation: A Q-method study. *International Journal of Hydrogen Energy*, *40*(8), 3111–3121. doi:10.1016/j.ijhydene.2014.06.171

Block, J. (1961). *The q-sort method in personality assessment and psychiatric research*. Springfield, IL: Bannerstone House. doi:10.1037/13141-000

Bracken, S. S., & Fischel, J. E. (2006). Assessment of preschool classroom practices: Application of Q-sort methodology. *Early Childhood Research Quarterly*, *21*(4), 417–430. doi:10.1016/j.ecresq.2006.09.006

Brard, M., & Lê, S. (2018). Adaptation of the Q-methodology for the characterization of a complex concept through a set of products: From the collection of the data to their analysis. *Food Quality and Preference*, *67*, 77–86. doi:10.1016/j.foodqual.2017.06.010

Brown, S. R. (1980). *Political subjectivity*. New Haven, CT: Yale University Press. Retrieved Jan. 23, 2019, from https://qmethodblog.files.wordpress.com/2016/01/brown-1980-politicalsubjectivity.pdf

Brown, S. R. (1993, April/July). A primer on Q Methodology. *Operant Subjectivity*, *16*(3/4), 91–138.

Bryant, L. D., Green, J. M., & Hewison, J. (2006). Understandings of Down's syndrome: A Q methodological investigation. *Social Science & Medicine*, *63*(5), 1188–1200. doi:10.1016/j.socscimed.2006.03.004 PMID:16644080

Bueno, P. F., & Schiavetti, A. (2019). The influence of fisherman scale in the resilience of socio-ecological systems: An analysis using Q methodology. *Ocean and Coastal Management*, *169*, 214–224. doi:10.1016/j.ocecoaman.2018.12.008

Byrne, R., Byrne, S., Ryan, R., & O'Regan, B. (2017). Applying the Q-method to identify primary motivation factors and barriers to communities in achieving decarbonisation goals. *Energy Policy*, *110*, 40–50. doi:10.1016/j.enpol.2017.08.007

Chang, S. O., Kim, J. H., Kong, E. S., Kim, C. G., Ahn, S. Y., & Cho, N. O. (2008). Exploring ego-integrity in old adults: A Q-methodology study. *International Journal of Nursing Studies*, *45*(2), 246–256. doi:10.1016/j.ijnurstu.2006.07.020 PMID:16982055

Chapman, R., Tonts, M., & Plummer, P. (2015). Exploring perceptions of the impacts of resource development: A Q-methodology study. *The Extractive Industries and Society*, *2*(3), 540–551. doi:10.1016/j.exis.2015.04.008

Courcoux, P., Qannari, E.M., & Faye, P. (2015). Free sorting as a sensory profiling technique for product development. *Rapid Sensory Profiling Techniques and Related Methods,* 153 – 185.

Cross, R. M. (2005, April). Exploring attitudes: The case for Q methodology. *Health Education Research, 20*(2), 206–213. doi:10.1093/her/cyg121 PMID:15385430

Cross-Sudworth, F., Williams, A., & Herron-Marx, S. (2011). Maternity services in multi-cultural Britain: Using Q methodology to explore the views of first- and second-generation women of Pakistani origin. *Midwifery, 27*(4), 458–468. doi:10.1016/j.midw.2010.03.001 PMID:21036439

Cuppen, E., Bosch-Rekveldt, M. G. C., Pikaar, E., & Mehos, D. C. (2016). Stakeholder engagement in large-scale energy infrastructure projects: Revealing perspectives using Q methodology. *International Journal of Project Management, 34*(7), 1347–1359. doi:10.1016/j.ijproman.2016.01.003

Cuppen, E., Breukers, S., Hisschemöller, M., & Bergsma, E. (2010). Q methodology to select participants for a stakeholder dialogue on energy options from biomass in the Netherlands. *Ecological Economics, 69*(3), 579–591. doi:10.1016/j.ecolecon.2009.09.005

Davies, B. B., & Hodge, I. D. (2012). Shifting environmental perspectives in agriculture: Repeated Q analysis and the stability of preference structures. *Ecological Economics, 83*, 51–57. doi:10.1016/j.ecolecon.2012.08.013

Doody, D. G., Kearney, P., Barry, J., Moles, R., & O'Regan, B. (2009). Evaluation of the Q-method as a method of public participation in the selection of sustainable development indicators. *Ecological Indicators, 9*(6), 1129–1137. doi:10.1016/j.ecolind.2008.12.011

Duenckmann, F. (2010). The village in the mind: Applying Q-methodology to re-constructing constructions of rurality. *Journal of Rural Studies, 26*(3), 284–295. doi:10.1016/j.jrurstud.2010.01.003

Durning, D. (1999). The transition from traditional to postpositivist policy analysis: A role for Q-Methodology. *Journal of Policy Analysis and Management, 18*(3), 389–410. doi:10.1002/(SICI)1520-6688(199922)18:3<389::AID-PAM4>3.0.CO;2-S

Eden, S., Donaldson, A., & Walker, G. (2005). Structuring subjectivities? Using Q methodology in human geography. *Area, 37*(4), 413–422. doi:10.1111/j.1475-4762.2005.00641.x

Ellingsen, I. T., Størksen, I., & Stephens, P. (2010, December). Q methodology in social work research. *International Journal of Social Research Methodology*, *13*(5), 395–409. doi:10.1080/13645570903368286

Ellis, G., Barry, J., & Robinson, C. (2007). Many ways to say 'no', different ways to say 'yes': Applying Q-methodology to understand public acceptance of wind farm proposals. *Journal of Environmental Planning and Management*, *50*(4), 517–551. doi:10.1080/09640560701402075

Evelina, B. C., & Nadia, B. C. (2014). The Q-sort technique used in identifying the level of methodological skills of the prospective teachers. In the proceedings of the EPC-TKS 2013. *Procedia: Social and Behavioral Sciences*, *128*, 60–65. doi:10.1016/j.sbspro.2014.03.118

Forouzani, M., Karami, E., Zamani, G. H., & Moghaddam, K. R. (2013). Agricultural water poverty: Using Q-methodology to understand stakeholders' perceptions. *Journal of Arid Environments*, *97*, 190–204. doi:10.1016/j.jaridenv.2013.07.003

Forrester, J., Cook, B., Bracken, L., Cinderby, S., & Donaldson, A. (2015). Combining participatory mapping with Q-methodology to map stakeholder perceptions of complex environmental problems. *Applied Geography (Sevenoaks, England)*, *56*, 199–208. doi:10.1016/j.apgeog.2014.11.019

Frantzi, S., Carter, N. T., & Lovett, J. C. (2009). Exploring discourses on international environmental regime effectiveness with Q methodology: A case study of the Mediterranean Action Plan. *Journal of Environmental Management*, *90*(1), 177–186. doi:10.1016/j.jenvman.2007.08.013 PMID:18079046

Gamelas, A. M., & Aguiar, C. (2014). Preschool teachers' ideas about practices to promote peer relations: Using Q methodology to determine viewpoints. In the Proceedings of WCLTA 2013. *Procedia: Social and Behavioral Sciences*, *141*, 1304–1308. doi:10.1016/j.sbspro.2014.05.223

Gaskin, J. (2015, Sept. 24). Q-sort using Qualtrics. *YouTube*. Retrieved Jan. 27, 2019, from https://youtu.be/ZEqPJoKxo2w

Grijpma, J. W., Tielen, M., van Staa, A. L., Maasdam, L., van Gelder, T., Berger, S. P., ... Massey, E. K. (2016). Kidney transplant attitudes towards self-management. *Patient Education and Counseling*, *99*, 836–843. doi:10.1016/j.pec.2015.11.018 PMID:26682972

Ha, E.-H. (2014). Attitudes toward video-assisted debriefing after simulation in undergraduate nursing students: An application of Q methodology. *Nurse Education Today*, *34*(6), 978–984. doi:10.1016/j.nedt.2014.01.003 PMID:24467864

Ha, E.-H. (2015). Attitudes toward clinical practice in undergraduate nursing students: A Q- methodology study. *Nurse Education Today*, *35*(6), 733–739. doi:10.1016/j.nedt.2015.01.013 PMID:25660267

Ha, E.-H. (2018). Experience of nursing students with standardized patients in simulation-based learning: Q-methodology study. *Nurse Education Today*, *66*, 123–129. doi:10.1016/j.nedt.2018.04.023 PMID:29702441

Hermelingmeier, V., & Nicholas, K. A. (2017). Identifying five different perspectives on the ecosystem services concept using Q Methodology. *Ecological Economics*, *136*, 255–265. doi:10.1016/j.ecolecon.2017.01.006

Howard, R. J., Tallontire, A. M., Stringer, L. C., & Marchant, R. A. (2016). *Which 'fairness,' for whom,* and why? An empirical analysis of plural notions of fairness in Fairtrade Carbon Projects, using Q methodology. *Environmental Science & Policy*, *56*, 100–109. doi:10.1016/j.envsci.2015.11.009

Hu, B. Y., Yang, Y., & Ieong, S. S. L. (2016). Chinese urban and suburban parents' priorities for early childhood education practices: Applying Q-sort methodology. *Children and Youth Services Review*, *64*, 100–109. doi:10.1016/j.childyouth.2016.03.010

Hugé, J., Velde, K. V., Benitez-Capistros, F., Japay, J. H., Satyanarayana, B., Ishak, M. N., ... Dahdouh-Guebas, F. (2016). Mapping discourses using Q methodology in Matang Mangrove Forest, Malaysia. *Journal of Environmental Management*, *183*, 988–997. doi:10.1016/j.jenvman.2016.09.046 PMID:27692515

Iofrida, N., De Luca, A. I., Gulisano, G., & Strano, A. (2018). An application of Q-methodology to Mediterranean olive production—Stakeholders' understanding of sustainability issues. *Agricultural Systems*, *162*, 46–55. doi:10.1016/j.agsy.2018.01.020

Jaung, W., Putzel, L., Bull, G. Q., Kozak, R., & Markum. (2016). Certification of forest watershed services: A Q methodology analysis of opportunities and challenges in Lombok, Indonesia. *Ecosystem Services*, *22*, 51–59. doi:10.1016/j.ecoser.2016.09.010

Jedeloo, S., van Staa, A., Latour, J. M., & van Exel, N. J. A. (2010). Preferences for health care and self-management among Dutch adolescents with chronic conditions: A Q-methodological investigation. *International Journal of Nursing Studies*, *47*(5), 593–603. doi:10.1016/j.ijnurstu.2009.10.006 PMID:19900675

Kelly, S. L., & Young, B. W. (2017). Examining undergraduates' library priorities through Q methodology. *Journal of Academic Librarianship*, *43*(3), 170–177. doi:10.1016/j.acalib.2017.04.002

Kerr, N., Gouldson, A., & Barrett, J. (2018). Holistic narratives of the renovation experience: Using Q-methodology to improve understanding of domestic energy retrofits in the United Kingdom. *Energy Research & Social Science*, *42*, 90–99. doi:10.1016/j.erss.2018.02.018

Kim, I.-J., & Shim, H.-W. (2018). Subjectivity about turnover intention among male nurses in South Korea: A Q-Methodological study. *Asian Nursing Research*, *12*(2), 113–120. doi:10.1016/j.anr.2018.04.002 PMID:29660490

Kim, K. Y., & Lee, B. G. (2015). Marketing insights for mobile advertising and consumer segmentation in the cloud era: A Q-R hybrid methodology and practices. *Technological Forecasting and Social Change*, *91*, 78–92. doi:10.1016/j.techfore.2014.01.011

Kim, T.-Y., & Shin, D.-H. (2017). The survival strategy of branded content in the over-the-top (OTT) environment: Eye-tracking and Q-methodology approach in digital product placement. *Telematics and Informatics*, *34*(7), 1081–1092. doi:10.1016/j.tele.2017.04.016

Kraak, V. I., Swinburn, B., Lawrence, M., & Harrison, P. (2014). A Q methodology study of stakeholders' views about accountability for promoting healthy food environments in England through the Responsibility Deal Food Network. *Food Policy*, *49*, 207–218. doi:10.1016/j.foodpol.2014.07.006

Lansing, D. M. (2013). Not all baselines are created equal: A Q methodology analysis of stakeholder perspectives of additionality in a carbon forestry offset project in Costa Rica. *Global Environmental Change*, *23*(3), 654–663. doi:10.1016/j.gloenvcha.2013.02.005

Lee, J.-H. (2019). Conflict mapping toward ecotourism facility foundation using spatial Q methodology. *Tourism Management*, *72*, 69–77. doi:10.1016/j.tourman.2018.11.012

Li, T., Petrini, M. A., & Stone, T. E. (2018). Baccalaureate nursing students' perspectives of peer tutoring in simulation laboratory, a Q methodology study. *Nurse Education Today*, *61*, 235–241. doi:10.1016/j.nedt.2017.12.001 PMID:29268198

Lin, F., He, Y., Ni, Z., Olive, R., Ren, M., Yao, L., & Ye, Q. (2017). Individualized intervention to reduce anxiety in adult orthodontic patients based on Q methodology. *American Journal of Orthodontics and Dentofacial Orthopedics*, *152*(2), 161–170. doi:10.1016/j.ajodo.2016.12.015 PMID:28760278

Liu, C.-C., & Chen, J. C. H. (2013). Using Q methodology to explore user's value types on mobile phone service websites. *Expert Systems with Applications*, *40*(13), 5276–5283. doi:10.1016/j.eswa.2013.03.036

Mahmoodi, H., Sarbakhsh, P., & Shaghaghi, A. (2018). Barriers to adopt the Health Promoting Hospitals (HPH) initiative in Iran: The Q method derived perspectives of front line practitioners. *Patient Education and Counseling*, 1–8. PMID:30442484

Mandolesi, S., Nicholas, P., Naspetti, S., & Zanoli, R. (2015). Identifying viewpoints on innovation in low-input and organic dairy supply chains: A Q-methodological study. *Food Policy*, *54*, 25–34. doi:10.1016/j.foodpol.2015.04.008

Matinga, M. N., Pinedo-Pascua, I., Vervaeke, J., Monforti-Ferrario, F., & Szabó, S. (2014). Do African and European energy stakeholders agree on key energy drivers in Africa? Using Q methodology to understand perceptions on energy access debates. *Energy Policy*, *69*, 154–164. doi:10.1016/j.enpol.2013.12.041

Militello, M., & Benham, M. K. P. (2010). 'Sorting out' collective leadership: How Q-methodology can be used to evaluate leadership development. *The Leadership Quarterly*, *21*(4), 620–632. doi:10.1016/j.leaqua.2010.06.005

Mokry, S., & Dufek, O. (2014). Q method and its use for segmentation in tourism. In the proceedings of the Enterprise and the Competitive Environment 2014 Conference. Mar. 6 – 7, 2014. Brno, Czech Republic. *Procedia Economics and Finance*, *12*, 445–452. doi:10.1016/S2212-5671(14)00366-9

Morecroft, C., Cantrill, J., & Tully, M. P. (2006). Individual patient's preferences for hypertension management: A Q-methodological approach. *Patient Education and Counseling*, *61*(3), 354–362. doi:10.1016/j.pec.2005.04.011 PMID:15896942

Nahm, A. Y., Rao, S. S., Solis-Galvan, L. E., & Ragu-Nathan, T. S. (2002, Winter). The Q-sort Method: Assessing reliability and construct validity of questionnaire items at a pre-testing stage. *Journal of Modern Applied Statistical Methods; JMASM, 1*(1), 114–125. doi:10.22237/jmasm/1020255360

Naspetti, S., Mandolesi, S., & Zanoli, R. (2016). Using visual Q sorting to determine the impact of photovoltaic applications on the landscape. *Land Use Policy, 57*, 564–573. doi:10.1016/j.landusepol.2016.06.021

Newman, I., & Ramlo, S. (2010). Using Q methodology and Q factor analysis in mixed methods research. Sage handbook of mixed methods in social and behavioral research, 505-530.

Nguyen, B. N., Boruff, B., & Tonts, M. (2018). Indicators of mining in development: A Q-methodology investigation of two gold mines in Quang Nam province, Vietnam. *Resources Policy, 57*, 147–155. doi:10.1016/j.resourpol.2018.02.014

Niedziałkowski, K., Komar, E., Pietrzyk-Kaszyńska, A., Olszańska, A., & Grodzińska-Jurczak, M. (2018). Discourses on public participation in protected areas governance: Application of Q methodology in Poland. *Ecological Economics, 145*, 401–409. doi:10.1016/j.ecolecon.2017.11.018

Nijnik, M., Nijnik, A., Sarkki, S., Muñoz-Rojas, J., Miller, D., & Kopiy, S. (2018). Is forest related decision-making in European treeline areas socially innovative? A Q-methodology enquiry into the perspectives of international experts. *Forest Policy and Economics, 92*, 210–219. doi:10.1016/j.forpol.2018.01.001

Ormerod, K. J. (2017). Common sense principles governing potable water recycling in the southwestern US: Examining subjectivity of water stewards using Q methodology. *Geoforum, 86*, 76–85. doi:10.1016/j.geoforum.2017.09.004

Øverland, K., Thorsen, A. A., & Størksen, I. (2012). The beliefs of teachers and daycare staff regarding children of divorce: A Q methodological study. *Teaching and Teacher Education, 28*(3), 312–323. doi:10.1016/j.tate.2011.10.010

Pagnussatt, D., Petrini, M., dos Santos, A. C. M. Z., & da Silveira, L. M. (2018). What do local stakeholders think about the impacts of small hydroelectric plants? Using Q methodology to understand different perspectives. *Energy Policy, 112*, 372–380. doi:10.1016/j.enpol.2017.10.029

Paige, J. B. (2014). Making sense of methods and measurement: Q-methodology— Part I—philosophical background. *Clinical Simulation in Nursing, 10*(12), 639–640. doi:10.1016/j.ecns.2014.09.008

Paige, J. B. (2015a). Making sense of methods and measurement: Q-methodology— Part II—Methodological procedures. *Clinical Simulation in Nursing, 11*(1), 75–77. doi:10.1016/j.ecns.2014.10.004

Paige, J. B., & Morin, K. H. (2015b). Using q-methodology to reveal nurse educators' perspectives about simulation design. *Clinical Simulation in Nursing, 11*(1), 11–19. doi:10.1016/j.ecns.2014.09.010

Park, Y., Yeun, E. J., & Hwang, Y. Y. (2016). Subjectivity about sexual ethics among Korean undergraduate students using Q Methodology. *Asian Nursing Research, 10*(2), 143–149. doi:10.1016/j.anr.2016.05.002 PMID:27349672

Pederson, D. R., Moran, G., Sitko, C., Campbell, K., Ghesquire, K., & Acton, H. (1990, December). Maternal sensitivity and the security of infant-mother attachment: A Q-sort study. *Child Development, 61*(6), 1974–1983. doi:10.2307/1130851 PMID:2083509

Pereira, M. A., Fairweather, J. R., Woodford, K. B., & Nuthall, P. L. (2016). Assessing the diversity of values and goals amongst Brazilian commercial-scale progressive beef farmers using Q-methodology. *Agricultural Systems, 144*, 1–8. doi:10.1016/j. agsy.2016.01.004

Prabakaran, R., Seymour, S., Moles, D. R., & Cunningham, S. J. (2012). Motivation for orthodontic treatment investigated with Q-methodology: Patients' and parents' perspectives. *American Journal of Orthodontics and Dentofacial Orthopedics, 142*(2), 213–220. doi:10.1016/j.ajodo.2012.03.026 PMID:22858331

Rajé, F. (2007). Using Q methodology to develop more perceptive insights on transport and social inclusion. *Transport Policy, 14*(6), 467–477. doi:10.1016/j. tranpol.2007.04.006

Risdon, A., Eccleston, C., Crombez, G., & McCracken, L. (2003). How can we learn to live with pain? A Q-methodological analysis of the diverse understandings of acceptance of chronic pain. *Social Science & Medicine, 56*(2), 375–386. doi:10.1016/ S0277-9536(02)00043-6 PMID:12473322

Schall, D., Lansing, D., Leisnham, P., Shirmohammadi, A., Montas, H., & Hutson, T. (2018). Understanding stakeholder perspectives on agricultural best management practices and environmental change in the Chesapeake Bay: A Q methodology study. *Journal of Rural Studies*, *60*, 21–31. doi:10.1016/j.jrurstud.2018.03.003

Serfass, D. G., & Sherman, R. A. (2013). A methodological note on ordered Q-Sort ratings. *Journal of Research in Personality*, *47*(6), 853–858. doi:10.1016/j.jrp.2013.08.013

Shields, A., & Cicchetti, D. (1997). Emotion regulation among school-age children: The development and validation of a new criterion Q-sort Scale. *Developmental Psychology*, *33*(6), 906–916. doi:10.1037/0012-1649.33.6.906 PMID:9383613

Shin, H. S., Kim, J. H., & Ji, E. S. (2018). Clinical nurses' resilience skills for surviving in a hospital setting: A Q-methodology study. *Asian Nursing Research*, *12*(3), 175–181. doi:10.1016/j.anr.2018.06.003 PMID:29964201

Silvius, A. J. G., Kampinga, M., Paniagua, S., & Mooi, H. (2017). Considering sustainability in project management decision making: An investigation using Q-methodology. *International Journal of Project Management*, *35*(6), 1133–1150. doi:10.1016/j.ijproman.2017.01.011

Sklarwitz, S. (2017). Assessing global citizenship attitudes with Q Methodology. *Journal of Social Studies Research*, *41*(3), 171–182. doi:10.1016/j.jssr.2016.09.001

Steelman, T. A., & Maguire, L. A. (1999). Understanding participant perspectives: Q-methodology in national forest management. *Journal of Policy Analysis and Management*, *18*(3), 361–388. doi:10.1002/(SICI)1520-6688(199922)18:3<361::AID-PAM3>3.0.CO;2-K

Stenner, P. H. D., Cooper, D., & Skevington, S. M. (2003). Putting the Q into quality of life; the identification of subjective constructions of health-related quality of life using Q methodology. *Social Science & Medicine*, *57*(11), 2161–2172. doi:10.1016/S0277-9536(03)00070-4 PMID:14512246

Stephenson, W. (1936). Introduction to inverted factor analysis, with some applications to studies in orexis. *Journal of Educational Psychology*, *27*(5), 353–367. doi:10.1037/h0058705

Stephenson, W. (1993, October). Introduction to Q-Methodology. *Operant Subjectivity*, *17*(1/2), 1–13.

Stone, T. E., Kang, S. J., Cha, C., Turale, S., Murakami, K., & Shimizu, A. (2016). Health beliefs and their sources in Korean and Japanese nurses: A Q-methodology pilot study. *Nurse Education Today*, *36*, 214–220. doi:10.1016/j.nedt.2015.10.017 PMID:26577748

Sung, K. (2011). Exploring wisdom in the Korean elderly: A Q methodology study. *Asian Nursing Research*, *5*(2), 128–140. doi:10.1016/S1976-1317(11)60021-2 PMID:25030262

Sung, P., & Akhtar, N. (2017). Exploring preschool teachers' perspectives on linguistic diversity: A Q study. *Teaching and Teacher Education*, *65*, 157–170. doi:10.1016/j.tate.2017.03.004

Sy, M. M., Rey-Valette, H., Simier, M., Pasqualini, V., Figuières, C., & De Wit, R. (2018). Identifying consensus on coastal lagoons ecosystem services and conservation priorities for an effective decision making: A Q approach. *Ecological Economics*, *154*, 1–13. doi:10.1016/j.ecolecon.2018.07.018

Vaas, J., Driessen, P. P. J., Giezen, M., van Laerhoven, F., & Wassen, M. J. (2018). (in press). 'Let me tell you your problems'. Using Q methodology to elicit latent problem perceptions about invasive alien species. *Geoforum*, 1–12.

van Exel, J., Baker, R., Mason, H., Donaldson, C., & Brouwer, W. (2015). Public views on principles for health care priority setting: Findings of a European cross-country study using Q methodology. *Social Science & Medicine*, *126*, 128–137. doi:10.1016/j.socscimed.2014.12.023 PMID:25550076

van Exel, J., & De Graaf, G. (2005). *Q methodology: A sneak preview*. Retrieved Jan. 24, 2019, from http://www.jobvanexel.nl

van Exel, J., de Graaf, G., & Brouwer, W. (2007). Care for a break? An investigation of informal caregivers' attitudes toward respite care using Q-methodology. *Health Policy (Amsterdam)*, *83*(2-3), 332–342. doi:10.1016/j.healthpol.2007.02.002 PMID:17367892

van Hooft, S. M., Dwarswaard, J., Jedeloo, S., Bal, R., & van Staa, A. (2015). Four perspectives on self-management support by nurses for people with chronic conditions: A Q-methodological study. *International Journal of Nursing Studies*, *52*(1), 157–166. doi:10.1016/j.ijnurstu.2014.07.004 PMID:25107442

Van IJzendoorn, M. H., Verejken, C. M. J. L., Bakermans-Kranenburg, M. J., & Riksen-Walraven, J. M. (2004). Assessing attachment security with the Attachment Q Sort: Meta-analytic evidence for the validity of the Observer AQS. *Child Development*, *75*(4), 1188–1213. doi:10.1111/j.1467-8624.2004.00733.x PMID:15260872

Vaughn, B. E., & Waters, E. (1990, December). Attachment behavior at home and in the laboratory: Q-sort observations and strange situation classifications of one-year-olds. *Child Development*, *61*(6), 1965–1973. doi:10.2307/1130850 PMID:2083508

Vikström, P., Carlsson, I., Rosén, B., & Björkman, A. (2018). Patients' views on early sensory relearning following nerve repair—A Q-methodology study. *Journal of Hand Therapy*, *31*(4), 443–450. doi:10.1016/j.jht.2017.07.003 PMID:28967458

Vizcaíno, A., García, F., Villar, J. C., Piattini, M., & Poerillo, J. (2013). Applying q-methodology to analyze the success factors in GSD. (global software development). *Information and Software Technology*, *55*, 1200–1211. doi:10.1016/j.infsof.2013.01.003

Walder, P., & Kantelhardt, J. (2018). The environmental behavior of farmers—Capturing the diversity of perspectives with a Q methodological approach. *Ecological Economics*, *143*, 55–63. doi:10.1016/j.ecolecon.2017.06.018

Waters, E., & Deane, K. E. (1985). Defining and assessing individual differences in attachment relationships: Q-methodology and the organization of behavior in infancy and early childhood. *Monographs of the Society for Research in Child Development*, *50*(1/2), 41–65. doi:10.2307/3333826

Watts, S., & Stenner, P. (2005). Doing Q methodology: Theory, method and interpretation. *Qualitative Research in Psychology*, *2*(1), 67–91. doi:10.1191/1478088705qp022oa

Weldegiorgis, F. S., & Ali, S. H. (2016). Mineral resources and localized development: Q-methodology for rapid assessment of socioeconomic impacts in Rwanda. *Resources Policy*, *49*, 1–11. doi:10.1016/j.resourpol.2016.03.006

Westen, D., Muderrisoglu, S., Fowler, C., Shedler, J., & Koren, D. (1997). Affect regulation and affective experience: Individual differences, group differences, and measurement using a Q-sort procedure. *Journal of Consulting and Clinical Psychology*, *65*(3), 429–439. doi:10.1037/0022-006X.65.3.429 PMID:9170766

Work, J., Hensel, D., & Decker, K. A. (2015). A Q methodology student of perceptions of poverty among midwestern nursing students. *Nurse Education Today*, *35*(2), 328–332. doi:10.1016/j.nedt.2014.10.017 PMID:25466797

Yarar, N., & Orth, U. R. (2018). Consumer lay theories on healthy nutrition: A Q methodology application in Germany. *Appetite*, *120*, 145–157. doi:10.1016/j.appet.2017.08.026 PMID:28851558

Yeun, E. (2005). Attitudes of elderly Korean patients toward death and dying: An application of Q-methodology. *International Journal of Nursing Studies*, *42*(8), 871–880. doi:10.1016/j.ijnurstu.2004.12.002 PMID:16210025

Yeun, E. J., Bang, H. Y., Ryoo, E. N., & Ha, E.-H. (2014). Attitudes toward simulation-based learning in nursing students: An application of Q methodology. *Nurse Education Today*, *34*(7), 1062–1068. doi:10.1016/j.nedt.2014.02.008 PMID:24629271

Zanoli, R., Carlesi, L., Danovaro, R., Mandolesi, S., & Naspetti, S. (2015). Valuing unfamiliar Mediterranean deep-sea ecosystems using visual Q-methodology. *Marine Policy*, *61*, 227–236. doi:10.1016/j.marpol.2015.08.009

Zhang, T. (2018). Graduate students identities in the intercultural practices on a U.S. campus: A Q inquiry. *International Journal of Intercultural Relations*, *64*, 77–89. doi:10.1016/j.ijintrel.2018.03.005

KEY TERMS AND DEFINITIONS

Concourse: A full created selection of possible statements (from which a subset or "Q sample" is drawn for the q-sort activity).

Factor Analysis: A quantitative statistical analysis approach to identify underlying (latent) factors or components in observed or survey data to understand the most influential factors on a construct.

Factor Interpretation: The definition and framing of an identified factor from a statistical factor analysis based on its component parts.

Factor Scores: A numerical value showing a respondent's relative standing on a factor.

Graphic Elicitation: Visual elicitation, the use of a visual construct to elicit responses from research respondents.

P-Set: Respondents in a Q-methodology study.

Q-Methodology: A standard research methodology to identify insider/people's self-reported "subjectivities" through a q-sort method.

Q-Sample: The statements that will be presented to Q-methodology research participants (a selective portion of the larger concourse).

Q-Sort: The research participant work of sorting the statements/cards in the Q-Methodology research.

Q-Sort Grid (Q-Sort Score Sheet, Q-Sort Template, Q-Sort Card Grid, Q-Board): The visual table or grid on which q-set statement cards (or other information objects) are sorted.

APPENDIX

The following contains the q-sort text from the trial q-sort survey. The earlier parts with the informed consent and demographic data elicitations were not included. (Some of the open-shared demographics blocks of questions were created by Qualtrics. While they are for customer use, it is not clear if the survey contents are copyrighted or not.) Also, the text eliciting responses here was set up mostly as placeholder text, without in-depth consideration of the "condition of instructions" (Paige, 2015a, p. 76), which are critical for the research.

Q26

The Q-Sort.

Box 1.

Q27

Directions: In Table 8, there are 52 items that need to be placed in the categories in the table header. Notice that the categories have limits in terms of how many may be placed in each. If there are overages, the responses will not be considered valid for the q-sort. Make sure that all of the 52 items are placed before moving on to the second part of the q-methodology study.

> End of Block: QSort
> Start of Block: Debriefing

Q28

Q-Methodology Debriefing.

Table 8. In graduate-level higher education studies research related to educational technologies, the research project should...

Strongly agree (3 total only)	Agree (5 total only)	Somewhat agree (8 total only)	Neither agree nor disagree (20 total only)	Somewhat disagree (8 total only)	Disagree (5 total only)	Strongly disagree (3 total only)
_____ include full saturation in the literature review (1)	_____ include full saturation in the literature review (1)	_____ include full saturation in the literature review (1)	_____ include full saturation in the literature review (1)	_____ include full saturation in the literature review (1)	_____ include full saturation in the literature review (1)	_____ include full saturation in the literature review (1)
_____ include partial review of the literature (2)	_____ include partial review of the literature (2)	_____ include partial review of the literature (2)	_____ include partial review of the literature (2)	_____ include partial review of the literature (2)	_____ include partial review of the literature (2)	_____ include partial review of the literature (2)
_____ involve other co-researchers (3)	_____ involve other co-researchers (3)	_____ involve other co-researchers (3)	_____ involve other co-researchers (3)	_____ involve other co-researchers (3)	_____ involve other co-researchers (3)	_____ involve other co-researchers (3)
_____ be a stand-alone research work (4)	_____ be a stand-alone research work (4)	_____ be a stand-alone research work (4)	_____ be a stand-alone research work (4)	_____ be a stand-alone research work (4)	_____ be a stand-alone research work (4)	_____ be a stand-alone research work (4)
_____ be aligned with the graduate advisor's research (5)	_____ be aligned with the graduate advisor's research (5	_____ be aligned with the graduate advisor's research (5)	_____ be aligned with the graduate advisor's research (5)	_____ be aligned with the graduate advisor's research (5)	_____ be aligned with the graduate advisor's research (5)	_____ be aligned with the graduate advisor's research (5)
_____ involve multimodal informational resources (6)	_____ involve multimodal informational resources (6)	_____ involve multimodal informational resources (6)	_____ involve multimodal informational resources (6)	_____ involve multimodal informational resources (6)	_____ involve multimodal informational resources (6)	_____ involve multimodal informational resources (6)
_____ include multiple educational technologies (7)	_____ include multiple educational technologies (7)	_____ include multiple educational technologies (7)	_____ include multiple educational technologies (7)	_____ include multiple educational technologies (7)	_____ include multiple educational technologies (7)	_____ include multiple educational technologies (7)
_____ include well known educational technologies (8)	_____ include well known educational technologies (8)	_____ include well known educational technologies (8)	_____ include well known educational technologies (8)	_____ include well known educational technologies (8)	_____ include well known educational technologies (8)	_____ include well known educational technologies (8)
_____ include open-source educational technologies (9)	_____ include open-source educational technologies (9)	_____ include open-source educational technologies (9)	_____ include open-source educational technologies (9	_____ include open-source educational technologies (9)	_____ include open-source educational technologies (9)	_____ include open-source educational technologies (9)
_____ be novel (10)	_____ be novel (10)	_____ be novel (10)	_____ be novel (10)	_____ be novel (10)	_____ be novel (10)	_____ be novel (10)
_____ be publishable (11)	_____ be publishable (11)	_____ be publishable (11)	_____ be publishable (11)	_____ be publishable (11)	_____ be publishable (11)	_____ be publishable (11)
_____ involve educational technology testing (12)	_____ involve educational technology testing (12)	_____ involve educational technology testing (12)	_____ involve educational technology testing (12)	_____ involve educational technology testing (12)	_____ involve educational technology testing (12)	_____ involve educational technology testing (12)
_____ relate to the student researcher's biographical history (13)	_____ relate to the student researcher's biographical history (13)	_____ relate to the student researcher's biographical history (13)	_____ relate to the student researcher's biographical history (13)	_____ relate to the student researcher's biographical history (13)	_____ relate to the student researcher's biographical history (13)	_____ relate to the student researcher's biographical history (13
_____ be personally meaningful to the student researcher (14)	_____ be personally meaningful to the student researcher (14)	_____ be personally meaningful to the student researcher (14)	_____ be personally meaningful to the student researcher (14)	_____ be personally meaningful to the student researcher (14)	_____ be personally meaningful to the student researcher (14)	_____ be personally meaningful to the student researcher (14)

continued on following page

Table 8. Continued

Strongly agree (3 total only)	Agree (5 total only)	Somewhat agree (8 total only)	Neither agree nor disagree (20 total only)	Somewhat disagree (8 total only)	Disagree (5 total only)	Strongly disagree (3 total only)
_____ be low cost (15)	_____ be low cost (15)	_____ be low cost (15)	_____ be low cost (15)	_____ be low cost (15)	_____ be low cost (15)	_____ be low cost (15)
_____ be high cost (16)	_____ be high cost (16)	_____ be high cost (16)	_____ be high cost (16)	_____ be high cost (16)	_____ be high cost (16)	_____ be high cost (16)
_____ involve inherited (non-self-generated) datasets (17)	_____ involve inherited (non-self-generated) datasets (17)	_____ involve inherited (non-self-generated) datasets (17)	_____ involve inherited (non-self-generated) datasets (17)	_____ involve inherited (non-self-generated) datasets (17)	_____ involve inherited (non-self-generated) datasets (17)	_____ involve inherited (non-self-generated) datasets (17)
_____ involve established research methods (18	_____ involve established research methods (18)	_____ involve established research methods (18)	_____ involve established research methods (18)	_____ involve established research methods (18)	_____ involve established research methods (18)	_____ involve established research methods (18)
_____ involve established data analytics methods (19)	_____ involve established data analytics methods (19)	_____ involve established data analytics methods (19)	_____ involve established data analytics methods (19)	_____ involve established data analytics methods (19)	_____ involve established data analytics methods (19)	_____ involve established data analytics methods (19)
_____ involve new research methods (20)	_____ involve new research methods (20)	_____ involve new research methods (20)	_____ involve new research methods (20)	_____ involve new research methods (20)	_____ involve new research methods (20)	_____ involve new research methods (20)
_____ involve new data analytics methods (21)	_____ involve new data analytics methods (21)	_____ involve new data analytics methods (21)	involve new data analytics methods (21)	involve new data analytics methods (21)	involve new data analytics methods (21)	involve new data analytics methods (21)
_____ be about a "hot" current issue (22)	_____ be about a "hot" current issue (22	_____ be about a "hot" current issue (22)	_____ be about a "hot" current issue (22)	_____ be about a "hot" current issue (22)	_____ be about a "hot" current issue (22)	_____ be about a "hot" current issue (22)
_____ be funded by the government (23)	_____ be funded by the government (23)	_____ be funded by the government (23)	_____ be funded by the government (23)	_____ be funded by the government (23)	_____ be funded by the government (23)	_____ be funded by the government (23)
_____ be funded by industry (24)	_____ be funded by industry (24)	_____ be funded by industry (24)	_____ be funded by industry (24)	_____ be funded by industry (24)	_____ be funded by industry (24)	_____ be funded by industry (24)
_____ be secret and enbargoed (25)	_____ be secret and enbargoed (25)	_____ be secret and enbargoed (25)	_____ be secret and enbargoed (25)	_____ be secret and enbargoed (25)	_____ be secret and enbargoed (25)	_____ be secret and enbargoed (25)
_____ be achieved within deadline (26)	_____ be achieved within deadline (26)	_____ be achieved within deadline (26)	_____ be achieved within deadline (26)	_____ be achieved within deadline (26	_____ be achieved within deadline (26)	_____ be achieved within deadline (26)
_____ be closely supervised by the faculty advisory team (27)	be closely supervised by the faculty advisory team (27)	be closely supervised by the faculty advisory team (27)	be closely supervised by the faculty advisory team (27)	be closely supervised by the faculty advisory team (27)	be closely supervised by the faculty advisory team (27)	be closely supervised by the faculty advisory team (27)
_____ be distantly supervised by the faculty advisory team (28)	_____ be distantly supervised by the faculty advisory team (28)	_____ be distantly supervised by the faculty advisory team (28)	_____ be distantly supervised by the faculty advisory team (28)	_____ be distantly supervised by the faculty advisory team (28)	_____ be distantly supervised by the faculty advisory team (28)	_____ be distantly supervised by the faculty advisory team (28)
_____ be informed by a theory or theories (29)	_____ be informed by a theory or theories (29)	_____ be informed by a theory or theories (29)	_____ be informed by a theory or theories (29)	_____ be informed by a theory or theories (29)	_____ be informed by a theory or theories (29)	_____ be informed by a theory or theories (29)

continued on following page

143

Table 8. Continued

Strongly agree (3 total only)	Agree (5 total only)	Somewhat agree (8 total only)	Neither agree nor disagree (20 total only)	Somewhat disagree (8 total only)	Disagree (5 total only)	Strongly disagree (3 total only)
_____ be informed by a model or models (30)	_____ be informed by a model or models (30)	_____ be informed by a model or models (30)	_____ be informed by a model or models (30)	_____ be informed by a model or models (30)	_____ be informed by a model or models (30)	_____ be informed by a model or models (30
_____ be informed by a framework or frameworks (31)	_____ be informed by a framework or frameworks (31)	_____ be informed by a framework or frameworks (31)	_____ be informed by a framework or frameworks (31)	_____ be informed by a framework or frameworks (31)	_____ be informed by a framework or frameworks (31)	_____ be informed by a framework or frameworks (31)
_____ be practically applicable (32)	_____ be practically applicable (32)	_____ be practically applicable (32)	_____ be practically applicable (32)	_____ be practically applicable (32)	_____ be practically applicable (32)	_____ be practically applicable (32)
involve data visualizations (33)	involve data visualizations (33)	involve data visualizations (33)	involve data visualizations (33)	involve data visualizations (33)	involve data visualizations (33)	involve data visualizations (33)
_____ include diagrams and illustrations (34)	_____ include diagrams and illustrations (34)	_____ include diagrams and illustrations (34)	_____ include diagrams and illustrations (34)	_____ include diagrams and illustrations (34)	_____ include diagrams and illustrations (34)	_____ include diagrams and illustrations (34)
_____ be based on the graduate student researcher's ambition for a future career (35)	_____ be based on the graduate student researcher's ambition for a future career (35)	_____ be based on the graduate student researcher's ambition for a future career (35)	_____ be based on the graduate student researcher's ambition for a future career (35)	_____ be based on the graduate student researcher's ambition for a future career (35)	_____ be based on the graduate student researcher's ambition for a future career (35)	_____ be based on the graduate student researcher's ambition for a future career (35)
_____ involve travel (36)	_____ involve travel (36)	_____ involve travel (36)	_____ involve travel (36)	_____ involve travel (36)	_____ involve travel (36)	_____ involve travel (36)
_____ be related to the physical location of the university (37)	_____ be related to the physical location of the university (37)	_____ be related to the physical location of the university (37)	_____ be related to the physical location of the university (37)	_____ be related to the physical location of the university (37)	_____ be related to the physical location of the university (37)	_____ be related to the physical location of the university (37)
_____ involve a second language (38)	_____ involve a second language (38)	_____ involve a second language (38)	_____ involve a second language (38)	_____ involve a second language (38)	_____ involve a second language (38)	_____ involve a second language (38)
_____ be done in a first language (39)	_____ be done in a first language (39)	_____ be done in a first language (39)	_____ be done in a first language (39	_____ be done in a first language (39)	_____ be done in a first language (39)	_____ be done in a first language (39)
_____ include a byline with the masters or doctoral committee members when published (40)	_____ include a byline with the masters or doctoral committee members when published (40)	_____ include a byline with the masters or doctoral committee members when published (40)	_____ include a byline with the masters or doctoral committee members when published (40)	_____ include a byline with the masters or doctoral committee members when published (40)	_____ include a byline with the masters or doctoral committee members when published (40)	_____ include a byline with the masters or doctoral committee members when published (40)
_____ include some crediting of the masters or doctoral committee members (41)	_____ include some crediting of the masters or doctoral committee members (41)	_____ include some crediting of the masters or doctoral committee members (41)	_____ include some crediting of the masters or doctoral committee members (41)	_____ include some crediting of the masters or doctoral committee members (41)	_____ include some crediting of the masters or doctoral committee members (41)	_____ include some crediting of the masters or doctoral committee members (41)

continued on following page

Table 8. Continued

Strongly agree (3 total only)	Agree (5 total only)	Somewhat agree (8 total only)	Neither agree nor disagree (20 total only)	Somewhat disagree (8 total only)	Disagree (5 total only)	Strongly disagree (3 total only)
_____ capture the student researcher's personally as a signature (42)	_____ capture the student researcher's personally as a signature (42)	_____ capture the student researcher's personally as a signature (42)	_____ capture the student researcher's personally as a signature (42)	_____ capture the student researcher's personally as a signature (42)	_____ capture the student researcher's personally as a signature (42)	_____ capture the student researcher's personally as a signature (42)
_____ have the research costs borne by the university (43)	_____ have the research costs borne by the university (43)	_____ have the research costs borne by the university (43)	_____ have the research costs borne by the university (43)	_____ have the research costs borne by the university (43)	_____ have the research costs borne by the university (43)	_____ have the research costs borne by the university (43
_____ have the research costs borne by the student and the student's family (44)	_____ have the research costs borne by the student and the student's family (44)	_____ have the research costs borne by the student and the student's family (44)	_____ have the research costs borne by the student and the student's family (44)	_____ have the research costs borne by the student and the student's family (44)	_____ have the research costs borne by the student and the student's family (44)	_____ have the research costs borne by the student and the student's family (44)
_____ be prosocial (45)	_____ be prosocial (45)	_____ be prosocial (45)	_____ be prosocial (45)	_____ be prosocial (45)	_____ be prosocial (45)	_____ be prosocial (45)
_____ be revolutionary (46)	_____ be revolutionary (46)	_____ be revolutionary (46)	_____ be revolutionary (46)	_____ be revolutionary (46)	_____ be revolutionary (46)	_____ be revolutionary (46)
_____ lead to social change (47)	_____ lead to social change (47)	_____ lead to social change (47)	_____ lead to social change (47)	_____ lead to social change (47)	_____ lead to social change (47)	_____ lead to social change (47)
_____ protect the status quo (48)	_____ protect the status quo (48)	_____ protect the status quo (48)	_____ protect the status quo (48)	_____ protect the status quo (48)	_____ protect the status quo (48)	_____ protect the status quo (48)
_____ include patent-able discoveries (49)	_____ include patent-able discoveries (49)	_____ include patent-able discoveries (49)	_____ include patent-able discoveries (49)	_____ include patent-able discoveries (49)	_____ include patent-able discoveries (49)	_____ include patent-able discoveries (49)
_____ provide research instruments available at no charge to other researchers (50)	_____ provide research instruments available at no charge to other researchers (50)	_____ provide research instruments available at no charge to other researchers (50)	_____ provide research instruments available at no charge to other researchers (50)	_____ provide research instruments available at no charge to other researchers (50)	_____ provide research instruments available at no charge to other researchers (50)	_____ provide research instruments available at no charge to other researchers (50)
_____ provide research instruments for-pay to other researchers (51)	_____ provide research instruments for-pay to other researchers (51)	_____ provide research instruments for-pay to other researchers (51)	_____ provide research instruments for-pay to other researchers (51)	_____ provide research instruments for-pay to other researchers (51)	_____ provide research instruments for-pay to other researchers (51)	_____ provide research instruments for-pay to other researchers (51)
_____ challenge an existing model (52)	_____ challenge an existing model (52)	_____ challenge an existing model (52)	_____ challenge an existing model (52)	_____ challenge an existing model (52)	_____ challenge an existing model (52)	_____ challenge an existing model (52)

Q29

An important part of the q-methodology involves having the respondent explain his / her responses to the q-sort...in three main categories: the high agreement, the high disagreement, and the neutral issues.

Q30

Please review your responses in the q-sort step just prior. Please explain your "strongly agree," "agree" and "somewhat agree" selections in the text box below.
    You can use the back arrow to review your recorded responses.

_____
_____
_____
_____
_____

Q31

Please review your responses in the q-sort step above. Please explain your "neither agree nor disagree" selections in the text box below.
    You can use the back arrow to review your recorded responses.

_____
_____
_____
_____
_____

Q32

Please review your responses in the q-sort step above. Please explain your "strongly disagree," "disagree" and "somewhat disagree" selections in the text box below.
    You can use the back arrow to review your recorded responses.

_____
_____
_____
_____
_____

End of Block: Debriefing

Section 3
Analyzing Online Survey Data

Chapter 7

Using Computational Text Analysis to Explore Open-Ended Survey Question Responses

ABSTRACT

To capture a broader range of data than close-ended questions (often defined and delimited by the survey instrument designer), open-ended questions, such as text-based elicitations (and file-upload options for still imagery, audio, video, and other contents) are becoming more common because of the wide availability of computational text analysis, both within online survey tools and in external software applications. These computational text analysis tools—some online, some offline—make it easier to capture reproducible insights with qualitative data. This chapter explores some analytical capabilities, in matrix queries, theme extraction (topic modeling), sentiment analysis, cluster analysis (concept mapping), network text structures, qualitative cross-tabulation analysis, manual coding to automated coding, linguistic analysis, psychometrics, stylometry, network analysis, and others, as applied to open-ended questions from online surveys (and combined with human close reading).

DOI: 10.4018/978-1-5225-8563-3.ch007

INTRODUCTION

The popularization of online surveys has meant that a wide range of different questions are ask-able, with the integration of still visuals, audio, video, web links, and other elements. Invisible or hidden questions enable the collection of additional information, such as time spent per question, devices used to access the survey, geographical information, and other data. File upload question types enable respondents to share imagery, audio, video, and other digital file types as a response. Integrations with online tools enable outreaches through social media for broader audiences through crowd-sourcing and commercial survey panels. Automation enables customizing survey experiences with uses of names, question answers, piped text from a number of sources, expanded question elicitations (like through loop & merge techniques, and others), branching logic, and randomizers, among others. And many online research suites, designed as all-in-one shops, enable the automated analyses of text, quantitative data in cross-tabulation analyses, and other approaches.

Yet, in the midst of all these changes, a simple confluence of technological capabilities has suggested an even more fundamental change: the sophistication of computational text analysis (computer-aided text analysis) means that open-ended text-based survey question responses may be better harnessed and exploited for information than in the recent past. Computational text analysis enables the identification of a range of data patterns: matrix queries, theme extraction (topic modeling), sentiment analysis, cluster analysis (concept mapping), network text structures, qualitative cross-tabulation analysis, manual coding to automated coding, linguistic analysis, psychometrics, stylometry, network analysis, and others. These computational text analysis approaches harness quantitative, qualitative and mixed methods approaches, and all include "humans in the loop" for the analyses.

While some all-in-one online survey systems are expanding to built-in text analyses, the available tools look to be simplistic presently, with commercial software tools enabling more sophisticated text analysis. Those with the technology skills and statistical know-how stand to exploit the capabilities of open-ended survey questions and freeform respondent comments and insights. Going to "machine reading" (or "distant reading" through various forms of computational text analysis) does not remove the human from the loop. There is still the need for human "close reading" of the findings and of some of the original raw data. (In some cases, all of the original text may be read depending on the size of the text corpus.)

Technology Tools Used

The software tools highlighted in this work include Qualtrics®, NVivo 12 Plus, Linguistic Inquiry and Word Count (LIWC2015), and Network Overview, Discovery and Exploration for Excel (NodeXL).

REVIEW OF THE LITERATURE

The main strength of surveys is that they capture elicited information from human respondents, but that fact is also its main weakness. There is a wide body of literature that shows that people's responses to surveys may depend on social relationships, design features of how questions are presented and asked, the types of technologies used, and other factors, which "intervene" and "interfere" with respondents' offering their truest thinking. Besides these factors, the respondent himself/herself has limitations, in terms of built-in cognitive biases (confirmative bias, anchoring biases, priming effects, and others) and limited working memory. And yet, surveys are sometimes the only way to capture respondent experiences, preferences, imaginations, and opinions, even with the limitations of self-reportage.

Surveys are delivered in various ways. Surveys may be delivered in person or remotely, to respondents who are alone or in the company of others. They may be other-administered or self-administered. They may be delivered through various modalities: via telephone (Arnon & Reichel, Apr. 2009) or paper (postal or face-to-face) or computer, offline or online, and so on. There are some survey sequences that involve various mixes of the prior variables. Some classic Delphi survey methods began with face-to-face (F2F) meetings followed by distance-based interactions, for example.

Modalities and Respondent Responsiveness

Researchers have studied to understand differences between various modalities of surveys, such as between mail (postal) and web ones (Kwak & Radler, 2002). Various studies have found some differences in response rates to surveys based on their modality, but others have found "no significant differences"—but these vary depending on the specific research contexts and respondents. The differences in survey modes are generally thought to be a source of instability in terms of responses, with potential effects on both respondents and on responses. The ideal is to achieve "measurement equivalence" (Andrews, Nonnecke, & Preece, 2003, p. 190), so modality does not affect outcomes.

In early years, researchers found wide discrepancies between open-ended vs. closed questions in a postal survey (Falthzik & Carroll, 1971), with only 27% responding to open-ended questions and 78% for closed question. Each approach has its strengths and weaknesses. One study suggests that the "mode effect" between paper and electronic surveys did not result in any statistically significant difference in the length of answers to open-ended questions (Denscombe, Aug. 2008). One study that found that fifth graders responded more in-depth to open-ended questions on computerized versions than paper ones (Love, Butz, Usher, & Waiters, 2018), which may be a result of generational differences.

In-person open-ended survey responses may be unduly influenced by the interviewer and his / her preferences, resulting in measurement error:

The average survey has a vast number of opportunities for measurement error resulting from the interaction between an interviewer and a respondent. Even in the case of simple forced-choice questions, subtle cues delivered by the interviewer become a part of the stimulus situation and lend credibility to the hypothesis that the responses solicited in the interview are due, in part, to the particular interviewer who collected them. In the case of open-ended survey questions the opportunities for interview bias increase substantially, since such questions give rise to a prolonged social interaction in which cues are actively sought and parsimoniously delivered. (Shapiro, Autumn 1970, p. 412)

Those who would build survey instruments will not be interacting with the survey respondents directly, but the constructed survey instrument may have unplanned effects on respondent feedback. To mitigate for this, research on survey designs has focused on such influences, such as the order of response options (ascending or descending), user interface effects, question layout (horizontal and vertical), and sizes of answer boxes for open-ended questions (Maloshonok & Terentev, 2016, pp. 506 - 507). One research team studied the prior elements to see if these aspects of survey questions affect "data quality" (based on whether responses are "substantive" or informational, and the amounts of feedback in open-ended questions) (p. 507). Radio buttons in the survey design work better to lower the selection of non-substantive answers like "Don't know" than slider response and text-box interfaces (p. 506). While some researchers suggest that the "primacy effect" influences the ratings that people apply to scalar questions, such as that going from negative ratings to positive ones (ascending order) "significantly reduces the share of positive answers," this effect was not found in another study (p. 507). There is also the idea that descending (from positive to negative scale measures) order format "increases the number of respondents who choose neutral response categories" p. 507). Larger text boxes do seem to encourage more commentary for native speakers of the survey language for "narrative questions" (Maloshonok & Terentev, 2016, pp. 514 - 515).

In an earlier study, just the availability of "more space for responses to an open-ended question produced marginally more words and ideas per response, but did not generate a greater total number of ideas" (Gendall, Menelaou, & Brennan, 1996, p. 1). So more contents do not mean more quality responses per se. The uses of encouragement to respondents "to write positive or negative comments to an open-ended question did not produce either more words or more ideas" (Gendall, Menelaou, & Brennan, 1996, p. 1). The question cue does influence "the number and content of the responses received" (Gendall, Menelaou, & Brennan, 1996, p. 1), which suggests the importance of thoughtful question design and testing of those designs for responsiveness and data quality. A later study found that the sizes of answer boxes with "extra verbal instructions" had an effect on response quality, with quality defined as including "response length, number of themes reported, elaboration on themes, response time, and item nonresponse" (Smyth, Dillman, Christian, & McBride, May 2009, p. 5).

To avoid low response rates, survey designers need to avoid creating "high-burden Web interactions" that may lower response rates to online surveys (Crawford, Coupler, & Lamias, Summer 2001, p. 146). Some interventions to encourage response include the following: "a progress indicator, automating password entry, varying the timing of reminder notices to nonrespondents, and using a prenotification report on the anticipated survey length" to "vary the burden (perceived or real) of the survey request" (Crawford, Coupler, & Lamias, Summer 2001, p. 146).

Another test of modality potentially affecting responses focused on sequences—such as beginning from the quantitative methods to the qualitative and then vice versa, to see if the respective survey respondent groups responded differently. They found: "The sequence of data collection did not greatly affect the participants' responses to the close-ended questions (survey items) or the open-ended questions (interview questions)" (Covell, Sidani, & Ritchie, 2012, p. 664). That is not to say that the researchers did not find some risks of unduly influencing some open-ended question results:

That is, participants' descriptions of the phenomenon of interest will be affected by the domains, dimensions, and / or aspects captured and / or covered by those assessed with the quantitative measure; therefore, the qualitative responses may not accurately or solely reflect their perspective. These recommendations are logical; however, they are not empirically based. No empirical evidence could be found from investigations that supports or refutes the influence of the sequence of data collection in concurrent mixed methods designs on the participants' responses to close-ended questions (e.g., items on surveys) or open-ended questions (e.g. interview questions) when data are collected at the same phase of a study. (Covell, Sidani, & Ritchie, 2012, p. 665)

How questions are set up can also frame respondent understandings of the purposes of the questions and the scope. "Response alternatives" frame understandings for respondents and affect their provided answers (Schwarz, Feb. 1999, p. 95) and help respondents contextualize their own behavior (Schwarz, Hippler, Deutsch, & Strack, Autumn 1985, p. 389). Response scales to close-ended questions are informational to survey respondents Schwarz, Hippler, Deutsch, & Strack, Autumn 1985, p. 394), and they systematically affect respondent choices: "An examination of respondents' behavioral reports indicates that those who were presented the low range scale tended to choose categories in the middle of the list, whereas respondents who were presented the high range scale tended to endorse the first category provided" Schwarz, Hippler, Deutsch, & Strack, Autumn 1985, p. 390). When offered a list of numbers, most survey respondents tend to choose those "near the middle of the list" (Payne, 1951, p. 80, as cited in Schwarz, Hippler, Deutsch, & Strack, Autumn 1985, p. 389), with respondents preferring "usual" behavior (and not the polar extremes). Researchers note that question design requires some directiveness, so respondents understand what researchers are interested in, but the options should be inclusive of the range of alternatives without unduly leading respondents to certain responses.

Survey question design involves defining objectives for the question and creating question cues that achieve those objectives without bias.

Uses of Open-Ended Questions in Online Surveys

Historically, the most common open-ended question in surveys were as a catch-all question. However, while this information was captured, researchers apparently did not always analyze these.

The habitual 'any other comments' general open question at the end of structured questionnaires has the potential to increase response rates, elaborate responses to closed questions, and allow respondents to identify new issues not captured in the closed questions. However, we believe that many researchers have collected such data and failed to analyze or present it. (O'Cathain & Thomas, 2004, p. 1)

Researchers suggest that if survey designers are more strategic in building "general open questions at the end of structure questionnaires," they may more effectively elicit useful insights (O'Cathain & Thomas, 2004, p. 1). They identify four basic types of open-ended questions—to extend existing close-ended questions (such as with "Other, please specify"), to substitute for a closed question, to expand on an answer given to a prior close-ended question, and to "elaborate on their general experience in relation to the overall topic of the survey" (O'Cathain & Thomas, 2004, p. 3). These refer to open-ended questions in relationship to close-ended ones. In more recent work, open-ended survey questions are strategically designed to capture original insights not available otherwise, without any necessary direct tie to close-ended questions.

Open-ended questions may serve various question roles. In one study, they were used to assess respondent senses of the questionnaire, and one involved eliciting information conceived as private in many cultures (Leidich, Jayaweera, Arcara, Clawson, Chalker, & Rochat, 2018). Open-ended questions may be used to measure non-expert respondent competence (Brugidou, 2003; Reynolds, Bostrom, Read, & Morgan, 2010). Another study used open-ended questions to identify "sub-corpora by group" which may inform on segments of the respondents (Deneulin, Le Fur, & Bavaud, 2016, p. 289), or audience / consumer category / population segmentation.

A core feature is that open-ended questions enable a wide range of responses for questions about which the survey designer may not directly anticipate the full range of possible responses.

In one study, researchers identified a negativity bias in open-ended responses (in terms of employee surveys) (Poncheri, Lindberg, Thompson, & Surface, July 2008). To balance against "strategic misrepresentations of values in open-ended stated preference surveys," researchers have explored positive and negative reinforcement to mitigate these tendencies (Dit Sourd, Zawojska, Mahieu, & Louviere, 2018, p. 153). Interventions have included sharing of information, recoding values, structuring incentives (for "consequential" surveys with opportunities for gain or loss), and other efforts.

Manifest or Latent Information

An important differentiation is to understand whether the online survey research is in pursuit of manifest or latent information, which some have referred to as "breadth" vs. "depth." The research team explains:

Another methodological question at the outset is whether a study will examine the **manifest** *(visible at the surface level or literally present in the text) or* **latent** *(having a deeper meaning implied in the text) content of the text or a combination. Manifest content is identified using coding and key word searches and can be recorded in frequencies such as word counts. Latent content, although amenable to objective* *coding processes, is more complex and requires developing constructs and drawing conclusions to add broader meaning to the text. It is generally easier to conduct a CA (content analysis) of the manifest content of a message, but latent content is often the more interesting and debatable aspect of communication. (Kondracki, Wellman, & Amundson, 2002, p. 225)*

In some ways, making a case for what is manifest may be somewhat easier than what is latent, but there are data analytics methods and software tools that make the latter easier and more arguable.

Who Responds to Online Surveys?

A range of methodological studies suggest varying reasons why people do or do not respond to surveys in general and to open-ended questions in particular. In terms of who will respond to online surveys, this depends on various factors, such as the types of research, the incentives designed into the survey, the access to information, and other factors. In some cases, targeted surveys may go out to an organization's membership, and there may be higher response rates to these than to others. Non-response error affects how representative the captured data sample is.

In theory, the Internet enables access to all those who are engaged online, but Internet research surveys have strengths and weaknesses. While online surveys may seem more efficient in "cost and speed," that may not be so accurate in terms of a "significantly shorter survey fielding period" (Fricker & Schonlau, 2012, p. 356). A common challenge may be a "coverage error" for representative population (Fricker & Schonlau, 2012, p. 357), and because there are some "hard-to-involve Internet users" who are "nonpublic participants of online communities (also known as 'lurkers')" (Andrews, Nonnecke, & Preece, 2003, p. 185). Online it is difficult to distinguish one's survey from others (Fricker & Schonlau, 2012, p. 365). People who are highly motivated to engage in a particular topic are found to respond to web surveys (Holland & Christian, May 2009, p. 196), but that characteristic already suggests some bias in the data collected. Internet penetration does not reach all possible respondents who may have insights on a topic because of the simple reality that "not all persons in the United States can be reached using the Internet" (Crawford, Coupler, & Lamias, Summer 2001, p. 146). There is also the reality that many surveys online are incentivized by micropayments, which may attract people who are willing to share their thoughts for very small amounts of money. Sampling options for electronic surveys include the following: "non-probabilistic methods: self-selection; volunteer panels of Internet users; probability-based methods: intercept; list-based, high coverage; mixed-mode design with choice of completion method; prerecruited panels of Internet users; (and) probability samples of full populations" (Couper, 2000, as cited Andrews, Nonnecke, & Preece, 2003, p. 185). [Non-probabilistic approaches deal with samples that are not necessarily "representative," and many of these are convenience samples. Self-selection methods include opt-in to participate in advertised surveys. Volunteer panels are those who opt-in based on expertise or micropayments, or other incentives. The probabilistic methods include the following: "Intercept surveys target visitors at a particular Web site, asking every nth visitor to participate, similar to an election exit poll. Invitation presentation timing problems may increase nonresponse. With the sampling option, list-based sampling, everyone on a list is sent an invitation to increase coverage. However, this approach does not address nonresponses. With prerecruited Internet user panels, panel members are recruited using probability sampling methods such as random digital dialing. Here, nonresponse can occur at any stage of the recruitment and survey process. The last sampling method, probability samples of full populations, requires that participants can be provided with the PCs and Internet access necessary to participate (Andrews, Nonnecke, & Preece, 2003, p. 190).]

More Responsive "Types" to Open-Ended Questions

Multiple studies suggest that particular demographic features may predispose some to be more sensitive to some survey design features than others. Open-ended questions allow respondents to reply "in their own words" (Glasow, April, 2005, p. 2-7), which requires some contemplation and effort. The cognitive load required is higher than for making selections from pre-defined options.

A different research team suggests that "large answer boxes earn higher item nonresponse than small answer boxes regardless of the usage of a motivation text" (Zuell, Menold, & Körber, 2015, p. 115). One explanation for this is that open-ended questions incur a "higher cognitive burden" for respondents even as these help "gain additional, more sophisticated information from respondents" (Zuell, Menold, & Körber, 2015, p. 115). In this study, those from the "social sciences" as a field of study and females…were more responsive to the open-ended questions (Zuell, Menold, & Körber, 2015, p. 115).

For example, "interactive probing" (elicitations for further elaboration) with web surveys seems to work well in particular contexts only and particular respondents:

We find that respondents' interest in the question topic significantly affects the responses to open-ended questions, and interactively probing responses to open-ended questions in web surveys can improve the quality of responses for some respondents, particularly for those very interested in the question topic. Nonresponse remains a significant problem for open-ended questions; we found high item nonresponse rates for the initial question and even higher nonresponse to the probe, especially for those less interested in the topic of the question. (Holland & Christian, May 2009, p. 196)

Text and Textual Analysis

Once open-ended questions have been designed and presented in as non-biased ways as possible, and sufficient responses captured, it is important to analyze the responses based on research design, particularly the intent and objectives of the open-ended questions. Textual data is fairly high dimensional in terms of semantic or meaning-bearing terms. It carries information through orthography, the conventions for writing a language (including spelling, punctuation, capitalization, and others). It carries information by author hands (signatures of authors). Researchers suggest that text analysis is not directly linked to a particular theoretical framework but cuts across multiple types. They write:

The assumption about the nature of text refers to the relationship between text data and reality. Positivist approaches assume language corresponds to an objective reality; that is, meaning is assumed to be objective—researchers merely need to find it. Linguistic approaches assume that language is not a neutral description of reality but rather an act that shapes reality. Linguistic approaches assume that reality emerges through language because reality does not exist independent of language. Interpretivist approaches assume that the meaning of language is subjective—the speaker, listener, and observer may all ascribe different meanings to language. (Lacity & Janson, Fall 1994, p. 139) (Note: The numerical citations have been removed from the prior paragraph.)

A text analysis approach encapsulates these different types of approaches depending on the researcher, the theoretical frameworks, the research context, and other factors. Regardless of the initial text analysis findings, validity checks are assumed to follow (Lacity & Janson, Fall 1994, p. 141). More modern approaches assume some level of validation checking as well.

Concurrent Mixed Methods Research

Classic survey data was generally quantitative and amenable to a variety of statistical analysis methods. With the inclusion of open-ended questions, capturing "interview" data, the data also became qualitative, amenable to qualitative analytics methods through interpretive lenses and without claims of objectivity.

Sufficient Data

A quality response, generically, is seen as achieving "data saturation" [described as the point at which few other changes are made to the codebook (Trans, Porcher, Falissard, & Ravaud, 2016, p. 88) or the point that no new information is available]. In one meta-analytic study, data saturation was achieved with greater than 150 participants for the full range of identifiable themes (Tran, Porcher, Falissard, & Ravaud, 2016). This study was based on Monte Carlo simulations on data:

In the literature, 85% of researchers used a convenience sample, with a median size of 167 participants (interquartile range [IQR] = 69 – 406). In our simulation study, the probability of identifying at least one new theme for the next included subject was 32%, 24%, and 12% after the inclusion of 30, 50, and 100 subjects, respectively. The inclusion of 150 participants at random resulted in the identification of 92% themes (IQR = 91 – 93%) identified in the original study. (Trans, Porcher, Falissard, & Ravaud, 2016, p. 88)

Having sufficient respondents enables quality because these may help mitigate over-estimations and under-estimations, to get closer to accurate data.

Depth of Responses

Another data quality approach involves the depth or complexity of the textual responses, with research indicating that it is better in some cases and worse in others, in case-based studies. In self-administered questionnaires, open-ended questions involved reduced responses as compared to the same questions in face-to-face interviews (Sudman & Bradburn, 1974, pp. 35 – 36). Open-ended questions elicited more of a response when the subject matter was "threatening" (Sudman & Bradburn, 1974, p. 47). And open-ended questions seemed to be more protected against social desirability effects (Sudman & Bradburn, 1974, p. 47).

One study focused on recognizing respondent motivations (not as "mono" or single-channel but multi-channel) (Espina & Figueroa, 2017). To achieve these, the question cues need to enable respondents to process information at the semantic or meaning-based levels (not the orthographic or the phonological ones, or the ones based on language rules or sounds) (Burgess & Weaver, 2003, as cited in Gardner, 2018, p. 7).

In online survey systems, there is coding of text data done in system for close-ended questions but not open-ended ones (Van Selm & Jankowski, 2006), but this may be changing with later-generation systems. A common approach to summative content analysis involves "counting and comparisons, usually of keywords or content" (Hsieh & Shannon, Nov. 2005, p. 1277). Frequency counts may seem simplistic on the surface, but such an approach enables some pithy research insights. The data from open-ended surveys are also analyzed using concept mapping to summarize the text responses in the aggregate (Jackson & Trochim, Oct. 2002). In offline qualitative analytics software, the enablements may include the following: *"text impo*rt and management; *exploration*; *dictionaries, categorization schemes, and coding*; and *export operations"* (Kondracki, Wellman, & Amundson, 2002, p. 227), and more.

COMPUTATIONAL TEXT ANALYSIS TO EXPLORE OPEN-ENDED SURVEY QUESTION RESPONSES

Before focusing on the various available types of computational text analyses for open-ended survey question responses, it helps to explore the steps to setting up an online survey with open-ended questions. This segment integrates some of the research findings addressed in the prior section and information related to some of the functionalities in Qualtrics®. Setting up a research survey generally involves the following eight somewhat-recursive semi-sequential steps:

1. Research Design
2. Survey Design
3. Deployment
4. Data Capture
5. Data Cleaning
6. Data Analysis
7. Write-up
8. Presentation

These related steps are depicted in Figure 1, with the nominal steps highlighted. The respective steps will require different amounts of effort and time depending on the research context and focus. A brief summary of each step follows. (This summary is not to replace more thorough works describing various aspects of the work but is intended merely to set a context for the discussion of computational text analysis of open-ended questions from online surveys.)

A brief summary of the eight steps follow.

1. Research Design

The design of an online survey requires the definition of some basic elements, which may be addressed in part by the following questions:

- **Published Research:** What sorts of prior published research inform the research design, and why?
- **Research Objectives:** What is/are the objective/s of the survey? (If the survey is part of more complex research, what are the objectives of that research, and how does the survey part fit within that larger context?)
- **Data and Information:** What informational content is needed?
  - What are optimal ways to attain this information?
  - Are there extant survey instruments that are available for use to elicit this information? If not, what are the unique needs for this particular research?
- **Target Respondents:** Who are the target respondents for the survey research?
  - Do the respondents have access the requisite information?
  - How will these respondents be reached? How will they be sufficiently sampled for statistical power in the research? For sufficient data saturation?
  - What incentives will be used to elicit their responses?
  - Are there vulnerable populations being accessed? How can their interests be protected?
- **Designed Elicitations:** What sorts of questions, prompts, and elicitations will be most effective in this context? Will there by hypotheticals? Stories? Vignettes? Images? Video? Simulations?
  - What are ways to ensure that questions are single-barreled for easier analytics?
  - If in-depth prompts are needed, how should these be designed? What stimuli should be used? What (non-leading) memory aids?

Figure 1. General online survey design, development, and deployment sequence

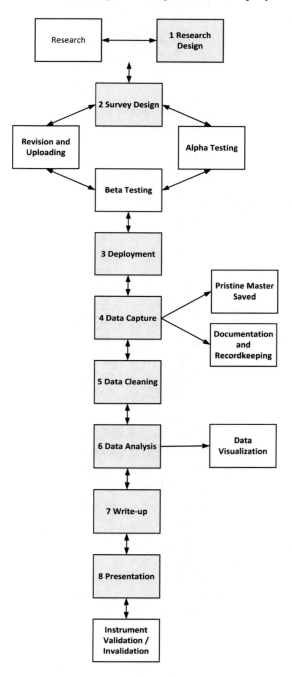

General Online Survey Design, Development, and Deployment Sequence

- ◦ When will different modalities of questions be deployed, and why?
- ◦ What sequences will be most effective?
- ◦ If there are branching logic sequences, what are the rationales for these, and how should these be designed? What are ways to ensure that the branches are fitting and do not fail to capture information from the respective respondents?
- ◦ If latent or hidden understandings and patterns are a focus, how will these be elicited? How will the data be captured? How will the data be analyzed?
- ◦ Will demographic data be captured? If so, which ones? Why, or why not? How will demographic data be used? What are ways to elicit such data without turning off survey respondents (or creating a sense of invasion of privacy)?

- **Accessibility:** How can the online survey be made fully accessible for all potential respondents (and in alignment with federal laws requiring accessibility)?
- **Ethical, Legal, and Professional Considerations:** What are ethical considerations for this survey? Legal ones? Professional requirements considerations?
- **Data Handling:** How will the data be managed? Why?
- **Data Analytics:** How will the data be analyzed? Why?
  - ◦ What sorts of quantitative, qualitative, and mixed methods analytics methods will be applied, and why?
  - ◦ What statistical techniques will be applied, and why?
  - ◦ How will the data be value-coded? Why?
  - ◦ What data visualization techniques will be applied, and why?
- **Pilot Testing:** How will the survey instrument be pilot tested? Which subject matter experts may be brought in for the testing? Which target respondents?
  - ◦ How will the instrument be validated/invalidated?
  - ◦ How will its reliability be tested?
  - ◦ How will potential response biasing be identified and mitigated for?
  - ◦ How will the neutrality of the survey instrument be ensured?
- **Technology Identification:** How well will this survey be deployed on the particular online research platform, and why? What functionalities will be required for the particular platform?
  - ◦ What about the technologies needed for the computational text analyses?

Depending on the ambitions of the research, other questions may also need to be included.

2. Survey Design

Based on the prior research design, the survey is set up with the elicitations. The open-ended questions may be included in any part of the designed sequences (Figure 2). The sequences matter because the prior contents of the survey may set up respondents to address particular issues or to have particular thoughts top-of-mind. A survey, in all its parts—from the name, the informed consent, the textual and other descriptors, the questions, the prompts, the sequences—inform respondents about what is relevant and what the researcher(s) wants to know. If poorly designed, the information will be leading and affect the acquired feedback.

In general, conceptually, open-ended questions may appear in various ways in survey sequences. There may be none used; one or few used, such as at the end, beginning, or middle of a survey; interspersed open-ended and close-ended questions in surveys, or surveys with open-ended questions used throughout. If there were a

Figure 2. Some variations on placements of open-ended questions in online surveys

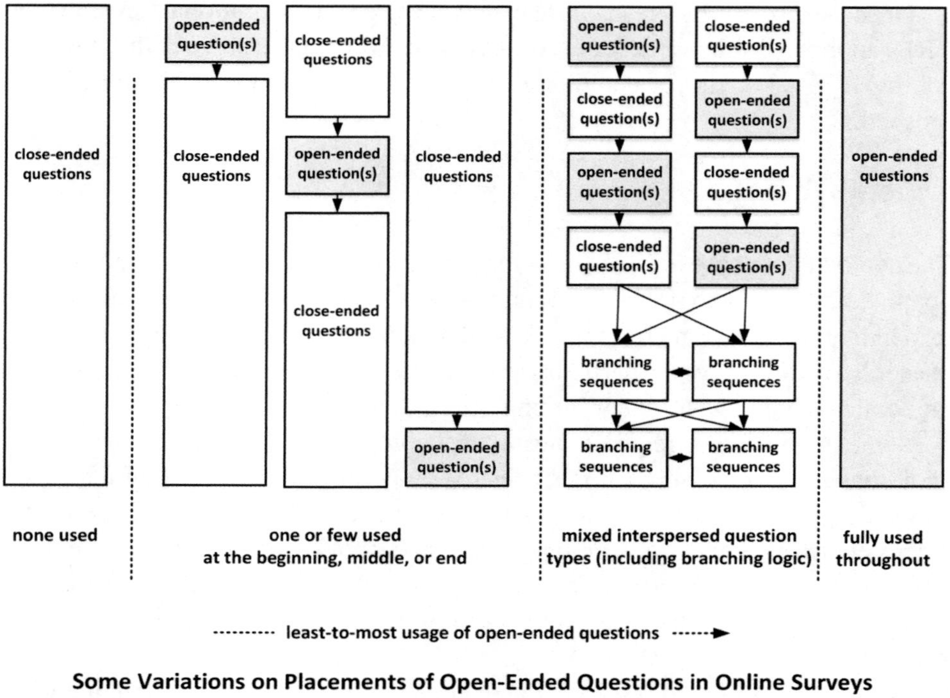

Some Variations on Placements of Open-Ended Questions in Online Surveys

typical use case, it might be those in the two middle categories of Figure 2, where a few are placed at the beginning, middle, or end, or a few are interspersed with close-ended questions.

When the draft instrument is completed and polished, it is uploaded to the survey platform and tested for all functionalities (including with faux auto-created data… to ensure that the information will be captured in a usable format). Then, a live link is sent to pilot testers. Content experts evaluate the instrument to ensure that it is sufficiently comprehensive and representational of the constructs under study. Target respondents experience the survey to ensure that it is understandable and adaptable to their respective experiences. To test for undue design influences, variants of the survey may be tested to assess for systematic biases based on question types, question sequences, answer designs for close-ended questions, and other details. How to test open-ended questions requires a little more work than for close-ended ones because of the polysemous nature of language and the openness of a text box-based response. Auto-generated data only creates garble text on online research systems, so both experts and target respondents engaged in the pilot test would do well to fully flesh out their responses in open-ended questions, and avoid placeholder text.

Once the researcher or research team has acquired the Institutional Review Board (IRB) approval for the work (or exemption from oversight), and gone through other approvals based on the local authorizing environment, then the actual research can proceed.

3. Deployment

The deployment phase involves launching the online survey—via a closed list or an open-access link (with invites to various populations of possible respondents). The respondents should come from the defined populations suitable for the survey. This phase also involves inviting participation. In some cases, this may include conducting randomized drawings for the awarding of prizes to participants.

Some monitoring is required during the deployment given the changeability of cloud-based survey platforms. Changes made by the company hosting the survey may affect the survey's availability and performance. (Author note: For example, when Qualtrics retracted its "conjoint analysis" feature in September 2018, a number of surveys using this feature were rendered inoperable. The company had not given its users any warning that they had decided to retract this feature and move it to a different conjoint analysis suite.)

In some multi-phased research, the deployment may involve multiple iterations of survey phase deployments.

4. Data Capture

The captured data from online surveys consist of both structured and semi-structured and unstructured data. Structured data refers to labeled data, such as those in a classic data table (Table 01). The column data are demographic data and question data. The row data represent each of the respondents. Structured data can be downloaded as comma separated values (.csv), tab-separated values (.tsv), extensible markup language (.xml), and data formats for common statistical analysis tools like SPSS (.sav), and others. More complex questions like ranking questions, matrix table questions, slider questions, may have their data downloaded separately for more in-depth analysis. Visual questions like hotspot questions and heat map questions, which enable selection of particular regions on a 2D image or map or figure also do well with unique per question data downloads for enriched data analytics and visual representations of the summary data.

Semi-structured and unstructured data refers to imagery, text, audio, video, and multimodal data formats. The capturing of this data requires their artful downloading to maintain their formatting and ride-along metadata.

The data capture phase should include archival of the pristine master sets of data with proper labeling, so that if lossy methods of data cleaning and manipulation occur, there is always a pristine unedited master set to draw from.

5. Data Cleaning

Data cleaning for quantitative data generally involves removing multiple responses if one individual responded multiple times. It involves managing incomplete responses (because some statistical analysis techniques and machine learning techniques cannot run with blanks in data fields). For textual data, data cleaning may involve

Table 1. Typical data structure of online survey responses

	Demographic Data	Question 1	Question 2	Question 3	Question 4...
Respondent 1					
Respondent 2					
Respondent 3					
Respondent 4					
Respondent 5					
Respondent 6					

correction of misspellings, interpretation of confusing text, and other factors. If some text files are uploaded portable document format (.pdf) files, these have to be machine readable, so some of these will have to be run through optical character recognition (OCR) scans if these were captured as image files.

In addition to the data cleaning, how the various text sets are thin-sliced will affect the types of askable questions about the textual data (with some of the software tools). For example, some of the lighter-weight software tools require the manual separation of the content in respective text sets to enable comparisons and contrasts. To ask other questions of the text, the various granular text corpora may have to be recombined with others. For example, if a researcher wanted to compare how female and male respondents engaged a particular question, using a lighter weight text analysis software tool, then there has to be a text set representing each group (female and male respondents) for the particular question. With the respective sets, various analyses may be run. (More on this will follow.)

More sophisticated qualitative analytics tools enable the coding of contents into separate nodes, which can then be compared and contrasted (such as through matrix table queries, sentiment analysis, qualitative cross-tabulation analysis, and other tools).

For audio and video, these have to be transcribed for the text analysis to be applied. Likewise, imagery has to be turned into an informational textual format to be queried, coded, and included in qualitative computational text analysis.

Some tools treat text analyses somewhat naively. N-grams (contiguous sequences of words) may not be accurately recognized and coded. For example, some do not see words as more than unigrams or one-grams; they do not consider bi-grams or digrams (two words in contiguous order like "computational linguistics"), tri-grams (three words in contiguous order like "Latin numerical prefixes"), four-grams (four words in contiguous order like "longest common substring problem"), and others. If words are treated in a non-sticky way, names and phrases cannot be coded in a way that more accurately reflects the natural language usage in the world. Another naïve point is how sentiment is analyzed. More sophisticated algorithms will recognize negatives, and they will recognize irony and sarcasm. Many of the off-the-shelf qualitative analytics software tools lack such sophistication at present.

6. Data Analysis

In terms of open-ended text-based-response questions, computational text analysis enables multiple ways to approach the data: (1) exploratory queries, (2) manual coding, (3) auto-coding, and (4) mixed sequence analysis.

(1) "Exploratory" queries enable running of various text analytics methods against the text to provide overall summative data and descriptions of the data. Researchers can also zoom-in to particular terms, symbols, phrases, or other elements in the text and explore the contextual usage of every instance of the particular term (such as in an interactive word tree). Simple explorations may include word frequency counts (which may be depicted as word clouds, treemap diagrams, sunburst diagrams, Pareto charts, bar charts, and others). Word frequency counts may be explored not only for the most popular semantic terms used but also for the "long tail" or outlier topics with single or few mentions. Such outliers may shed light on unique topics of interest.

(2) "Manual" coding involves a researcher-created codebook or "codeframe" by which raw data may be coded for insights. A codebook may be created in a top-down way, based on theories, models, or frameworks. Or they may be created from the available data in a bottom-up way, based on "grounded theory" approaches. Or they may be created in a mixed top-down and bottom-up way, informed by concepts and by the available data. A manual codebook may be automated if there are sufficient examples of coded text to each codebook category and subcategories (nodes and subnodes). A researcher can code, say, 10% of the raw textual data and then have the computer code the rest of the data (with a Cohen's Kappa of 1, with very high interrater reliability). Manually created codebooks may be exported and used in other similar research contexts. These codebooks should contain the following, at minimum: the comprehensive list of codes, and the definitions for what belongs within each code category. It also helps to have a few paragraphs describing the origins of the manual codebook. All who contributed to the codebook should be listed based on their respective roles. The codebook should have a disambiguated and unique name for easy reference.

(3) "Autocoding" (in various forms of machine learning) may be applied to understand topic modeling, sentiment, psychometrics, stylometry, and other aspects of text. Topic modeling or theme extraction identifies the main topics and subtopics in a text set, and this method also captures a sense of the topic prevalence (based on counted mentions). Sentiment analysis involves the identification of how positive or negative non-neutral expressions are in the text set (and around particular topics). Psychometrics are measures of the amount of psychology related insights. Stylometry involves counts of various points of grammar and syntax that may be indicative of an author hand (as a "tell"). More on these will follow. The basic power of such auto coding is that such results are reproducible and repeatable (important values in quantitative data analysis).

(4) "Mixed sequence" analysis involves combining any of the prior in a mix of different queries. For example, computational sentiment analysis may be run on individual responses to a particularly controversial issue, and then those autocoded text sets (for very negative, moderately negative, moderately positive, and very positive) may be analyzed to explore different topics emplaced in the respective sentiment categories. Frequency counts may be run against the sets to understand the frequency of mentions in the respective sentiment sets. Or a cluster diagram (concept map) may be created from a word-frequency-based dendrogram to understand how related topics are interconnected, and the main categories may be analyzed to understand what is being discussed in relation to particular popular topics (and fat nodes). Or demographic data may be used to separate people by gender, class, geography, professions, age, and / or other features, to see how these might affect their perceptions of particular issues raised in the survey. (This may be done with qualitative cross-tabulation analyses, matrix queries, and others.)

Computational text analysis methods transform unstructured and semi-structured data into quantitative structured data. The questions asked in such computational methods are rich, and they shed light on issues that may not be capturable in other ways. The output data are representable in human-interpretable data visualizations. Further, these approaches enable the handling of vast amounts of data well beyond the capabilities of human close reading and human manual coding, so the scale factor is an important one.

Some Computational Text Analysis Approaches (by Function)

While it is beyond the purview of this work to describe the nuances of the various computational text analysis techniques, some of the more common methods are described here.

Matrix Queries

Matrices are rectangular arrays of quantities and / or expressions. A matrix query involves the definition of contents for any of the variables in columns or rows and the viewing of the resulting overlapping data cells to understand frequencies. For example, the cell which is the overlap between Column Header A and Row Header A will be populated with frequency data, and matrices will represent as color intensity-highlighted cells to show the interrelationships. To create such matrices, the data have to be properly set up and coded. (Table 2)

Table 2. An empty generic data matrix

	Column Header A	**Column Header B**	**Column Header C**	**Column Header D**
Row Header A				
Row Header B				
Row Header C				
Row Header D				

Theme Extraction (Topic Modeling)

Theme extraction or topic modeling is an automated process by which the software program extracts the main focuses (topics and related subtopics) of particular text sets (whether documents, articles, text corpora, or other).

Sentiment Analysis

Sentiment is conceptualized as a polar dimension, either positive or negative. While a majority of natural language is not sentiment-laden but "neutral," the text in a text set that is seen to carry a sentiment value is coded in a pre-existing dictionary with a certain direction (positive or negative) and intensity, and the comparison of words in a text set against this dictionary enables coding to sentiment (either as a binary positive or negative category, or as a continuum, such as the "very negative, moderately negative, moderately positive, and very positive" categories mentioned earlier).

Cluster Analysis (Concept Mapping)

Concept mapping by showing interrelationships between main semantic terms in a text set provides an aggregate summary sense of the text. Clustering can be used in other ways, too, with individuals sharing messaging on a social media platform clustered based on "shared messaging" and shared interests (or at least shared engagement around particular topics). Clustering is based on a number of different algorithms, some identifying likeness, others identifying word proximities, and so on.

Network Text Structures

Network text structures capture structured relationships of various types. Social relationships may be those between individuals intercommunicating across a social media platform or a learning management system or an online survey research platform (with collaborative surveying). Or it may indicate relationships between co-occurring folk tags on an image sharing platform. Or it may show relationships between co-occurring terms within a certain size proximity. Essentially, network text structures are comprised of terms and their interrelationships.

Qualitative Cross-Tabulation Analysis

A qualitative cross-tabulation analysis enables the identification of large-scale patterns in survey data including open-ended text-response questions. One form of this analysis is to use the captured demographic features of the respondents in the row headers to find what relationships there may be among those dimensions and particular commenting on certain topics, certain sentiments, and other variables in the research. (Table 3)

Another common setup of a qualitative cross-tabulation analysis has the respective individual cases in the row headers column. The qualitative cross-tabulation analysis does not use the calculations of chi-squared calculations and degrees of freedom and critical values found in the quantitative version, but the cells are mostly filled with straight counts.

Table 3. One setup of a qualitative cross-tabulation analysis

Demographic Features of Respondents	Topic	Topic	Topic	Sentiment	Other Variables

Manual Coding to Automated Coding

Manual codebooks and codeframes may highlight particular aspects of the raw data as a form of systematic content analysis, "coding raw messages (ie, textual material, visual images, illustrations) according to a classification scheme" (Kondracki, Wellman, & Amundson, 2002, p. 224).

Linguistic Analysis

Computational text analysis tools enable the capturing of various dimensions of textual contents. For example, normed scores for text features may be captured to understand how analytic, clout or authoritative-based, authentic (emotionally warm), and positive (tone) a particular text or text set may be normed against known corpora. There are various types of linguistic analyses for particular general and customized purposes.

Psychometrics

Some tools have built-in psychometric assessments (backed up by validity and reliability scores), for positive and negative emotions, social focuses, cognitive processes, perceptual features, bodily references, human drives, time references, physics relativity references, lifestyle references, informalisms, and netspeak, among others.

Stylometry

Basic linguistic analyses may be run for basic counts of various word types and punctuation types, to enable stylometry (the metrics of style), to understand authorship. Each human writer's authorship is composed of a particular mix of word combinations, in a way that is often hidden to the unique author (and so is less directly manipulate-able).

Network Analysis

Multiple tools enable the capturing of interrelationships between words, people inter-communicating, folk tags, and other relational angles.

Query Sequences

Each of the above computational text analyses techniques may be applied in different sequential orders to ask particular questions and acquire particular informational data.

In each of the sequences above, there are various options for data cleaning, parameter setting, data visualizations, and other ways to customize the approaches.

7. Write-Up

In terms of the write-up of the text analyses, the methods should be described in depth, along with the parameter settings and the technologies used (and the versions of the technologies. Certainly, the findings need to be human-analyzed and the findings and implications of those findings described in depth.

8. Presentation

The prior section gives a sense of some of the capabilities of commercial and freeware tools for text analysis. These are not from a comprehensive list of software, and there are many others out in the public space. Still, this gives a sense of some of the approaches to the analysis of text responses from online surveys. Many of the findings are reproducible (and repeatable) in terms of outcomes, which is an important part of quantitative data analytics.

DISCUSSION

Many who design surveys usually use close-ended questions (T/F, multiple-choice, ranking, and other structured alternative options) to elicit responses from respondents because the responses are easy to represent and the summary data are readily available on most online survey platforms. On occasion, one of the multiple-choice selections may include "Other" and text fill-in options. Using close-ended questions can be limiting, however, based on the initial conceptualizations by the survey instrument creator. The potential of open-ended questions enriches what may be learned from survey respondents beyond the initial expectations of survey instrument creators. There is some early work on how to create elicitations that encourage more in-depth engagement by respondents. Some of these come from the learning space, with open-ended questions designed to develop cognitive skills and express their rationales for particular concepts (Lee, Kinzie, & Whittaker, 2012).

Applying computational text analytics to responses by the respective respondents not only informs on the target topic, but it may suggest ways to improve the survey instrument for later deployments. The answers may help survey designers elicit valuable data, ask difficult questions, iterate to acquire more in-depth data, encourage effusiveness (and data leakage) in respondents, trigger the subconscious and unconscious, and ultimately attain a wider range of textual responses.

Certainly, survey designs are not only evaluated for potential biasing from its structure, but there are implications external to the instrument. Researchers have to consider how to handle "sensitive" responses ethically from responses to open-ended questions (Lloyd & Devine, 2015). And political surveys have been found to have effects on the political opinions and actions of voters (Biondo, Pluchino, & Rapisarda, 2018), which have external implications on the research work.

If textual data is multi-faceted and informationally rich, "images are much higher dimensional, and typically more noisy than pure text" (Wu, Teney, Wang, Shen, Dick, & van den Hengel, 2017, p. 22). Further, "…images capture more of the richness of the real world, whereas natural language already represents a higher level of abstraction" (Wu, Teney, Wang, Shen, Dick, & van den Hengel, 2017, p. 22). Automated analyses of image sets, such as "visual question answering," which enables structured annotations of an image show a sense of promise for the future. The prompts to computers involve "an image and a question in natural language" (Wu, Teney, Wang, Shen, Dick, & van den Hengel, 2017, p. 21), and the computer programs combine machine vision and natural language processing to provide annotation of the images, with impressive accuracy. (In this context, the question to be answered was not created until runtime.)

The literature review, the description of the eight steps to building a survey with open-ended questions, and the cursory summary of some of the software tool functionalities for text analysis suggest that designing a survey purposefully with an understanding of how the data may be analyzed once captured is critical. At each of the eight steps, important knowledge and skills are required, to ensure that an online survey is comprehensive, ethical, professional, and effective.

FUTURE RESEARCH DIRECTIONS

This work makes a simple assertion that online surveys may be designed with more usable open-ended questions because of the computational text analyses that are possible. Eight steps have been suggested for the building of surveys based on quantitative, qualitative, and mixed methods approaches, specifically including open-ended questions.

1.   Research Design
2.   Survey Design
3.   Deployment
4.   Data Capture
5.   Data Cleaning
6.   Data Analysis
7.   Write-up
8.   Presentation

This work has addressed some common approaches, but there is a number of other tools in the commercial and open-source space that offer other ways to extract insights. Sequential ways of processing texts and conducting queries, and creating data visualizations may enable richer insights.

As various computational text analysis methods are harnessed for end-to-end online survey systems, their capabilities may also be studied for knowability.

With the prevalence of custom text analysis dictionaries and other light programs, the capabilities of these tools may also contribute to the field.

Another worthwhile angle may be to study the design of fully open-ended question surveys.

Visual question answering and other more sophisticated computational analysis techniques may enable the computational assessment of "file upload" questions, with the analysis of imagery and text with machine vision. These computational text and image analytics capabilities do not restrict human close reading, and the computational findings are still analyzed by the researcher. There is still the "human in the loop".

CONCLUSION

This chapter suggests that a broader strategic usage of open-ended questions in online surveys is warranted given the ability to manage and analyze such texts using computational text analyses.

REFERENCES

Andrews, D., Nonnecke, B., & Preece, J. (2003). Electronic survey methodology: A case study in reaching hard-to-involve Internet users. *International Journal of Human-Computer Interaction*, *16*(2), 185–210. doi:10.1207/S15327590IJHC1602_04

Arnon, S., & Reichel, N. (2009, April). Closed and open-ended question tools in a telephone survey about 'The Good Teacher.'. *Journal of Mixed Methods Research*, *3*(2), 172–196. doi:10.1177/1558689808331036

Biondo, A. E., Pluchino, A., & Rapisarda, A. (2018). Modeling surveys effects in political competitions. *Physica A*, *503*, 714–726. doi:10.1016/j.physa.2018.02.211

Brugidou, M. (2003). Argumentation and values: An analysis of ordinary political competence via an open-ended question. *International Journal of Public Opinion Research*, *15*(4), 413–430. doi:10.1093/ijpor/15.4.413

Covell, C. L., Sidani, S., & Ritchie, J. A. (2012). Does the sequence of data collection influence participants' responses to closed and open-ended questions? A methodological study. *International Journal of Nursing Studies*, *49*(6), 664–671. doi:10.1016/j.ijnurstu.2011.12.002 PMID:22204811

Crawford, S. D., Coupler, M. P., & Lamias, M. J. (2001, Summer). Web surveys: Perceptions of burden. *Social Science Computer Review*, *19*(2), 146–162. doi:10.1177/089443930101900202

Deneulin, P., Le Fur, Y., & Bavaud, F. (2016). Study of the polysemic term of minerality in wine: Segmentation of consumers based on their textual responses to an open-ended survey. *Food Research International*, *90*, 288–297. doi:10.1016/j.foodres.2016.11.004 PMID:29195884

Denscombe, M. (2008, August). The length of responses to open-ended questions: A comparison of online and paper questionnaires in terms of a mode effect. *Social Science Computer Review*, *26*(3), 359–368. doi:10.1177/0894439307309671

Dit Sourd, R. C., Zawojska, E., Mahieu, P.-A., & Louviere, J. (2018). Mitigating strategic misrepresentation of values in open-ended stated preference surveys by using negative reinforcement. *Journal of Choice Modelling*, *28*, 153–166. doi:10.1016/j.jocm.2018.06.001

Espina, A., & Figueroa, A. (2017). Why was this asked? Automatically recognizing multiple motivations behind community question-answering questions. *Expert Systems with Applications*, *80*, 126–135. doi:10.1016/j.eswa.2017.03.014

Falthzik, A. M., & Carroll, S. J. Jr. (1971). Rate of return for closed versus open-ended questions in a mail questionnaire survey of industrial organizations. *Psychological Reports*, *29*(3_suppl), 1121–1122. doi:10.2466/pr0.1971.29.3f.1121

Fricker, R. D., & Schonlau, M. (2012). Advantages and disadvantages of Internet research surveys: Evidence from the literature. In J. Hughes (Ed.), SAGE Internet Research Methods. London: SAGE Publications.

Gardner, M. K. (2018). The psychology of deep learning. In Z. Robert (Ed.), *Zheng's Strategies for Deep Learning with Digital Technology* (pp. 3–36). Hauppauge, NY: Nova Science Publishers, Inc.

Gendall, P., Menelaou, H., & Brennan, M. (1996). Open-ended questions: Some implications for mail survey research. *Marketing Bulletin*, *7*, 1–8.

Glasow, P.A. (2005, Apr.). Fundamentals of survey research methodology. *MITRE*, 1-1 to DI-1.

Holland, J. L., & Christian, L. M. (2009, May). The influence of topic interest and interactive probing on responses to open-ended questions in web surveys. *Social Science Computer Review*, *27*(2), 196–212. doi:10.1177/0894439308327481

Hsieh, H.-F., & Shannon, S. E. (2005, November). Three approaches to qualitative content analysis. *Qualitative Health Research*, *15*(9), 1277–1288. doi:10.1177/1049732305276687 PMID:16204405

Jackson, K. M., & Trochim, W. M. K. (2002, October). Concept mapping as an alternative approach for the analysis of open-ended survey responses. *Organizational Research Methods*, *5*(4), 307–336. doi:10.1177/109442802237114

Kondracki, N.L., Wellman, N.S., & Amundson, D.R. (2002). *Content analysis: Review of methods and their applications in nutrition education*. Report.

Kwak, N., & Radler, B. (2002). A comparison between mail and web surveys: Response pattern, respondent profile, and data quality. *Journal of Official Statistics*, *18*(2), 257–273.

Lacity, M. C., & Janson, M. A. (1994, Fall). Understanding qualitative data: A framework of text analysis methods. *Journal of Management Information Systems*, *11*(2), 137–155. doi:10.1080/07421222.1994.11518043

Lee, Y., Kinzie, M. B., & Whittaker, J. V. (2012). Impact of online support for teachers' open-ended questioning in pre-k science activities. *Teaching and Teacher Education*, *28*(4), 568–577. doi:10.1016/j.tate.2012.01.002

Leidich, A., Jayaweera, R., Arcara, J., Clawson, S., Chalker, C., & Rochat, R. (2018). Evaluating the feasibility and acceptability of sending pregnancy and abortion history surveys through SMS text messaging to help reach sustainable development goal 3. *International Journal of Medical Informatics*, *114*, 108–113. doi:10.1016/j.ijmedinf.2017.10.017 PMID:29100753

Lloyd, K., & Devine, P. (2015). The inclusion of open-ended questions on quantitative surveys of children: Dealing with unanticipated responses relating to child abuse and neglect. *Child Abuse & Neglect*, *48*, 200–207. doi:10.1016/j.chiabu.2015.03.021 PMID:25952476

Love, A. M. A., Butz, A. R., Usher, E. L., & Waiters, B. L. (2018). Open-ended response from early adolescents: Method matters. *Journal of Adolescence*, *67*, 31–34. doi:10.1016/j.adolescence.2018.05.007 PMID:29890346

Maloshonok, N., & Terentev, E. (2016). The impact of visual design and response formats on data quality in a web survey of MOOC students. *Computers in Human Behavior*, *62*, 506–515. doi:10.1016/j.chb.2016.04.025

O'Cathain, A., & Thomas, K. J. (2004). 'Any other comments?' Open questions on questionnaires—a bane or a bonus to research? *BMC Medical Research Methodology*, *4*(25), 1–7. PMID:15533249

Poncheri, R. M., Lindberg, J. T., Thompson, L. F., & Surface, E. A. (2008, July). A comment on employee surveys: Negativity bias in open-ended responses. *Organizational Research Methods*, *11*(3), 614–630. doi:10.1177/1094428106295504

Reynolds, T. W., Bostrom, A., Read, D., & Morgan, M. G. (2010). Now what do people know about global climate change? Survey studies of educated laypeople. *Risk Analysis*, *30*(10), 1520–1538. doi:10.1111/j.1539-6924.2010.01448.x PMID:20649942

Schwarz, N. (1999). Self-reports: How the questions shape the answers. *The American Psychologist*, *54*(2), 93–105. doi:10.1037/0003-066X.54.2.93

Schwarz, N., Hippler, H.-J., Deutsch, B., & Strack, F. (1985, Autumn). Response scales: Effects of category range on reported behavior and comparative judgments. *Public Opinion Quarterly*, *49*(3), 388–395. doi:10.1086/268936

Shapiro, M. J. (1970, Autumn). Discovering interviewer bias in open-ended survey responses. *Public Opinion Quarterly*, *34*(3), 412–415. doi:10.1086/267819

Smyth, J. D., Dillman, D. A., Christian, L. M., & McBride, M. (2009, May). Open-ended questions in web surveys: Can increasing the size of answer boxes and providing extra verbal instructions improve response quality? *Public Opinion Quarterly, 73*(2), 325–337. doi:10.1093/poq/nfp029

Sudman, S., & Bradburn, N. M. (1974). *Response effects in surveys: A review and synthesis.* Chicago: Aldine Publishing Company.

Tran, V.-T., Porcher, R., Falissard, B., & Ravaud, P. (2016). Point of data saturation was assessed using resampling methods in a survey with open-ended questions. *Journal of Clinical Epidemiology, 80*, 88–96. doi:10.1016/j.jclinepi.2016.07.014 PMID:27492788

Van Selm, M., & Jankowski, N. W. (2006). Conducting online surveys. *Quality & Quantity, 40*(3), 435–456. doi:10.100711135-005-8081-8

Wu, Q., Teney, D., Wang, P., Shen, C., Dick, A., & van den Hengel, A. (2017). Visual question answering: A survey of methods and datasets. *Computer Vision and Image Understanding, 163*, 21–40. doi:10.1016/j.cviu.2017.05.001

Zuell, C., Menold, N., & Körber, S. (2015). The influence of the answer box size on item nonresponse to open-ended questions in a web survey. *Social Science Computer Review, 33*(1), 115–122. doi:10.1177/0894439314528091

KEY TERMS AND DEFINITIONS

Close-Ended Questions: Questions that may be responded to with true/false, yes/no, or other multiple-choice options.

Cluster Analysis: Any of a class of statistical analysis techniques that group various contents (like words or data points) based on similarity or other forms of connectedness (often depicted in node-link graphs).

Codebook (Codeframe): The thematic categories that may be coded to that are relevant to a particular phenomenon or research target of interest (and these may be created from top-down coding as well as bottom-up coding).

Computational Text Analysis: The application of various counting, statistical analysis, dictionary comparison, and other techniques to capture information from natural language texts (and transcribed speeches).

Concept Map: A 2D diagram that shows interrelationships between words and concepts.

Coverage Error: A sampling error in survey deployment that does not involve sufficient random representation of the complete population's members.

Dendrogram: A data visualization that shows clustered words in structured interrelationships as branches on a tree (may be horizontal or vertical).

Dimensionality: The state of having multiple characteristics or attributes (with high dimensionality indicating many dimensions and low dimensionality indicating few dimensions).

Elicitation: The drawing out of information.

File-Upload Questions: Questions that may be responded to with the upload of any number of digital file types.

High-Burden: A descriptive term suggesting the level of investment needed for a survey respondent to engage with a survey instrument.

Linguistic Analysis: The scientific study of language.

Modality: A form or type (of survey, such as face-to-face, in-person; by telephone; by postal mail; by computer face-to-face; by paper face-to-face; online; mixed modal, and others).

N-Gram: A contiguous sequence of "n" items (words), from unigram (one-gram) to bigram, three-gram, four-gram, and so on.

Network Analysis: The depiction of objects and relationships.

Non-Substantive Option: A response of "don't know" on a survey that does not offer much in the way of informational value; the equivalent of avoiding an opportunity to answer or skipping an elicitation.

Open-Ended Questions: Questions that may be responded to with a variety of text responses (only limited by the length of the text).

Polysemous: Many-meaninged.

Population Segmentation: The partitioning of a human population to particular sub-groups with specified characteristics and preferences.

Psychometric: The objective measurement of various aspects of human personality.

Qualitative Cross-Tabulation Analysis: The integration of a cross-tabulation table with interview subjects/focus group speakers/survey respondents in the row data, and variables and themes in the column data to enable the identification of data patterns through computational means.

Semantic: Meaning-bearing (as in words in a language).

Sentiment Analysis: The labeling of words and phrases as positive or negative (in a binary way) or in various categories of positive to negative (on a continuum).

Stylometry: The statistical analysis (metrics) of style.

Text Corpus: A collection of written texts selected around particular topics and standards.

Theme Extraction: The identification of main ideas and/or topics from a text or collection of texts.

Topic Modeling: The extraction of topics within a piece of writing or set of written texts.

Treemap Diagram: A data visualization indicating the frequency of occurrence of particular words and/or n-grams.

Visual Question Answering: A new computational data analytics technique that enables computers to analyze an image or image sequence or set using computer vision and making observations of the target images.

Word Frequency Count: A computational technique that enables computers to count how many words of each time occur in a piece of writing or collection or text set.

Word Tree: A data visualization that depicts a target word or ngram/phrase and a number of lead-up and lead-away words to the target term to provide human users with a sense of the target word/phrase use contexts (for semantic meaning).

Chapter 8

Applying Qualitative Matrix Coding Queries and Qualitative Crosstab Matrices for Explorations of Online Survey Data

ABSTRACT

Two computation-enabled matrix-based analytics techniques have become more available for the analysis of text data, including from online surveys. These two approaches are (1) the qualitative matrix coding query and (2) the qualitative crosstab matrix, both in NVivo 12 Plus. The first approach enables insights about the coding applied to qualitative data, and the second enables the identification of data patterns based on case (ego or entity) attributes of survey respondents. The data analytics software has integrations with multiple online survey platforms (Qualtrics and Survey Monkey currently), and the automated coding of the data from these respective platforms and other software features enable powerful data analytics. This chapter provides insights as to some of what may be discoverable using both matrix-based techniques as applied to online survey data.

DOI: 10.4018/978-1-5225-8563-3.ch008

INTRODUCTION

Matrices, as exploratory data structures, have long been used in qualitative research to identify data patterns, surface fresh insights, and achieve other research and data analytics aims. They have been used to elicit information from survey respondents in visual ways (aka "graphic elicitation techniques") (Copeland & Agosto, 2012, pp. 514 – 517, pp. 519 - 524). For quantitative, qualitative, and mixed methods research, matrices have been a staple. In early days, they were completed manually, and in more recent years, they have been populated using computational means. Matrices are a basic data structure form: a rectangular (including) table consisting of row and column headers and then overlapping or intersecting cell data. For binary matrices, the cells are 1s (present) or 0s (not present); for intensity matrices, the cells are numbers, with higher numbers indicating higher intensities of counts or frequencies. Depending on their focuses and respective purposes in research, the different matrices have different names.

Since the early 1990s, qualitative data analytics suites have extended the power of computational matrices. These tools are referred to as a category of Computer Assisted Qualitative Data AnalysiS (CAQDAS). Software may be used to convert coding from qualitative data for statistical analysis in a mixed methods approach:

Such integration (of mixed methods studies data) is seen as occurring: (a) when text and numeric data are **combined** *in an analysis; (b) when data are* **converted** *from one form to another during analysis; or (c) when combination and conversion occur together iteratively or in generating blended data for further analyses. (Bazeley, Spring 2006, p. 64)*

These enablements broaden the types of available knowledge and askable questions in qualitative research. They complement the theory-based top-down-coded research by enabling reproducible research with objectively supported data.

This work introduces two core matrix applications in the NVivo 12 Plus software tool: (1) the qualitative matrix coding query and (2) the qualitative crosstab matrix. It also includes some references to some other lesser-known matrix queries (like Coding Comparison queries (based on a similarity matrix). [QSR International (Qualitative Solutions and Research) is the maker of NVivo, which was initially known as NUD*IST or "Non numerical Unstructured Data Indexing Searching and Theorizing software." NVivo originated in 1999.]

REVIEW OF THE LITERATURE

Matrices have over a 150 years of historical priors. An early precursor would be a mathematical array of numbers, represented in a rectangular form. These mathematics-based matrices have been around since the 1850s. They have been harnessed for quantitative data analysis for a number of applications, and these applications are integrated in any number of quantitative data analytics packages. These data matrices or data arrays may involve millions of variables that are managed through spreadsheet programs and statistical packages (and some databases).

At core, a matrix is just a basic structure. There are column headers representing columns of data, and there are row headers representing rows of data, and the intersecting cells between the row and the columns indicate intersections or overlaps between the particular column and row. (Table 1) These intersections show "associations" and suggest at a kind of relationship between the two variables (in the Column and Row), but much more needs to be understood for further understandings and further definitions of relationship (Positive association? Negative association? Curvilinear association? Causation? Precursor? Leading indicator? Lagging indicator? Orthogonal non-relationship? Others?)

Qualitative and mixed methods researchers harnessed matrices for qualitative data analytics (Miles & Huberman, May 1984, p. 24). By comparisons, these qualitative ones contain fewer variables and data cells but require much more analytical depth and theorizing for sensemaking. Qualitative matrices may be "matrix displays for words" (Miles & Huberman, May 1984, p. 26). This form may serve as a notetaking device for researchers, who may make observations and fill in the particular matrix cells. In these latter usages, descriptive matrices may contain more than numeric data:

The rows and columns of the matrix can include almost any aspect of the data: time periods, persons, groups, roles, event classes, settings, processes, key variables,

Table 1. A basic matrix structure

researcher or respondent explanations. The cell entries can be equally diverse, ranging from direct-quote raw data excerpts to key phrases, summaries, or quasi-scaled judgments. Such matrices both force and support analysis; rows and columns can be reordered, combined, or separated as new avenues of significance open up. Local contexts are seen holistically, not lost in dispersed narrative. (Miles & Huberman, May 1984, p. 26)

Sometimes, there is no *a priori* awareness of what will go into the matrix, based on theory, models, or frameworks. Other researchers observe: "The lists forming the matrix can be of individuals, roles, sites, topics, or properties of these, and can be organized in numerous ways, creating a large number of different types of matrices" (Maxwell & Miller, 2008, p. 469). The matrices may be "similarity-based and contiguity-based display…" (Maxwell & Miller, 2008, p. 469), with respective similar-variable segments placed in particular similar categories. The respective lists of "mutually exclusive categories" are created, and then researchers cross these "to create cells" (Maxwell & Miller, 2008, p. 469). In the analysis work, researchers may zoom in to look at a particular cell and the overlap between the particular column and row data. In qualitative crosstabulation matrices, there are also views based on the aggregated data (even if degrees of freedom, chi-squared measures, and p-values are not necessarily calculated).

In other cases, there are clearly determined approaches in the usages of the matrices. Even for mere description matrices, set up to "display categorized data in individual cells, just to observe what appears" (Averill, July 2002, p. 856), these may serve a lot of complex aims for research and analytics. The selection of data for particular purposes may be targeted for particular aims:

The range of descriptive matrix types is broad. In addition to the **checklist matrix** *(with indicators of a single-underlying variable), qualitative analysts have begun to explore* **time-ordered matrices** *displaying phenomena as they occurred chronologically; role-ordered matrices distributing data according to their sources (and/or targets) of attention; and* **conceptually-clustered matrices** *bringing together variables connected by theoretical ideas (e.g., a set of motives and attitudes relevant to innovation adoption). (Miles & Huberman, May 1984, p. 26)*

Some are "*conceptually-clustered matrices* bringing together variables connected by theoretical ideas" (Miles & Huberman, May 1984, p. 26). Such thematic analysis are traditionally theory-informed and top-down, but with the advancement of computational topic-modeling, bottom-up thematic analysis is also possible (albeit disconnected from a theoretical framework in the latter case unless a human-created customized coding dictionary is applied computationally). Some theme extractions involve word counting techniques, which are also part of qualitative research data analysis (Ryan & Bernard, 2003, p. 97).

Some matrices are "explanatory" ones set up to support "sorting out explanations, reasons, and causes for observed phenomena" (Miles & Huberman, May 1984, p. 26), based on respondent feedback. There are matrices set up to understand processes. Others are set up to understand system effects. Some are "process-outcome matrices" with some predictive applications. There are "reflective coding matrix" types (Scott & Howell, 2008). Regardless, qualitative matrices do require several core aspects of qualitative research: the identification of themes and the definition of a relevant unit of analysis.

Identifying Themes in Qualitative and Mixed Methods Research

Coding themes itself is a challenging and difficult process, much less coding within the constraints of a qualitative matrix. This coding work requires expertise in the field and in content analysis, along with deductive, inductive, and abductive logic. Coding involves the identification of what is important from the raw data. The coding phase is of central importance in qualitative data analysis (Wong & Ping, 2008). Said another way: "Codes are the building blocks for theory or model building and the foundation on which the analyst's arguments rest. Implicitly or explicitly, they embody the assumptions underlying the analysis" (MacQueen, McLellan, Kay, & Milstein, June 1998, p. 31). Manual codebooks, human-created ones, ideally contain six components: "the code, a brief definition, a full definition, guidelines for when to use the code, guidelines for when not to use the code, and examples" (MacQueen, McLellan, Kay, & Milstein, June 1998, p. 32). Ideally, they should achieve saturation, or inclusion of all the concepts that are relevant to the studied phenomenon (at least via the available acquired data).

One research team points to the many angles that may be taken in understanding "themes" is a particular domain:

What other kinds of relationships might be of interest? Casagrande and Hale (1967) suggested looking for attributes (e.g., X is Y), contingencies (e.g., if X, then Y), functions (e.g., X is a means of affecting Y), spatial orientations (e.g., X is close to Y), operational definitions (e.g., X is a tool for doing Y), examples (e.g., X is an instance of Y), comparisons (e.g., X resembles Y), class inclusions (X is a member of class Y), synonyms (e.g., X is equivalent to Y), antonyms (e.g., X is the negation of Y), provenience (e.g., X is the source of Y), and circularity (e.g., X is defined as X). (Ryan & Bernard, 2003, p. 92)

As researchers have noted, there are no simple understandings of how to create themes. Sometimes, what is not seen in a dataset is as relevant as what is observable (Ryan & Bernard, 2003, pp. 92 - 93).

In many cases, the identified themes are coded as "nodes" in qualitative and mixed methods data analytics suites. These codes (themes) themselves may be analyzed for "code frequencies, code-co-occurrences, (and) saliency" or how often code is applied to text segments or are related to particular respondents, "isolated pairs of codes applied to text segment and associated with a unique respondent," and "number of times that a code occurred within a combination of codes delineated by either text segments or respondents" (Guest & McLellan, May 2003, p. 191). Analyzing code matrices may provide meta-awareness of particular data patterns and may shed light on the research itself.

Identifying the Unit of Analysis

In qualitative analytics, the definition of the "unit of analysis" affects "the credibility of content analysis" (Elo, et al., Jan. – Mar. 2014, p. 5). If the unit is too coarse, the understandings may be too polysemic; if the unit is too narrow, "fragmentation" may result (p. 5). One authoring team writes, "The most suitable unit of analysis will be sufficiently large to be considered as a whole but small enough to be a relevant meaning unit during the analysis process" (Elo, et al., Jan. – Mar. 2014, p. 5). In computational analytics systems, the levels of granularity on which code may be applied may be cells (for spreadsheet program data), sentences, and paragraphs, from the smallest to the largest (NVivo 12 Plus). A unit may also be the level at which qualitative data (usually in textual format or proxy textual format) may be at the level of a node (in codebooks that may have hierarchical codes, with parent nodes, child nodes, grandchild nodes, and so on). How notes are abstracted into codes determines units of analyses. Qualitative crosstabulation analyses based on respondent attributes sets up each human case (ego or entity, individual or group) as a unit of analysis; these are also referred to as "contingency tables" that enable "correspondence analysis". How the data is set up and then how the queries are created in the respective matrices determine what questions are "askable" and with what level of certitude.

Related Data Visualizations

Also, qualitative, quantitative and mixed methods matrices do not just have to be represented as data arrays in table format. They can be represented in data visualizations of various types, such as cluster analyses (Guest & McLellan, May 2003) in 2D and 3D, treemap diagrams, dendrograms (horizontal and vertical), ring lattice graphs, bar charts, pareto charts, pie charts, sunburst diagrams, and others.

Matrix Quality

A matrix may be partially specified and shed light on one aspect of research work or the studied phenomenon. For a full research study, a number of matrix queries may have to be created for informational value. In other cases, the matrix may be at the heart of the research, and its variables may include full saturation, with all related variables included. Matrices may be used for (1) the research (notetaking, visual elicitation) and for (2) the data analytics (data reduction, matrix coding queries, qualitative crosstab analyses, and similarity matrices, among others). Matrix analysis may even be used to assess the quality of the research study (3) "an ancillary strategy…in assessing the trustworthiness of a qualitative study (March, 1990, as cited in Averill, July 2002, p. 856).

The basic binary matrix contains either 1's (present) or 0's (not present) in the intersecting cells. Similarity matrices are tables of scores "that express numerical distances—or likeness—between data points" (Namey, Guest, Thairu, & Johnson, 2008, p. 147). Case-based matrices may be built around individual respondents as well as aggregated cases which are similar (Namey, Guest, Thairu, & Johnson, 2008, p. 147). Matrices enable "multidimensional scaling" for differing levels of granularity to coarseness. The matrix analysis serves "as a complementary analytic strategy in qualitative inquiry" (Averill, July 2002, p. 855).

Classic matrices contained structured data, data labeled by the respective data label in the column header. Qualitative matrices may contain numbers and textual data in qualitative research, but they may also include URLs (uniform resource locators), thumbnail and other imagery, and other types of semi-structured contents. (Some initially suggested that non-numerical data were "unstructured," but this term has fallen out of favor given the inherency of structure in text, imagery, audio, video, and so on.) This is partially because one of the core precepts of qualitative research is that virtually everything has informational value.

In qualitative and mixed methods research as in most forms of hard science research, there is no absolute assertion of absolute proof but a collection of evidence that may suggest a convergence to a pseudo-consensus. Conclusions are held lightly in qualitative data analytics: "The competent researcher holds these conclusions lightly, maintaining openness and skepticism, but the conclusions are still there, inchoate and vague at first, then increasingly explicit and grounded, to use the classic term of Glaser and Strauss (1967)" (Miles & Huberman, May 1984, p. 26). Where quantitative research strives for "internal validity, external validity, reliability, and objectivity," qualitative research strives for "credibility, transferability, dependability, and confirmability" respectively, to ensure research quality and rigor (Anfara, Brown, & Mangione, Oct. 2002, p. 30). There are weaknesses to qualitative matrices, too. If something was not observed by the researcher or not thought to be important, and if no data was collected about a particular phenomenon, that absence will not necessarily be seen in a qualitative matrix analysis. Some matrices may be sparse, with empty cells (representing no collected data), and how those should be handled will inform what can be asserted from matrix data.

In the research literature, some qualitative researchers have expressed skepticism of what computer software (via CAQDAS) may bring to qualitative data analysis. Qualitative and mixed methods data analytics software suites have been compared to an "efficient clerk, research assistant or Trojan horse" (Morison & Moir, 1998, p. 106). These are not necessarily a standard part of qualitative researcher practice, with many still using butcher paper, sticky notes, Sharpie pens, for engaging data viscerally and mentally. Others see CAQDAS techniques as enabling "matrix intersection search" (Bazeley, 2002, p. 232) and "truly integrated analysis" (Bazeley, 2002, p. 229), with more reproducibility and computational precision. A mixed quantitative and qualitative approach to research allows researchers to "analyze more than just a handful of cases" (Ragin, 1987, as cited in Rihoux, 2003, p. 353) and to not unthinkingly go to dichotomization but "theoretically informed" (Rihoux, 2003, p. 358). In qualitative matrices, the assumption is that the variables are non-parametric ones.

Certainly, it is not a small decision about whether to integrate qualitative analytics software into research. The choices of whether to go manual or electronic for coding qualitative data is "dependent on the size of the project, the funds and the time available, and the inclination and expertise of the researcher" among others (Basit, Spring 2003, p. 143). One team applied a systematized decision tree analysis to consider whether or not to analyze qualitative datasets using NVivo. They considered various factors including "training time, establishing inter-coder reliability, number and length of documents, coding time, coding structure, use of automated coding, and possible need for separate databases or additional supporting software" (Auld, et al., 2007, p. 37). The comfort level of the researchers is important. Qualitative data is "not fundamentally a mechanical or technical exercise. It is a dynamic, intuitive and creative process of inductive reasoning, thinking and theorizing" (Basit, Spring 2003, p. 143).

QUALITATIVE MATRIX CODING QUERIES AND QUALITATIVE CROSSTAB ANALYSES FROM ONLINE SURVEY DATA

A matrix is part of a research context and sequence. This is depicted in Figure 1, with three main applications of matrices—to engage in visual (or graphic) elicitation, to analyze data, and to evaluate the research. The two main matrix-creation approaches will be described—the matrix coding query and the crosstab analysis, but there are other types of matrix coding like autocoded topic modeling, sentiment analysis, coding comparison, and other types, which will be mentioned lightly.

Qualitative matrices may be used as part of hypothesizing, with *a priori* theory-supported concepts of what might be found in matrices. Qualitative matrices may be used in an exploratory way to search for data patterns. Autocoding methods may enable both answers to hypothesizing and scope for exploratory analysis. Also, abductive logic applied to research evidence may result in "new hypotheses and theories" (Timmermans & Tavory, 2012, p. 167), which suggests value to post-hoc hypothesizing.

Basic Steps

What are some basic steps to setting up a project in NVivo 12 Plus to enable qualitative matrix queries and explorations of both types (matrix coding queries, qualitative crosstab analyses) from online survey data?

1. First, capture the Qualtrics API Token from the user account.
2. Open up a project in NVivo 12 Plus. Go to the import tab, the Survey button, and Qualtrics.
3. Input the API token in the window.
4. The next window populates with the respective surveys by title, whether the survey is currently active or not, the date created, the date most recently modified, the numbers of recorded responses, and other information. Identify the survey of interest. Select it.

Figure 1. Matrices used in qualitative and mixed methods research involving online surveys

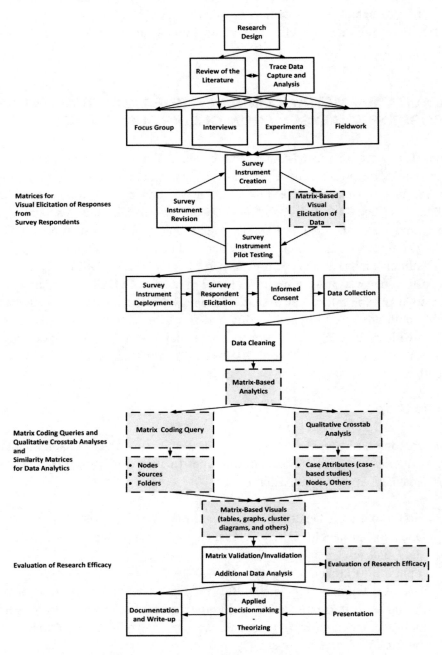

Matrices Used in Qualitative and Mixed Methods Research involving Online Surveys

5.   The software will offer to identify respondents as cases, close-ended questions as attributes, and open-ended questions as nodes (Figure 2).
6.   Follow through with the process. Lastly, allow the software to autocode the themes and the sentiment. (Figure 3)

The process is described within NVivo 12 Plus.

Figure 2. "Welcome to the survey import wizard" window in Nvivo 12 Plus

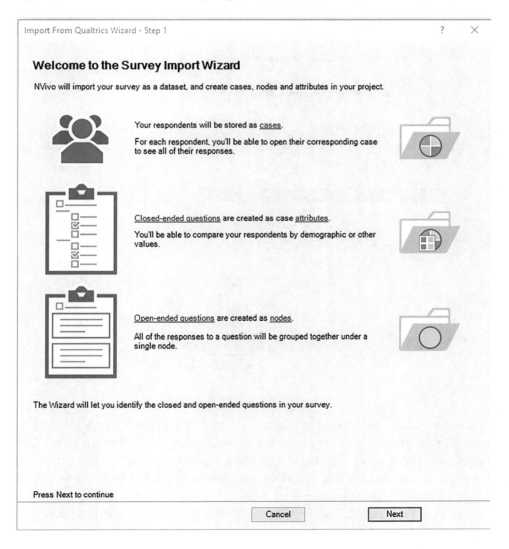

Figure 3. "Import from qualtrics wizard" and autocoding in NVivo 12 Plus

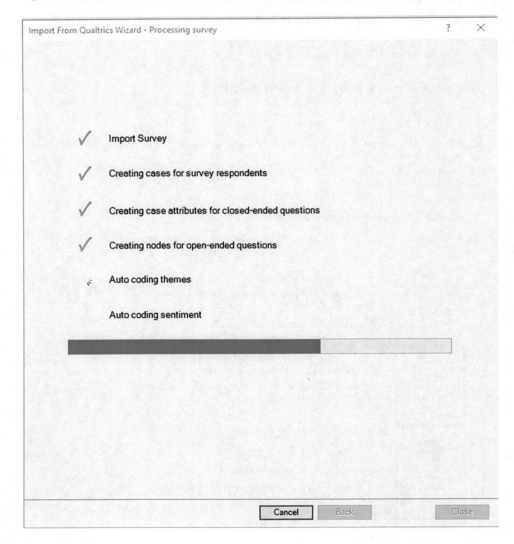

Before setting up the two matrix queries, it may help to see what results from the autocoding of the online survey contents. Figures 4 and 5 show three main top-level topics: bag, loss, and significant loss. The first is a sunburst diagram and only shows the top-level themes, and the latter is a treemap diagram that includes the related sub-topics. For example, under loss, there is "significant loss, significance loss, significance loss, weight," and others. Under "bag," there is "polypropylene bag,

Figure 4. Auto-extracted Top-level Topics from Open-ended Text-based Survey Responses (in a sunburst diagram)

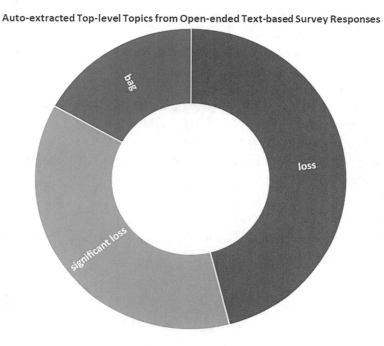

Figure 5. Auto-extracted top-level and related sub-level topics from open-ended text-based survey responses (in a treemap diagram)

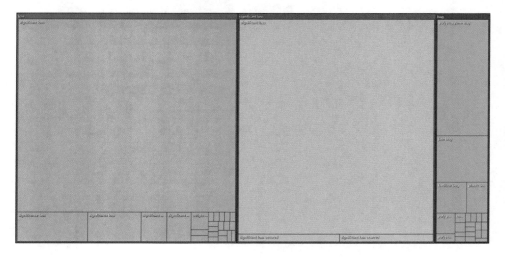

fertilizer bag, plastic bag," and others. (Misspelled words were treated as different phenomenon. If researchers need to, they may clean the data and then re-run these. For this chapter, the work was run in the raw.) The two data visualizations were derived from underlying autocoded data matrices.

In terms of sentiment, the text-responses of the survey takers were categorized first as either neutral or sentimental language, and the sentimental language was then categorized in one of four sets: very negative, moderately negative, moderately positive, and very positive. The intensity matrix shows a clustering of intensified sentiment ("moderately negative" and "moderately positive") around significant losses of crops (Figure 6). This figure was partially redacted.

A treemap diagram from this same sentiment data showed some negative sentiment around pesticide use (Figure 7).

Figure 6. Auto-extracted sentiment analysis of survey responses with an intensity of emotions around issues of crop loss

		A : Very negative	B : Moderately negative	C : Moderately positive	D : Very positive
1 : Nodes\\Crop~		0	0	0	0
2 : Nodes\\Crop~		1	4	0	0
3 : Nodes\\Crop~		1	1	0	1
4 : Nodes\\Crop~		0	0	1	0
5 : Nodes\\Crop~		0	1	0	0
6 : Nodes\\Crop~		1	6	0	0
7 : Nodes\\Crop~		0	0	0	0
8 : Nodes\\Crop~	nificant losse...	0	51	62	0
9 : Nodes\\Crop~	nificant losse...	0	7	17	0
10 : Nodes\\Crop~	gnificant loss...	2	58	34	0
11 : Nodes\\Crop~	gnificant loss...	2	46	36	0
12 : Nodes\\Crop~	gnificant loss...	1	34	46	0
13 : Nodes\\Crop~	gnificant loss...	0	9	24	0
14 : Nodes\\Crop~	gnificant loss...	0	67	80	1
15 : Nodes\\Crop~	gnificant loss...	0	64	59	0
16 : Nodes\\Crop~	gnificant loss...	3	44	24	0
17 : Nodes\\Crop~	gnificant loss...	0	70	72	0
18 : Nodes\\Crop~	gnificant loss...	1	64	81	2
19 : Nodes\\Crop~		0	0	0	0
20 : Nodes\\Crop~	other informat...	1	14	0	0
21 : Nodes\\Crop~	ved in the cur...	0	0	0	0
22 : Nodes\\Crop~	ume per day	0	0	0	0
23 : Nodes\\Crop~	in your grain fr...	0	0	0	0
24 : Nodes\\Crop~	asing control ...	0	2	3	1
25 : Nodes\\Crop~	te number of t...	0	0	0	0
26 : Nodes\\Crop~	to market for...	0	1	1	0
27 : Nodes\\Crop~	ame in a give...	0	0	0	0
28 : Nodes\\Crop~	ame in a give...	0	0	0	0
29 : Nodes\\Crop~	ame in a give...	0	0	0	0
30 : Nodes\\Crop~	ame in a give...	0	0	0	0
31 : Nodes\\Crop~	ame in a give...	0	0	0	0
32 : Nodes\\Crop~	ame in a give...	0	0	0	0
33 : Nodes\\Crop~	ame in a give...	0	0	0	0
34 : Nodes\\Crop~	ame in a give...	0	0	0	0
35 : Nodes\\Crop~	ame in a give...	0	0	0	0
36 : Nodes\\Crop~		0	0	0	0
37 : Nodes\\Crop~		0	0	0	0
38 : Nodes\\Crop~		0	0	0	0
39 : Nodes\\Crop~		0	0	0	0
40 : Nodes\\Crop~		0	1	0	0
41 : Nodes\\Crop~		0	0	0	0
42 : Nodes\\Crop~		0	0	0	0

Figure 7. Identifying negative sentiment around pesticide use

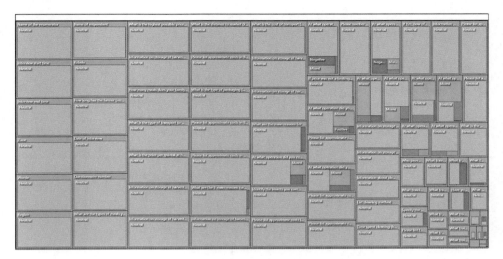

The software enables searching for particular commenting around terms of interest, like "fertilizer" or "crop." The resulting word trees are interactive and can bring researchers to the actual source to read the full context of the respective comments on the survey (Figures 8 and 9).

It is also possible to run a frequency word count (which results in a matrix) to export a word cloud (Figure 10) to capture a gist of the focuses of the textual contents. Had there been sufficient words, this data could be shown as a 2D or 3D cluster analysis, hierarchical word tree (dendrogram), or ring lattice graph, among others, within this software tool.

The Qualitative Matrix Coding Query

A matrix coding query enables a researcher to set up a matrix's rows and columns with various elements from the project. It enables asking particular questions, such as the following:

- Which sources provided the most insights for particular parts of the codebook?
- Which parts of the codebook resulted in the most coding?

Figure 8. "Fertilizer" word tree from online survey data responses

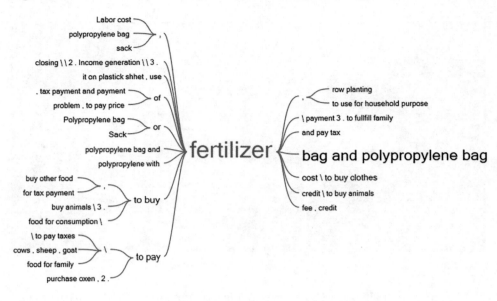

Figure 9. "Crop" word tree from online survey data responses

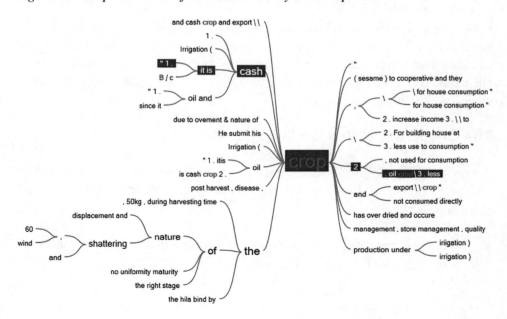

Figure 10. Word frequency count word cloud from open-ended survey questions (from a matrix table)

- If the data is longitudinal, what were the coding data patterns from time period to time period?
- And others…

Certainly, the researcher would also be asking, "Why?"

Figure 11 shows a resulting pareto chart from a qualitative coding query of autocoded themes and their frequency in terms of the whole set of online survey data responses.

Figure 11. Autocoded themes from the full set of survey respondents' text responses (in a pareto chart)

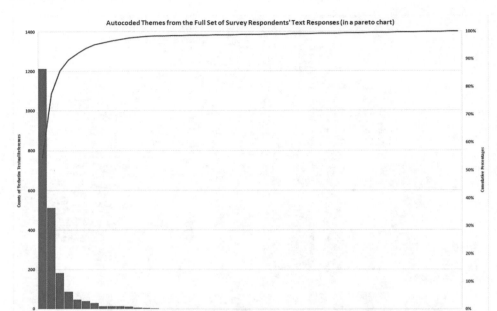

The Qualitative Crosstab Matrix

A qualitative crosstab matrix enables the creation of crosstabs based on respondent attributes (sociodemographic data, fixed opinions, and other features) and various captured coding. These types of matrices also require prior lead-up work in terms of the research, the capture of accurate sociodemographic data, the correct ingestion of data into the project, the prior (manual and / or computational) coding, and so on.

What are some askable questions using the computational qualitative crosstab matrix?

- What is the relationship between particular respondent attributes and observed expressed attitudes?
- Respondent attributes and general sentiments? Sentiments on particular questions? Sentiments on particular topics?

- Respondent attributes and topics of interest (based on particular question elicitations)?
- Individual cases and expressed attitudes, sentiments, and topics of interest?
- Combined groups and expressed attitudes, sentiments, and topics of interest?
- And others…

Figures 12 and 13 used as two attributes primary and secondary sources of income set against autoextracted themes from textual responses to open-ended question elicitations. One observation from this matrix is that those engaged in

Figure 12. Livestock as a primary source of income for those with observed concerns in survey responses (in column 8)

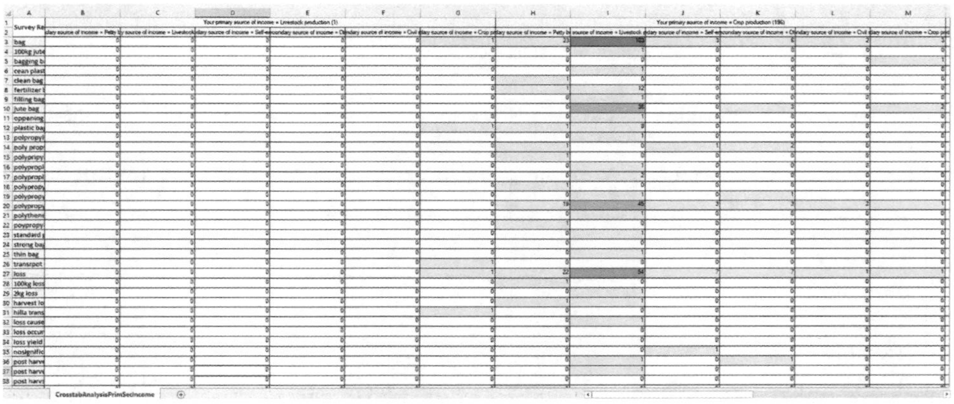

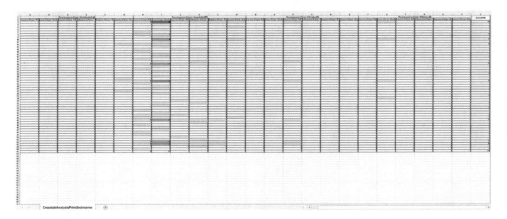

Figure 13. Primary and secondary sources of income in respondent attributes vs. autocoded topics

livestock production as a primary source of income have more outsized observations of concerns regarding crop loss and polypropylene bags. In this real world dataset, other attributes of the respondents may be studied such as the family sizes, education levels, lifestyle experiences, physical locations, specific crops, and others, compared against particular themes (auto-extracted and manually extracted), and so on. Both of the matrices here are multi-dimensional ones, but the software enables a zoomed-in view, down to two variables (one on the columns and one on the rows).

Another matrix approach is to run an inter-coder consistency (or similarity) matrix, comparing individual coders, or individual coding teams, or human coders and a machine coder… A basic similarity matrix looks like Table 2. The results of the similarity coding will report the data out in a matrix, with Cohen's Kappa and other calculations.

Table 2. The general structure of a similarity matrix

Coder 1/ Coder 2 (or Groups)	Variable / Attribute 1	Variable / Attribute 2	Variable / Attribute 3	Variable / Attribute 4	Variable / Attribute 5	Variable / Attribute 6
Variable / Attribute 1						
Variable / Attribute 2						
Variable / Attribute 3						
Variable / Attribute 4						
Variable / Attribute 5						
Variable / Attribute 6						
Total Counts						
Percentage Agreement or Disagreement						

DISCUSSION

This work provided walkthroughs of two types of common computationally-enabled matrix explorations using the NVivo 12 Plus qualitative data analytics software: (1) the qualitative matrix coding query and (2) the qualitative crosstab matrix.

As noted before, matrices may be used to...

- Elicit information visually,
- Identify patterns in data,
- Identify patterns in survey respondent answers to questions (based on sociodemographics, opinions, geography, and other attributes and / or mixed of attributes),
- Suggest decision making directions,
- Determine follow-on research, and others.

The software also enables other types of matrix setups such as from word frequency counts, coding comparison queries (built on similarity matrices), and others. While these enablements may not be as directly theoretically aligned as manual coding, these computational approaches build on the lead-up research and the manual coding of human researchers. These may complement manual coding.

Also, while matrices may not be used to present some data, there are benefits to understanding some of the maths going on behind these constructs and / or structural effects of such matrices. Also, all data tables in NVivo 12 Plus are exportable to Excel or SPSS formats, for additional data analysis and various other data visualizations.

FUTURE RESEARCH DIRECTIONS

Future research in this area may be to describe effective applications of just such manual- and computational enabled matrices in different research cases. Perhaps different software tools may be described with different enablements. Perhaps other sequences of matrix harnessing may be described from different research contexts.

CONCLUSION

This work focused on two main types of matrices in NVivo 12 Plus, a leading CAQDAS tool. This explored the qualitative matrix coding query and some of its basic capabilities as well as the qualitative crosstab matrix. As noted, there are word frequency count matrices, similarity matrices, sentiment analysis matrices, and others, enabled within this technology, in addition to a raft of other data analytics tools.

REFERENCES

Anfara, V. A. Jr, Brown, K. M., & Mangione, T. L. (2002, October). Qualitative analysis on stage: Making the research process more public. *Educational Researcher*, *31*(7), 28–38. doi:10.3102/0013189X031007028

Auld, G. W., Diker, A., Bock, M. A., Boushey, C. J., Bruhn, C. M., Cluskey, M., ... Zaghloul, S. (2007). Development of a decision tree to determine appropriateness of NVivo in analyzing qualitative data sets. *Journal of Nutrition Education and Behavior*, *39*(1), 37–47. doi:10.1016/j.jneb.2006.09.006 PMID:17276326

Averill, J. B. (2002, July). Matrix analysis as a complementary analytic strategy in qualitative inquiry. *Qualitative Health Research*, *12*(6), 855–866. doi:10.1177/104973230201200611 PMID:12109729

Basit, T. N. (2003, Summer). Manual or electronic: The role of coding in qualitative data analysis. *Educational Research*, *45*(2), 143–154. doi:10.1080/0013188032000133548

Bazeley, P. (2002). The evolution of a project involving an integrated analysis of structured qualitative and quantitative data: From N3 to NVivo. *International Journal of Social Research Methodology*, *54*(3), 229–243. doi:10.1080/13645570210146285

Bazeley, P. (2006, Spring). The contribution of computer software to integrating qualitative and quantitative data and analyses. *Research in the Schools*, *13*(1), 64–74.

Copeland, A. J., & Agosto, D. E. (2012). Diagrams and relational maps: The use of graphic elicitation techniques with interviewing for data collection, analysis, and display. *International Journal of Qualitative Methods*, *11*(5), 513–533. doi:10.1177/160940691201100501

Elo, S., Kääriäinen, M., Kanste, O., Pölkki, T., Utrainen, K., & Kyngäs, H. (2014, Jan. – Mar.). *Qualitative content analysis: A focus on trustworthiness*. SAGE Open. DOI: 10.1177/2150244014522633

Guest, G., & McLellan, E. (2003). Distinguishing the trees from the forest: Applying cluster analysis to thematic qualitative data. *Field Methods*, *15*(2), 186–201. doi:1 0.1177/1525822X03015002005

MacQueen, K. M., McLellan, E., Kay, K., & Milstein, B. (1998, June). Codebook development for team-based qualitative analysis. *Cultural Anthropology Methods*, *10*(2), 31–36.

Maxwell, J. A., & Miller, B. A. (2008). Categorizing and connecting strategies in qualitative data analysis. In P. Leavy & S. Hesse-Biber (Eds.), *Handbook of emergent methods*. New York: Guilford Press.

Miles, M. B., & Huberman, A. M. (1984, May). Drawing valid meaning from qualitative data: Toward a shared craft. *Educational Researcher*, *13*(5), 20–30. doi:10.3102/0013189X013005020

Morison, M., & Moir, J. (1998). The role of computer software in the analysis of qualitative data: Efficient clerk, research assistant or Trojan horse? *Journal of Advanced Nursing*, *28*(1), 106–116. doi:10.1046/j.1365-2648.1998.00768.x PMID:9687137

Namey, E., Guest, G., Thairu, L., & Johnson, L. (2008). Data reduction techniques for large qualitative data sets. *Handbook for Team-Based Qualitative Research*, *2*(1), 137–161.

Rihoux, B. (2003). Bridging the gap between the qualitative and quantitative worlds? A retrospective and prospective view on qualitative comparative analysis. *Field Methods*, *15*(4), 351–365. doi:10.1177/1525822X03257690

Ryan, G. W., & Bernard, H. R. (2003). Techniques to identify themes. *Field Methods*, *15*(1), 85–109. doi:10.1177/1525822X02239569

Scott, K. W., & Howell, D. (2008). Clarifying analysis and interpretation in grounded theory: Using a conditional relationship guide and reflective coding matrix. *International Journal of Qualitative Methods*, *7*(2), 1–15. doi:10.1177/160940690800700201

Timmermans, S., & Tavory, I. (2012). Theory construction in qualitative research: From grounded theory to abductive analysis. *Sociological Theory*, *30*(3), 167–186. doi:10.1177/0735275112457914

Wong, L. P., & Ping, W. L. (2008). Data analysis in qualitative research: A brief guide to using NVivo. *Malaysian Family Physician*, *3*(1), 14–20. PMID:25606106

KEY TERMS AND DEFINITIONS

Binary Matrix: A rectangular data table that records the absence or presence of a particular phenomenon in the cells indicating overlaps between the respective row and column headers.

Matrix: A data table with fixed numbers of rows and columns, with each representing a variable or attribute or other phenomenon, and the overlapping cells capturing the incidence or intensity of a phenomenon.

Matrix Coding Query: An exploratory query that involves defining row and column variables for a constructed matrix, which may include a combination of coding nodes, source contents, folder contents, and other contents in the project file.

Qualitative Matrix: A data table structure involving qualitative and/or mixed methods research data (often in textual format).

Relational Matrix: A data table with similar variables in the column headers and the row headers to enable the identification of the presence of a relationship between variables or not (in a binary matrix) or the intensity of a relationship between variables or not (in an intensity matrix); resulting data can be represented as a relational network graph.

Similarity Matrix: A data table that compares the amount of similarity and difference between the coding of two different coders or respective coding teams.

Conclusion

Sometimes, in thinking of future research potentials, one can do a back-of-the-napkin gaps analysis. It goes something like this: What has already been covered, and what has not yet been covered? Sometimes, depending on the topic, the space is so unexplored that such maps would be unnecessarily limiting. That seems to be the current case in terms of ways that people can design online surveys and exploit the available data from them. If pressed, I would have some ideas.

- What are creative graphic elicitation methods in research using online survey research suites?
- What are some full-text-response-only types of surveys out in the wild?
- What are effective ways to harness simulations in online survey research? Interactive videos?
- What are some effective ways to use automated agents in online survey research?
- What are some fully automated survey elicitations, and how are these used effectively?
- What are some methods for longitudinal survey-based research? Sequential survey-based research?
- What are some useful manual and semi-automated and fully automated codebooks that may be used against online survey data?
- What are some machine learning types of analytics applied to online survey data? Artificial intelligence applications?
- What are inventive methods for question design and item analysis?
- What are some inspired ways to validate/invalidate online survey research instruments?
- What are some innovative ways to conduct online conjoint analyses?
- What are some design methods for going global with online survey instruments?
- What are some ways to integrate an online survey with social media affordances for richer data elicitations and knowledge captures?

These are some early questions, and they are only a small part of what is clearly possible. With the respective platforms evolving all the time and innovative researchers creating new methods continuously, this space is a highly dynamic one. There are dedicated platforms to elicit insights about particular topics. There are data markets in which people vote on where they assume the world is going as a kind of predictive tool. "Surveying" in the traditional sense is evolving, along with a datafication environment that is harvesting information everywhere.

I look forward to seeing what others come up with in this space.

Shalin Hai-Jew
Kansas State University, USA
March 2019

Glossary

Attribute: A feature.

Binary Matrix: A rectangular data table that records the absence or presence of a particular phenomenon in the cells indicating overlaps between the respective row and column headers.

Branching Logic: Conditionals that determine the differentiated sequential paths of different survey respondents.

Close-Ended Questions: Questions that may be responded to with true/false, yes/no, or other multiple-choice options.

Cluster Analysis: Any of a class of statistical analysis techniques that group various contents (like words or data points) based on similarity or other forms of connectedness (often depicted in node-link graphs).

Codebook (Codeframe): The thematic categories that may be coded to that are relevant to a particular phenomenon or research target of interest (and these may be created from top-down coding as well as bottom-up coding).

Computational Text Analysis: The application of various counting, statistical analysis, dictionary comparison, and other techniques to capture information from natural language texts (and transcribed speeches).

Concept Map: A 2D diagram that shows interrelationships between words and concepts.

Concourse: A full created selection of possible statements (from which a subset or "Q sample" is drawn for the q-sort activity).

Conjoint Analysis: A type of choice-based experiment in which respondents indicate their preferences among a selection of attributes related to a particular choice-space (product, service, or other real-world and/or theoretical decision space).

Conjointedness: The combination of all factors involved.

Consensus: Consent, agreement.

Coverage Error: A sampling error in survey deployment that does not involve sufficient random representation of the complete population's members.

Cross-Tabulation Analysis: A data table or matrix that compares measures of the included variables (and that may be used to identify associational data patterns in a joint frequency distribution).

Crosswalk Analysis: A technique used to identify similarities and differences between two different systems (of a type or of different types) to aid in understandings, decision making, planning, and other applications; a bridging technique.

Data Pattern: Descriptive features and tendencies of focal data.

Debriefing: An elicitation of information to better understand a phenomenon or event.

Degrees of Freedom: The number of variables in a system (including in a cross-tabulation analysis or contingency table).

Delphi Study: A type of research involving experts, who engage in single- or multi-stage rounds of questions and other elicitations, in order to understand elusive future events or other topics.

Dendrogram: A data visualization that shows clustered words in structured interrelationships as branches on a tree (may be horizontal or vertical).

Dimensionality: The state of having multiple characteristics or attributes (with high dimensionality indicating many dimensions and low dimensionality indicating few dimensions).

Discussion Leader: Facilitator of a Delphi study.

Display Logic: Conditionals that determine whether particular survey respondents are able to view particular blocks or questions (or other parts of an online survey).

Dissensus: Dissent, disagreement.

E-Delphi Study: An electronic Delphi study deployed off of a socio-technical platform, such as a dedicated platform, an online survey platform, or social media platform.

Elicitation: The drawing out of information.

Expert Panel: The individuals who have varying levels of expertise in a particular domain, mixed-domain, or peripheral domain.

Factor Analysis: A quantitative statistical analysis approach to identify underlying (latent) factors or components in observed or survey data to understand the most influential factors on a construct.

Factor Interpretation: The definition and framing of an identified factor from a statistical factor analysis based on its component parts.

Factor Scores: A numerical value showing a respondent's relative standing on a factor.

File-Upload Questions: Questions that may be responded to with the upload of any number of digital file types.

Graphic Elicitation: Visual elicitation, the use of a visual construct to elicit responses from research respondents.

High-Burden: A descriptive term suggesting the level of investment needed for a survey respondent to engage with a survey instrument.

Linguistic Analysis: The scientific study of language.

Matrix: A data table with fixed numbers of rows and columns, with each representing a variable or attribute or other phenomenon, and the overlapping cells capturing the incidence or intensity of a phenomenon.

Matrix Coding Query: An exploratory query that involves defining row and column variables for a constructed matrix, which may include a combination of coding nodes, source contents, folder contents, and other contents in the project file.

MaxDiff (Maximum Difference Scaling, Best-Worst Scaling): A paired comparison method in which respondents identify their best and worst attributes among a set, which reveals a number of other ranked preferences among paired sets.

Modality: A form or type (of survey, such as face-to-face, in-person; by telephone; by postal mail; by computer face-to-face; by paper face-to-face; online; mixed modal, and others).

Network Analysis: The depiction of objects and relationships.

N-Gram: A contiguous sequence of "n" items (words), from unigram (one-gram) to bigram, three-gram, four-gram, and so on.

Non-Substantive Option: A response of "don't know" on a survey that does not offer much in the way of informational value; the equivalent of avoiding an opportunity to answer or skipping an elicitation.

Null Hypothesis: The assertion that the observed results of the research may be a result of random chance than anything else acting on the variables.

Online Survey: A structured information elicitation conducted online.

Open-Access Online Delphi Studies (OAODS): Often-continuous online (electronic) Delphi studies that involve open links that self-professed experts may access and respond to (requiring validation of expertise).

Open-Ended Questions: Questions that may be responded to with a variety of text responses (only limited by the length of the text).

Part-Worth (Attribute Importance Scores, Level Values, Utility Score, Part Utility): A utility measurement ("util") that shows a weighted preference for a particular attribute (or factor or dimension) in a product, service, or choice-space.

Polysemous: Many-meaninged.

Population Segmentation: The partitioning of a human population to particular sub-groups with specified characteristics and preferences.

P-Set: Respondents in a Q-methodology study.

Psychometric: The objective measurement of various aspects of human personality.

P-Value: A probability (p) value between 0 and 1 indicating a standard for statistical significance.

Q-Methodology: A standard research methodology to identify insider/people's self-reported "subjectivities" through a q-sort method.

Q-Sample: The statements that will be presented to Q-methodology research participants (a selective portion of the larger concourse).

Q-Sort: The research participant work of sorting the statements/cards in the Q-Methodology research.

Q-Sort Grid (Q-Sort Score Sheet, Q-Sort Template, Q-Sort Card Grid, Q-Board): The visual table or grid on which q-set statement cards (or other information objects) are sorted.

Qualitative Cross-Tabulation Analysis: The integration of a cross-tabulation table with interview subjects/focus group speakers/survey respondents in the row data, and variables and themes in the column data to enable the identification of data patterns through computational means.

Qualitative Matrix: A data table structure involving qualitative and/or mixed methods research data (often in textual format).

Real-Time Delphi Study: An online Delphi study with potentially only one round.

Relational Matrix: A data table with similar variables in the column headers and the row headers to enable the identification of the presence of a relationship between variables or not (in a binary matrix) or the intensity of a relationship between variables or not (in an intensity matrix); resulting data can be represented as a relational network graph.

Round: An iteration or "wave" of a Delphi study.

Self-Explicated Conjoint Analysis: A basic form of choice experiment in which respondents explicitly define their preferences from lists of attributes that comprise a particular product or service or real-world and/or theoretical choice-space.

Semantic: Meaning-bearing (as in words in a language).

Sentiment Analysis: The labeling of words and phrases as positive or negative (in a binary way) or in various categories of positive to negative (on a continuum).

Similarity Matrix: A data table that compares the amount of similarity and difference between the coding of two different coders or respective coding teams.

Stylometry: The statistical analysis (metrics) of style.

Text Corpus: A collection of written texts selected around particular topics and standards.

Theme Extraction: The identification of main ideas and/or topics from a text or collection of texts.

Topic Modeling: The extraction of topics within a piece of writing or set of written texts.

Treemap Diagram: A data visualization indicating the frequency of occurrence of particular words and/or n-grams.

Visual Question Answering: A new computational data analytics technique that enables computers to analyze an image or image sequence or set using computer vision and making observations of the target images.

Word Frequency Count: A computational technique that enables computers to count how many words of each time occur in a piece of writing or collection or text set.

Word Tree: A data visualization that depicts a target word or ngram/phrase and a number of lead-up and lead-away words to the target term to provide human users with a sense of the target word/phrase use contexts (for semantic meaning).

Related Readings

To continue IGI Global's long-standing tradition of advancing innovation through emerging research, please find below a compiled list of recommended IGI Global book chapters and journal articles in the areas of online research, survey data, and data analytics. These related readings will provide additional information and guidance to further enrich your knowledge and assist you with your own research.

Acharya, A. (2019). Ethnographic Study. In M. Gupta, M. Shaheen, & K. Reddy (Eds.), *Qualitative Techniques for Workplace Data Analysis* (pp. 246–271). Hershey, PA: IGI Global. doi:10.4018/978-1-5225-5366-3.ch011

Acharya, A., & Mohanty, P. K. (2019). Action Research. In M. Gupta, M. Shaheen, & K. Reddy (Eds.), *Qualitative Techniques for Workplace Data Analysis* (pp. 221–245). Hershey, PA: IGI Global. doi:10.4018/978-1-5225-5366-3.ch010

Akkarapatty, N., Muralidharan, A., Raj, N. S., & P., V. (2017). Dimensionality Reduction Techniques for Text Mining. In V. Bhatnagar (Ed.), *Collaborative Filtering Using Data Mining and Analysis* (pp. 49-72). Hershey, PA: IGI Global. doi:10.4018/978-1-5225-0489-4.ch003

Alok, S. (2019). Vignette Methodology: An Illustration From Conflict Research. In M. Gupta, M. Shaheen, & K. Reddy (Eds.), *Qualitative Techniques for Workplace Data Analysis* (pp. 117–143). Hershey, PA: IGI Global. doi:10.4018/978-1-5225-5366-3.ch006

Biba, M., Vajjhala, N. R., & Nishani, L. (2017). Visual Data Mining for Collaborative Filtering: A State-of-the-Art Survey. In V. Bhatnagar (Ed.), *Collaborative Filtering Using Data Mining and Analysis* (pp. 217–235). Hershey, PA: IGI Global. doi:10.4018/978-1-5225-0489-4.ch012

Boucher, M. L. Jr. (2018). Using Photo-Methods to Empower Participants in Education Research. In V. Wang & T. Reio Jr., (Eds.), *Handbook of Research on Innovative Techniques, Trends, and Analysis for Optimized Research Methods* (pp. 202–219). Hershey, PA: IGI Global. doi:10.4018/978-1-5225-5164-5.ch013

Brewer, E. W., Torrisi-Steele, G., & Wang, V. (2018). Addressing Survey Research. In V. Wang & T. Reio Jr., (Eds.), *Handbook of Research on Innovative Techniques, Trends, and Analysis for Optimized Research Methods* (pp. 341–359). Hershey, PA: IGI Global. doi:10.4018/978-1-5225-5164-5.ch020

Brewer, E. W., Torrisi-Steele, G., & Wang, V. X. (2015). Survey Research: Methods, Issues and the Future. *International Journal of Adult Vocational Education and Technology*, 6(4), 46–64. doi:10.4018/IJAVET.2015100106

Ceccaroni, L., Bowser, A., & Brenton, P. (2017). Civic Education and Citizen Science: Definitions, Categories, Knowledge Representation. In L. Ceccaroni & J. Piera (Eds.), *Analyzing the Role of Citizen Science in Modern Research* (pp. 1–23). Hershey, PA: IGI Global. doi:10.4018/978-1-5225-0962-2.ch001

Chambers, S., & Nimon, K. (2018). Conducting Survey Research Using MTurk. In V. Wang & T. Reio Jr., (Eds.), *Handbook of Research on Innovative Techniques, Trends, and Analysis for Optimized Research Methods* (pp. 258–288). Hershey, PA: IGI Global. doi:10.4018/978-1-5225-5164-5.ch016

Chapman, C., & Hodges, C. (2017). Can Citizen Science Seriously Contribute to Policy Development?: A Decision Maker's View. In L. Ceccaroni & J. Piera (Eds.), *Analyzing the Role of Citizen Science in Modern Research* (pp. 246–261). Hershey, PA: IGI Global. doi:10.4018/978-1-5225-0962-2.ch012

Cranton, P. (2018). Teachers as Researchers: Participatory and Action Research. In V. Wang & T. Reio Jr., (Eds.), *Handbook of Research on Innovative Techniques, Trends, and Analysis for Optimized Research Methods* (pp. 82–98). Hershey, PA: IGI Global. doi:10.4018/978-1-5225-5164-5.ch006

Deaton, C. C., & Malloy, J. A. (2018). Design-Based Case Study: Refining Interventions Through Systematic, Iterative Methods. In V. Wang & T. Reio Jr., (Eds.), *Handbook of Research on Innovative Techniques, Trends, and Analysis for Optimized Research Methods* (pp. 50–62). Hershey, PA: IGI Global. doi:10.4018/978-1-5225-5164-5.ch004

Dongre, S. S., & Malik, L. G. (2017). Data Stream Mining Using Ensemble Classifier: A Collaborative Approach of Classifiers. In V. Bhatnagar (Ed.), *Collaborative Filtering Using Data Mining and Analysis* (pp. 236–249). Hershey, PA: IGI Global. doi:10.4018/978-1-5225-0489-4.ch013

Dunkley, R. A. (2017). The Role of Citizen Science in Environmental Education: A Critical Exploration of the Environmental Citizen Science Experience. In L. Ceccaroni & J. Piera (Eds.), *Analyzing the Role of Citizen Science in Modern Research* (pp. 213–230). Hershey, PA: IGI Global. doi:10.4018/978-1-5225-0962-2.ch010

Esteves, M. G., Moreira de Souza, J., Uchoa, A. P., Pereira, C. V., & Antelio, M. (2017). Smart Activation of Citizens: Opportunities and Challenges for Scientific Research. In L. Ceccaroni & J. Piera (Eds.), *Analyzing the Role of Citizen Science in Modern Research* (pp. 262–284). Hershey, PA: IGI Global. doi:10.4018/978-1-5225-0962-2.ch013

Farmer, L. S. (2018). Extensions of Content Analysis in the Creation of Multimodal Knowledge Representations. In V. Wang & T. Reio Jr., (Eds.), *Handbook of Research on Innovative Techniques, Trends, and Analysis for Optimized Research Methods* (pp. 63–81). Hershey, PA: IGI Global. doi:10.4018/978-1-5225-5164-5.ch005

Gharesifard, M., & Wehn, U. (2017). What Drives Citizens to Engage in ICT-Enabled Citizen Science?: Case Study of Online Amateur Weather Networks. In L. Ceccaroni & J. Piera (Eds.), *Analyzing the Role of Citizen Science in Modern Research* (pp. 62–88). Hershey, PA: IGI Global. doi:10.4018/978-1-5225-0962-2.ch004

Gillingham, M. (2017). Surface Water Information Collection: Volunteers Keep the Great Lakes Great. In L. Ceccaroni & J. Piera (Eds.), *Analyzing the Role of Citizen Science in Modern Research* (pp. 285–301). Hershey, PA: IGI Global. doi:10.4018/978-1-5225-0962-2.ch014

Göbel, C., Cappadonna, J. L., Newman, G. J., Zhang, J., & Vohland, K. (2017). More Than Just Networking for Citizen Science: Examining Core Roles of Practitioner Organizations. In L. Ceccaroni & J. Piera (Eds.), *Analyzing the Role of Citizen Science in Modern Research* (pp. 24–49). Hershey, PA: IGI Global. doi:10.4018/978-1-5225-0962-2.ch002

Goyal, M., & Bhatnagar, V. (2017). A Classification Framework on Opinion Mining for Effective Recommendation Systems. In V. Bhatnagar (Ed.), *Collaborative Filtering Using Data Mining and Analysis* (pp. 180–194). Hershey, PA: IGI Global. doi:10.4018/978-1-5225-0489-4.ch010

Hai-Jew, S. (2019). *Methods for Analyzing and Leveraging Online Learning Data* (pp. 1–436). Hershey, PA: IGI Global. doi:10.4018/978-1-5225-7528-3

Haynes, C. A., & Shelton, K. (2018). Delphi Method in a Digital Age: Practical Considerations for Online Delphi Studies. In V. Wang & T. Reio Jr., (Eds.), *Handbook of Research on Innovative Techniques, Trends, and Analysis for Optimized Research Methods* (pp. 132–151). Hershey, PA: IGI Global. doi:10.4018/978-1-5225-5164-5. ch009

Hoffman, C., Cooper, C. B., Kennedy, E. B., Farooque, M., & Cavalier, D. (2017). SciStarter 2.0: A Digital Platform to Foster and Study Sustained Engagement in Citizen Science. In L. Ceccaroni & J. Piera (Eds.), *Analyzing the Role of Citizen Science in Modern Research* (pp. 50–61). Hershey, PA: IGI Global. doi:10.4018/978-1-5225-0962-2.ch003

Jain, A., Bhatnagar, V., & Sharma, P. (2017). Collaborative and Clustering Based Strategy in Big Data. In V. Bhatnagar (Ed.), *Collaborative Filtering Using Data Mining and Analysis* (pp. 140–158). Hershey, PA: IGI Global. doi:10.4018/978-1-5225-0489-4.ch008

Jambulingam, V. K., & Santhi, V. (2017). Knowledge Discovery and Big Data Analytics: Issues, Challenges, and Opportunities. In A. Singh, N. Dey, A. Ashour, & V. Santhi (Eds.), *Web Semantics for Textual and Visual Information Retrieval* (pp. 144–164). Hershey, PA: IGI Global. doi:10.4018/978-1-5225-2483-0.ch007

Jones, D. (2018). Research as Resistance: Activist Research as a Framework and Methodology for Social Change. In V. Wang & T. Reio Jr., (Eds.), *Handbook of Research on Innovative Techniques, Trends, and Analysis for Optimized Research Methods* (pp. 17–29). Hershey, PA: IGI Global. doi:10.4018/978-1-5225-5164-5. ch002

Ke, S., & Lee, W. (2017). Combining User Co-Ratings and Social Trust for Collaborative Recommendation: A Data Analytics Approach. In V. Bhatnagar (Ed.), *Collaborative Filtering Using Data Mining and Analysis* (pp. 195–216). Hershey, PA: IGI Global. doi:10.4018/978-1-5225-0489-4.ch011

Khan, N. I. (2019). Case Study as a Method of Qualitative Research. In M. Gupta, M. Shaheen, & K. Reddy (Eds.), *Qualitative Techniques for Workplace Data Analysis* (pp. 170–196). Hershey, PA: IGI Global. doi:10.4018/978-1-5225-5366-3.ch008

Related Readings

Kier, M., & Khalil, D. (2018). Critical Race Design: An Emerging Methodological Approach to Anti-Racist Design and Implementation. In V. Wang & T. Reio Jr., (Eds.), *Handbook of Research on Innovative Techniques, Trends, and Analysis for Optimized Research Methods* (pp. 30–49). Hershey, PA: IGI Global. doi:10.4018/978-1-5225-5164-5.ch003

Knox, C. H., Anderson-Inman, L., Terrazas-Arellanes, F. E., Walden, E. D., Strycker, L. A., & Hildreth, B. (2016). Strategies for Online Academic Research (SOAR): Digital Literacy for Middle School Students. *International Journal of Information Communication Technologies and Human Development*, 8(1), 42–68. doi:10.4018/IJICTHD.2016010103

Krishnamurthy, S., & Akila, V. (2017). Information Retrieval Models: Trends and Techniques. In A. Singh, N. Dey, A. Ashour, & V. Santhi (Eds.), *Web Semantics for Textual and Visual Information Retrieval* (pp. 17–42). Hershey, PA: IGI Global. doi:10.4018/978-1-5225-2483-0.ch002

Kumar, R., Pattnaik, P. K., & Pandey, P. (2017). Conversion of Higher into Lower Language Using Machine Translation. In A. Singh, N. Dey, A. Ashour, & V. Santhi (Eds.), *Web Semantics for Textual and Visual Information Retrieval* (pp. 92–107). Hershey, PA: IGI Global. doi:10.4018/978-1-5225-2483-0.ch005

Lal, S. B., Sharma, A., Chaturvedi, K. K., Farooqi, M. S., Kumar, S., Mishra, D. C., & Jha, M. (2017). State-of-the-Art Information Retrieval Tools for Biological Resources. In A. Singh, N. Dey, A. Ashour, & V. Santhi (Eds.), *Web Semantics for Textual and Visual Information Retrieval* (pp. 203–226). Hershey, PA: IGI Global. doi:10.4018/978-1-5225-2483-0.ch010

Lampoltshammer, T. J., & Scholz, J. (2017). Citizen-Driven Geographic Information Science. In L. Ceccaroni & J. Piera (Eds.), *Analyzing the Role of Citizen Science in Modern Research* (pp. 231–245). Hershey, PA: IGI Global. doi:10.4018/978-1-5225-0962-2.ch011

Leung, C. K., Jiang, F., Dela Cruz, E. M., & Elango, V. S. (2017). Association Rule Mining in Collaborative Filtering. In V. Bhatnagar (Ed.), *Collaborative Filtering Using Data Mining and Analysis* (pp. 159–179). Hershey, PA: IGI Global. doi:10.4018/978-1-5225-0489-4.ch009

Liu, H., & Kobernus, M. (2017). Citizen Science and Its Role in Sustainable Development: Status, Trends, Issues, and Opportunities. In L. Ceccaroni & J. Piera (Eds.), *Analyzing the Role of Citizen Science in Modern Research* (pp. 147–167). Hershey, PA: IGI Global. doi:10.4018/978-1-5225-0962-2.ch007

M., V., & K., T. (2017). History and Overview of the Recommender Systems. In V. Bhatnagar (Ed.), *Collaborative Filtering Using Data Mining and Analysis* (pp. 74-99). Hershey, PA: IGI Global. doi:10.4018/978-1-5225-0489-4.ch004

Mahajan, R. (2017). Review of Data Mining Techniques and Parameters for Recommendation of Effective Adaptive E-Learning System. In V. Bhatnagar (Ed.), *Collaborative Filtering Using Data Mining and Analysis* (pp. 1–23). Hershey, PA: IGI Global. doi:10.4018/978-1-5225-0489-4.ch001

Majumdar, A. (2019). Thematic Analysis in Qualitative Research. In M. Gupta, M. Shaheen, & K. Reddy (Eds.), *Qualitative Techniques for Workplace Data Analysis* (pp. 197–220). Hershey, PA: IGI Global. doi:10.4018/978-1-5225-5366-3.ch009

Malhotra, M., & Singh, A. (2017). A Study on Models and Methods of Information Retrieval System. In A. Singh, N. Dey, A. Ashour, & V. Santhi (Eds.), *Web Semantics for Textual and Visual Information Retrieval* (pp. 43–68). Hershey, PA: IGI Global. doi:10.4018/978-1-5225-2483-0.ch003

Malik, K. R., & Ahmad, T. (2017). Technique for Transformation of Data From RDB to XML Then to RDF. In A. Singh, N. Dey, A. Ashour, & V. Santhi (Eds.), *Web Semantics for Textual and Visual Information Retrieval* (pp. 70–91). Hershey, PA: IGI Global. doi:10.4018/978-1-5225-2483-0.ch004

McWhorter, R. R., & Ellinger, A. D. (2018). Qualitative Case Study Research: An Initial Primer. In V. Wang & T. Reio Jr., (Eds.), *Handbook of Research on Innovative Techniques, Trends, and Analysis for Optimized Research Methods* (pp. 185–201). Hershey, PA: IGI Global. doi:10.4018/978-1-5225-5164-5.ch012

Mittal, M., Sharma, R. K., Singh, V., & Mohan Goyal, L. (2017). Modified Single Pass Clustering Algorithm Based on Median as a Threshold Similarity Value. In V. Bhatnagar (Ed.), *Collaborative Filtering Using Data Mining and Analysis* (pp. 24–48). Hershey, PA: IGI Global. doi:10.4018/978-1-5225-0489-4.ch002

Mominó, J. M., Piera, J., & Jurado, E. (2017). Citizen Observatories as Advanced Learning Environments. In L. Ceccaroni & J. Piera (Eds.), *Analyzing the Role of Citizen Science in Modern Research* (pp. 192–212). Hershey, PA: IGI Global. doi:10.4018/978-1-5225-0962-2.ch009

Related Readings

Munn, S. L. (2018). Creating a Typology of Organizational Culture Using Cluster Analysis. In V. Wang & T. Reio Jr., (Eds.), *Handbook of Research on Innovative Techniques, Trends, and Analysis for Optimized Research Methods* (pp. 289–302). Hershey, PA: IGI Global. doi:10.4018/978-1-5225-5164-5.ch017

Narang, S. K., Kumar, S., & Verma, V. (2017). Knowledge Discovery From Massive Data Streams. In A. Singh, N. Dey, A. Ashour, & V. Santhi (Eds.), *Web Semantics for Textual and Visual Information Retrieval* (pp. 109–143). Hershey, PA: IGI Global. doi:10.4018/978-1-5225-2483-0.ch006

Nimon, K., Zientek, L. R., & Kraha, A. (2018). Conducting All-Possible-Subsets for MANOVA and Factorial MANOVA: No Longer a Weekend Project. In V. Wang & T. Reio Jr., (Eds.), *Handbook of Research on Innovative Techniques, Trends, and Analysis for Optimized Research Methods* (pp. 322–340). Hershey, PA: IGI Global. doi:10.4018/978-1-5225-5164-5.ch019

Nishani, L., & Biba, M. (2017). Statistical Relational Learning for Collaborative Filtering a State-of-the-Art Review. In V. Bhatnagar (Ed.), *Collaborative Filtering Using Data Mining and Analysis* (pp. 250–269). Hershey, PA: IGI Global. doi:10.4018/978-1-5225-0489-4.ch014

Norris, S. E. (2018). An Adaptive Leadership Approach to Adult Learning and Organizational Research. In V. Wang & T. Reio Jr., (Eds.), *Handbook of Research on Innovative Techniques, Trends, and Analysis for Optimized Research Methods* (pp. 99–114). Hershey, PA: IGI Global. doi:10.4018/978-1-5225-5164-5.ch007

Pal, A., & Kumar, M. (2017). Collaborative Filtering Based Data Mining for Large Data. In V. Bhatnagar (Ed.), *Collaborative Filtering Using Data Mining and Analysis* (pp. 115–127). Hershey, PA: IGI Global. doi:10.4018/978-1-5225-0489-4.ch006

Pandey, J. (2019). Deductive Approach to Content Analysis. In M. Gupta, M. Shaheen, & K. Reddy (Eds.), *Qualitative Techniques for Workplace Data Analysis* (pp. 145–169). Hershey, PA: IGI Global. doi:10.4018/978-1-5225-5366-3.ch007

Ravindranath, S. (2019). Behavioral Event Interview. In M. Gupta, M. Shaheen, & K. Reddy (Eds.), *Qualitative Techniques for Workplace Data Analysis* (pp. 73–95). Hershey, PA: IGI Global. doi:10.4018/978-1-5225-5366-3.ch004

Ravindranath, S., & Menachery, T. J. (2019). Storytelling. In M. Gupta, M. Shaheen, & K. Reddy (Eds.), *Qualitative Techniques for Workplace Data Analysis* (pp. 53–72). Hershey, PA: IGI Global. doi:10.4018/978-1-5225-5366-3.ch003

Rocco, T. S., Gionti, L. A., Plakhotnik, M. S., Munn, S. L., & Collins, J. C. (2018). Creating Support for Graduate Students' Writing and Publication Endeavors: A Case of a Writing Center. In V. Wang & T. Reio Jr., (Eds.), *Handbook of Research on Innovative Techniques, Trends, and Analysis for Optimized Research Methods* (pp. 360–376). Hershey, PA: IGI Global. doi:10.4018/978-1-5225-5164-5.ch021

Rose, A. D. (2018). Thinking Historically: Writing and Understanding Historical Research. In V. Wang & T. Reio Jr., (Eds.), *Handbook of Research on Innovative Techniques, Trends, and Analysis for Optimized Research Methods* (pp. 220–232). Hershey, PA: IGI Global. doi:10.4018/978-1-5225-5164-5.ch014

Saini, A. (2017). Big Data Mining Using Collaborative Filtering. In V. Bhatnagar (Ed.), *Collaborative Filtering Using Data Mining and Analysis* (pp. 128–138). Hershey, PA: IGI Global. doi:10.4018/978-1-5225-0489-4.ch007

Sangwan, N., & Dahiya, N. (2017). A Classification Framework Towards Application of Data Mining in Collaborative Filtering. In V. Bhatnagar (Ed.), *Collaborative Filtering Using Data Mining and Analysis* (pp. 100–114). Hershey, PA: IGI Global. doi:10.4018/978-1-5225-0489-4.ch005

Sedivy-Benton, A. L. (2018). Creating Meaningful Research for Graduate Students to Prevent Degree Abandonment. In V. Wang & T. Reio Jr., (Eds.), *Handbook of Research on Innovative Techniques, Trends, and Analysis for Optimized Research Methods* (pp. 152–171). Hershey, PA: IGI Global. doi:10.4018/978-1-5225-5164-5.ch010

Shaheen, M., Pradhan, S., & Ranajee. (2019). Sampling in Qualitative Research. In M. Gupta, M. Shaheen, & K. Reddy (Eds.), *Qualitative Techniques for Workplace Data Analysis* (pp. 25-51). Hershey, PA: IGI Global. doi:10.4018/978-1-5225-5366-3.ch002

Shelton, K., Haynes, C. A., & Creghan, K. A. (2018). Fundamentals of Delphi Research Methodology. In V. Wang & T. Reio Jr., (Eds.), *Handbook of Research on Innovative Techniques, Trends, and Analysis for Optimized Research Methods* (pp. 233–257). Hershey, PA: IGI Global. doi:10.4018/978-1-5225-5164-5.ch015

Singh, A., Dey, N., & Ashour, A. S. (2017). Scope of Automation in Semantics-Driven Multimedia Information Retrieval From Web. In A. Singh, N. Dey, A. Ashour, & V. Santhi (Eds.), *Web Semantics for Textual and Visual Information Retrieval* (pp. 1–16). Hershey, PA: IGI Global. doi:10.4018/978-1-5225-2483-0.ch001

Related Readings

Singh, A., & Sharma, A. (2017). Web Semantics for Personalized Information Retrieval. In A. Singh, N. Dey, A. Ashour, & V. Santhi (Eds.), *Web Semantics for Textual and Visual Information Retrieval* (pp. 166–186). Hershey, PA: IGI Global. doi:10.4018/978-1-5225-2483-0.ch008

Subirats, L., Simoes, J., & Steblin, A. (2017). Geographical Information Systems in Modern Citizen Science. In L. Ceccaroni & J. Piera (Eds.), *Analyzing the Role of Citizen Science in Modern Research* (pp. 117–146). Hershey, PA: IGI Global. doi:10.4018/978-1-5225-0962-2.ch006

Tarab, S. (2019). Becoming Familiar With Qualitative Research. In M. Gupta, M. Shaheen, & K. Reddy (Eds.), *Qualitative Techniques for Workplace Data Analysis* (pp. 1–24). Hershey, PA: IGI Global. doi:10.4018/978-1-5225-5366-3.ch001

Tiago, P. (2017). Social Context of Citizen Science Projects. In L. Ceccaroni & J. Piera (Eds.), *Analyzing the Role of Citizen Science in Modern Research* (pp. 168–191). Hershey, PA: IGI Global. doi:10.4018/978-1-5225-0962-2.ch008

Vela, L. A., Bocciolesi, E., Lombardi, G., & Urquhart, R. M. (2017). The Social Function of Citizen Science: Developing Researchers, Developing Citizens. In L. Ceccaroni & J. Piera (Eds.), *Analyzing the Role of Citizen Science in Modern Research* (pp. 89–116). Hershey, PA: IGI Global. doi:10.4018/978-1-5225-0962-2.ch005

Vijayakumar, S., Dasari, N., Bhushan, B., & Reddy, R. (2017). Semantic Web-Based Framework for Scientific Workflows in E-Science. In A. Singh, N. Dey, A. Ashour, & V. Santhi (Eds.), *Web Semantics for Textual and Visual Information Retrieval* (pp. 187–202). Hershey, PA: IGI Global. doi:10.4018/978-1-5225-2483-0.ch009

Watkins, K. E., Nicolaides, A., & Marsick, V. J. (2018). Action Research Approaches. In V. Wang & T. Reio Jr., (Eds.), *Handbook of Research on Innovative Techniques, Trends, and Analysis for Optimized Research Methods* (pp. 1–16). Hershey, PA: IGI Global. doi:10.4018/978-1-5225-5164-5.ch001

Wright, U. T., Rocco, T. S., & McGill, C. M. (2018). Exposing Oppressive Systems: Institutional Ethnography as a Research Method in Adult and Workforce Education. In V. Wang & T. Reio Jr., (Eds.), *Handbook of Research on Innovative Techniques, Trends, and Analysis for Optimized Research Methods* (pp. 115–131). Hershey, PA: IGI Global. doi:10.4018/978-1-5225-5164-5.ch008

Yan, Y., Dongmei, Z., & Weining, Y. (2019). Role of Platform, Supplier and Medium in Online Trust Formation. *International Journal of Business Data Communications and Networking*, *15*(1), 58–70. doi:10.4018/IJBDCN.2019010104

Yang, Y. (2018). A Brief Preview of Q Methodology. In V. Wang & T. Reio Jr., (Eds.), *Handbook of Research on Innovative Techniques, Trends, and Analysis for Optimized Research Methods* (pp. 303–321). Hershey, PA: IGI Global. doi:10.4018/978-1-5225-5164-5.ch018

Zeba, F., & Mohanty, P. K. (2019). Personal Diary Method: A Way of Collecting Qualitative Data. In M. Gupta, M. Shaheen, & K. Reddy (Eds.), *Qualitative Techniques for Workplace Data Analysis* (pp. 96–116). Hershey, PA: IGI Global. doi:10.4018/978-1-5225-5366-3.ch005

Zimmerman, A. S., & Kim, J. (2018). Storytelling as an Invitation to Become a Self in the World: The Promise of Narrative Inquiry. In V. Wang & T. Reio Jr., (Eds.), *Handbook of Research on Innovative Techniques, Trends, and Analysis for Optimized Research Methods* (pp. 172–184). Hershey, PA: IGI Global. doi:10.4018/978-1-5225-5164-5.ch011

About the Author

Shalin Hai-Jew works as an instructional designer at Kansas State University (K-State). She has taught at the university and college levels for many years (including four years in the People's Republic of China) and was tenured at Shoreline Community College but left tenure to pursue instructional design work. She has Bachelor's degrees in English and psychology, a Master's degree in Creative Writing from the University of Washington (Hugh Paradise Scholar), and an Ed.D in Educational Leadership with a focus on public administration from Seattle University (where she was a Morford Scholar). She tested into the University of Washington at 14. She reviews for several publishers and publications. She has worked on a number of instructional design projects, including public health, biosecurity, one health, mental health, PTSD, grain science, turfgrass management, social justice, and others. She has authored and edited a number of books. Hai-Jew was born in Huntsville, Alabama, in the U.S. Shalin is working on multiple book projects currently, related to learner profiling, form/function/style in instructional design, and the maintaining of human worth in times of automated work.

Index

Ensure Quality Research is Introduced to the Academic Community

Become an IGI Global Reviewer for Authored Book Projects

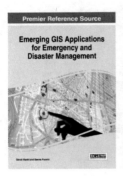

Premier Reference Source

Emerging GIS Applications for Emergency and Disaster Management

Premier Reference Source

Managerial Strategies and Green Solutions for Project Sustainability

Premier Reference Source

Comparative Approaches to Using R and Python for Statistical Data Analysis

Premier Reference Source

Solutions for High-Touch Communications in a High-Tech World

The overall success of an authored book project is dependent on quality and timely reviews.

In this competitive age of scholarly publishing, constructive and timely feedback significantly expedites the turnaround time of manuscripts from submission to acceptance, allowing the publication and discovery of forward-thinking research at a much more expeditious rate. Several IGI Global authored book projects are currently seeking highly qualified experts in the field to fill vacancies on their respective editorial review boards:

Applications may be sent to:
development@igi-global.com

Applicants must have a doctorate (or an equivalent degree) as well as publishing and reviewing experience. Reviewers are asked to write reviews in a timely, collegial, and constructive manner. All reviewers will begin their role on an ad-hoc basis for a period of one year, and upon successful completion of this term can be considered for full editorial review board status, with the potential for a subsequent promotion to Associate Editor.

If you have a colleague that may be interested in this opportunity,
we encourage you to share this information with them.

Printed in the United States
By Bookmasters